P9-DXK-820

CUJO

CUJO

THE UNTOLD STORY OF MY LIFE ON AND OFF THE ICE

CURTIS JOSEPH

with KIRSTIE McLELLAN DAY

HarperCollins*Publishers*Ltd

Cujo
Copyright © 2018 by Curtis Joseph and Kirstie McLellan Day
All rights reserved.

Published by HarperCollins Publishers Ltd

First edition

No part of this book may be used or reproduced in any manner whatsoever
without the prior written permission of the publisher, except in the case
of brief quotations embodied in reviews.

Unless otherwise noted, photos are courtesy Curtis Joseph.

HarperCollins books may be purchased for educational, business,
or sales promotional use through our Special Markets Department.

HarperCollins Publishers Ltd
Bay Adelaide Centre, East Tower
22 Adelaide Street West, 41st Floor
Toronto, Ontario, Canada
M5H 4E3

www.harpercollins.ca

Library and Archives Canada Cataloguing in Publication
information is available upon request.

ISBN 978-1-4434-5596-1

Printed and bound in the United States
LSC/H 9 8 7 6 5 4 3 2 1

To Madi, Taylor, Tristan, Luke, Kailey, Jason and Kensie Shayne.
Your love makes me the luckiest man in the world.

And to Stephanie, the love of my life,
thank you for bringing down the walls.

Contents

FOREWORD

HOCKEY IS, WITHOUT a doubt, just a wonderful game. Eighteen players get a chance to do their very best every single time they step out onto the ice. It's funny how we don't ever stop to think about the goalies. The rest of the team shifts on and off, but because there are just two goaltenders, they often play a whole sixty-minute game by themselves. No other player does that.

I was lucky enough to be part of Curtis Joseph's career. When I coached in Phoenix, I got to be part of the fun he had there. He was just a first-rate pro who practised hard and played hard with not such a good team. Never heard him complain, ever. In fact, he played so well, he wound up being team MVP.

And when I was putting together the 2002 Canadian men's Olympic hockey team, I knew that Curtis was the best goalie in the NHL that year. Curtis was unreal, so there was no question in our minds he was going to be a big part of the team. One of the things that made him great was that he was the kind of goaltender who liked to play the big games. He loved the challenge of the playoffs—that's when I saw him play his best.

The other side of knowing Curtis says more to me about the man, not the goalie. Things don't always go in our favour, and when you are a goalie, that means having to sit out games. Curtis was a huge part of our 2002 Olympic gold medal win, even though he didn't play the final game. I know it was really tough for him, but he didn't let it show. He put the team first and stayed really positive, standing behind every single player on our team. And you know what? I think we still would've had the same results had Curtis been in net. He's just that good a goalie.

As with every great player, it was always Curtis's attitude that made him invaluable to the team, whether it was St. Louis, Edmonton, Toronto, Detroit, Phoenix, Calgary or Team Canada. I don't know a lot about goaltending and the pressure goalies feel or the lives they live, but I do know one thing. Curtis was a team guy all the way!

Enjoy his book. He is a good man with a remarkable story.

—Wayne Gretzky

PROLOGUE

By the time I was ten years old, I was living on a steady diet of stale cookies, processed cheese slice sandwiches and frozen institutional hamburgers—God knows what they were made of. Every night, I'd throw one on a dirty old barbecue we kept outside the kitchen door. My bed was a mattress on the floor. It was tough to find a dry corner because Mom's cats peed and shit all over it. I didn't have sheets or anything, just an old blanket. In the winter, I'd sleep in an old coat that one of the men in the house had thrown out. Mom treated her animals better than she treated us kids.

I'm going to tell you all about my childhood, and my life. A lot of the early stuff is not good, but listen, I wouldn't change a thing. It made me who I am. It made me tough. It made me driven and it made me appreciate life. Think about it. There was no direction to go but up, right? Every day, everything kept getting better and better. Meeting my friends at school and in sports and going home with them and seeing how normal families lived filled me with awe. I'm a glass-half-full kind of guy. I loved watching the moms and dads and brothers and sisters and all the love between them. I'd think, "Wow, this is awesome." They inspired me to want to live in a family like they had.

I also found family in the game. No question. It was probably to my advantage that I didn't have a solid family life growing up because when, all of a sudden, I was surrounded by these wonderful human beings, I appreciated every single one of them. We were all part of this big group. We spent more time together than we did at home. We looked after one another. We had each other's backs. We called one another if somebody slept in. We travelled together. We ate together, we talked about the game together, we were going to win together and lose together. We were more than friends, so yes, we were a family. A hockey family.

Today, I have four great kids from my first marriage—Madison, Taylor, Tristan and Luke—and two from my second, Kailey and Kensie Shayne, plus Jason. He's our nephew and we're raising him too. Luke said to me, "Dad, you should write a book. If you can change one kid's life, help one kid continue on, overcome and turn things around, it's worth it."

All of my kids are thoughtful and funny too. They kill me. I was cleaning up and found a trophy our team won back when I was twelve. It's about the size of a small pickle jar and says ALL-ONTARIO CHAMPIONS—SINGLE A. I showed it to my oldest boy, Taylor, who was eighteen, and I said, "Taylor, look at this!" I pointed to the "Single A" part because, now that I am comfortable with my history, I'm proud of the fact that at that age, I was still playing single-A hockey. Nowadays, for somebody playing at that level at that age, the chances of making it to the NHL are absolutely slim to none. Taylor looked at the trophy and he nodded. "Nineteen seventy-nine. Wow, you're old."

When I retired from hockey, my kids asked me, "Dad, who owned you? C'mon, you can tell us." I try to be funny. We all try to be funny and joke around a lot. I pretended to think about it, and then I responded, "Uh . . . nobody!" And so they said, "Okay, Dad, we'll just look it up." They grabbed the computer and started googling, and I'm watching them, thinking, "Oooh, I wonder who did score on me most?" We looked at the stats and they went, "Oh . . . Teemu Selanne *owned you*! He had thirty-five goals or something crazy like that." And I said, "Ohhhh yeah," and I started to remember all those times

I played against him in the Western Conference and how many big goals he scored on me.

Selanne was so fast and just a pure goal scorer. When I played in Edmonton in 1995–96, we gave up a lot of chances and a lot of goals, so it was tough. But he was the guy who scored the most on me. There's probably a few other goalies who can say the same thing about him, right?

Flash-forward to the outdoor game in Winnipeg in 2016—the Heritage Classic alumni game. I was playing for Edmonton. Wayne Gretzky was playing too, and it was a big deal for Winnipeg because the Oilers used to beat the Jets all the time. There was a big crowd—31,000 fans. It was beautiful outside because it was Manitoba in October.

It was the third period and Selanne had four points already—the first goal, on a penalty shot, and three assists. Bill Ranford and Dwayne Roloson played goal in each of the first two periods, and I took over for the third. With 3.6 seconds on the clock and the score tied 5–5, Teemu was tripped in the Jets' end, which meant another penalty shot. He came in on me and he scored. How fitting. I got back to the locker room and my phone was buzzing. *Zzzt zzzt.* Somebody was texting me. I didn't even have my equipment off yet. I was sweating and frustrated that Teemu had scored on me. I always hated getting scored on. I looked, and the text was from my son Tristan, who makes me laugh because he's dry and funny and smart, but he's also the kid who tried to run beer through the Keurig machine. I picked up my phone and read the message. It said, "He still owns you, Dad."

CHAPTER 1

999

EVERYBODY USED TO call it Nine Ninety-Nine, because it was located at 999 Queen Street West in Toronto. And then in the 1970s, it got to be known by locals by its new address—1001 Queen Street West. Its proper name was the Queen Street Mental Health Centre. It was a mental institution. A big one.

During the 1970s, inmates whose conditions reached a stage where they could be managed by medication were moved on to halfway houses. One of these was a place called Martin Acres, located on a piece of farmland at the northeast corner of Leslie Street and Green Lane in Sharon, Ontario—now part of the town of East Gwillimbury, about forty-five minutes north of Toronto, right next to Newmarket. Martin Acres housed about seventeen men at a time. And it was my home. The place where I grew up.

The house was a big, red-brick "rehabilitation centre," but the men who went there never left. Outside, it was L-shaped with a couple of wings. One wing ran north-south, and the other from east to west. The shorter, newer wing was built over a triple-car garage. It was a maze. One wrong turn and you'd come to a wall.

You walked through the front door into the vestibule, and the first thing that hit your nose was the smell. Soup and cigarettes mixed with sweater dandruff from all the men who just sat around all day. All the men's bedrooms were upstairs. Downstairs, there was a kitchen, or as we called it, the "cafeteria." There was a bathroom between it and the room where they watched TV, played cards or just stared out the window.

Our family basically lived in a two-room apartment in the cen- tre of the house. Come in and turn right, and you were in my mom's kitchen. The flooring everywhere was this cheap lino, and on top of that were these industrial-sized plastic runners. You'd hear a slapping sound under your socks when you ran or played ball hockey. One step up from our kitchen was the dining room, which led to our living room and Mom's bedroom. It was all red carpet under the runners, but it was so old and worn, flat and hard, there was no give.

I remember the frogs. Mom collected them. Crystal frogs on the organ, huge cast-iron frogs on the floor, pewter frogs, ceramic frogs, piggy-bank frogs. Frogs covering the windowsills. Frogs everywhere you looked.

You could've used a spoon to scrape the nicotine off the walls in that house. Seventeen men and my mom, chain-smoking, day and night. Mom's husband, Harold, spent all of his spare time pounding out church songs on his big Wurlitzer organ in our little living room. The music would make Mom's dog, Bear, bark. Sometimes that woke up the men in the bedrooms that surrounded mine. They'd grunt and groan and talk out loud in their sleep. They didn't get up and come into my room at night, though. They were too heavily medicated. There was a smorgasbord of medications in the house—barbiturates, tranquilizers, antipsychotics, sedatives, you name it. That's why Mom stayed in her room all the time. She was in charge of giving the med- ications out to the patients, and she helped herself to a lot of it too.

CHAPTER 2

"I'll Take the Hit"

I HAD A weird life. Two moms, three dads and I grew up in a home full of mentally ill patients run by a crazy person. The last thing anybody expected was that I would someday make a living playing hockey—any kind of living, in any kind of minor league, let alone playing with the Toronto Maple Leafs and Edmonton Oilers and St. Louis Blues in the NHL, even making Team Canada. Coming from where I did, starting as late as I did, it seemed impossible to even dream about it.

Mom's name was Jeanne—pronounced Jan. She had this gravelly voice from years of smoking that would break into a loose cough when she laughed, and she'd tell people, "I'm from Paris, France." Ha, ha, wheeze, cough.

In truth, she was French Canadian. Her skin was white, but darker. Maybe she was Métis. I don't know, she made up a lot of stories. I do know she was from a small farm east of Sudbury. In rural areas like that, if the family was poor, they'd often send one or two of the girls to a nearby Roman Catholic convent. When Mom was four years old, her family handed her over to the convent in North Bay and she was raised to become a nursing nun. She was a novitiate and took her first set of vows but ran away before her final vows or "taking the veil," as they call it. She was working as a waitress at the Shamrock restaurant in Toronto when she met my first dad, Howard Eakins.

When I came along, Mom and Howard Eakins already had two grown kids, both of whom were out and on their own—Karen and Ron. We lived in Keswick in a house on Riveredge Drive. I was Howard's little buddy. He called me Tiger and carried me everywhere and would sit me on his knee to watch *Hockey Night in Canada*. In fact, one of the first words I ever spoke was "score!" Maybe that's why I always wanted to be a goal scorer in the NHL when I grew up.

Mom was short—five foot two—and portly. Her hair was long, straight and black, with hard grey streaks. She wore black glasses, thick and square, and dressed the same way every day, in pants and a tank top. Nothing special. Dark colours. She always wore bright red lipstick. Two bloody-coloured slashes across her mouth.

Three things stick out, like the way Mom sat in a chair. Legs apart, body bent forward, chin in her hand. Not feminine at all. I remember her hands. Old and veiny and covered in rings—several stacked on each finger. And she was strong. She had a black belt in karate, or so she said. One time, one of the new patients had a meltdown, and while the police were being called, she took the guy down. Pinned him to the floor until the police arrived.

I was scared of her. There were always threats, and she'd always overreact. If you made noise or did something she didn't like, she might take a swing at you with a brush or spoon or whatever she had in her hand. She spanked and grabbed too. When my older brother Grant and I were little, our arms and shoulders were often covered in purple fingerprint bruises.

Howard didn't have it easy with Mom. For her, the grass was always greener. She left him a couple of times before leaving him for good and marrying Harold Joseph, my second dad.

Harold Austin Joseph wasn't my natural father, but he raised me from the age of two. Mom wasn't my natural mother either. It's complicated, and I'll get to that in a bit. Harold was a Black man, but his eyes were light. He was tall, over six feet, and fit, with a round face and hair like boxing promoter Don King—a wild Afro, dyed black with silver roots. The ends of his hair stood up and were see-through, like a plum tree in the winter with all the leaves blown away. He was well groomed, a Brylcreem/Aqua Velva kind of guy. He wore a close shave and tidy pants with an ironed collared shirt and a sweater. Always a sweater. Harold was a real solid individual. Salt-of-the-earth kind of guy. He would tell silly jokes. They seemed to tickle his funny bone.

"Did you hear about the accident at the pharmacy?"

"No, Harold, what happened?"

"Well, there was a hearse and it smashed into another car. The back door popped open and the coffin came flying out. It flew right through the drugstore and landed right at the pharmacist's counter. The corpse sat up and said, 'Have you got anything to stop this coffin?'"

That's a Harold joke. He was very soft-spoken. Mild. He would do anything that anybody would tell him to do, which worked well for my mom.

In 1968, when I was almost a year old, Mom was working as a hospice nurse, taking care of Harold's wife, Ruth, who had cancer. Ruth had been a go-getter, the head of the family. She was a music teacher, a very successful one. She worked hard, and Harold did too. They weren't wealthy, but Ruth was innovative. Together they managed to buy an acreage out by Preston Lake, near Newmarket. On it was a nice bungalow made out of two wartime houses. She and Harold paid twenty-five dollars each for them and made the whole thing beautiful. Eleven rooms, including three bedrooms. Mom would sometimes take me with her to work. I remember playing with cars on Ruth's bedsheets and lying on the floor at their home, watching wrestling on an old black-and-white TV.

When Ruth died, Mom left my first dad, Howard, the guy who called me Tiger, and took up with Harold. Harold wouldn't have had an affair with a married woman, so he waited until she and Howard were divorced. Harold was a man of principle, a godly man. Mom told Howard to stay away from us. She was like that. Wilful. Domineering. If she wanted something, she took it.

You have to have some compassion for Mom. She did not have a good life, and I think she married Howard for security because he was a very solid guy. He went to work, he was very predictable, he came home at the same time every day, he handed her the paycheque, he got his allowance and he was happy. He had his dinner, he read the newspaper, he played a game or two with his kids, watched a bit of TV and went to bed at the same time every night. Mom, meanwhile, wanted a bigger chunk out of life because she'd been shut away her entire childhood. She was a welder during the war and then she had gone on to work as a nurse. She learned to play the organ and the guitar. She was very outgoing, while Howard was very steady, loving and quiet. I think her issue was that she couldn't get enough of life. She'd always been unwanted, so she didn't understand how to love. How do you learn to love someone? You learn to love somebody else by loving yourself. If you don't love yourself first, you can't love anybody else. It's not possible. I don't think she had any love for herself, so how in the world was she ever going to become a loving person?

Long before we lived at Martin Acres, we moved into Harold's house in Gormley, Ontario, and Harold became my new dad. I never saw Howard again. My stepsister, Karen, who was Howard's daughter, told me later that Howard was devastated. Not because Mom left, but because she took me. But Howard wasn't one to fight over things. He didn't see the point in setting up a tug-of-war over a child because he knew Mom would make his life and mine hell. Howard told Karen, "I'm the adult. I'll take the hit." And that's exactly what he did.

I was two years old. It had been two years since Mom brought me home from the hospital. Took me right out of the arms of my birth mother.

CHAPTER 3

Bad People

LIKE I SAID, by the time I came along and Mom took me in, she already had two adult children, Karen and Ron, and she'd adopted Grant, who was six years older than me. He was her sister's grandson. Grant's parents lived above a barbershop on Gerrard Street in Toronto—not the best area at the time.

The way Karen remembers it is that she and Mom first met Grant when they went down to visit. He was eighteen months old and was being fed a steady diet of chocolate bars.

There was a strange dichotomy about Mom. On one side, she was mean and angry and petty, and on the other, she was compassionate. When she saw Grant in that state, she rescued him. She told her niece, "I'm takin' him home and if you try to stop me, I'm gonna phone the Children's Aid." They begged her not to turn them in, and so Mom said, "Well, then, pack him up."

Mom, Grant and I moved in with Harold and his daughters, Frederica (Freddy) and Jeanette, and Harold's seven-year-old son, Victor. Jeanette was only seventeen when Mom told her to leave. She said she was trying to build a family for the boys and needed the bedroom. Jeanette was an excellent student and had just finished high school. She had already been accepted at York University and was determined to go. That summer, she moved down to Toronto, got on student welfare and started working twelve-hour night shifts at a factory from 7 p.m. to 7 a.m., seven days a week, to save enough for tuition and food and rent.

Freddy left us about six months earlier. At eighteen, she was a smart, quiet, athletic girl who was still reeling from her mother's death. But she had a great smile and a huge heart and spent a lot of time with me.

Living with Mom was a culture shock for Freddy, Jeanette and Victor because they grew up in the Baptist religion. No smoking or alcohol in the house, and Mom smoked and drank big time. She didn't hold her liquor very well either. When I was older, Karen, who was twenty-three years older than me, told me about the times she would come home from school and before they went inside, her older brother, Ron, would say, "Okay, you wait out here on the sidewalk. I'm gonna go in first and count the empty beer bottles on the kitchen counter." If there were more than four, they'd go to the neighbours' and wait for Howard to come home to clear the way.

Freddy had just graduated high school a year earlier and was working downtown in Toronto at an insurance company. She'd walk in the front door after work and Mom would tell her to fix dinner for the family. It was Freddy's job to clean the house and do the laundry. She was like Cinderella.

It was the last straw for Freddy when Mom raised her rent. She was almost twenty by this time, making $72 a week, and Mom wanted it all. Every penny. So, Freddy decided to move out. I was just a little guy crawling around when they had a fight about it after supper one night. Mom flew into one of her terrifying rages and started screaming and throwing things. Freddy ran out of the kitchen, scooping me up from the dining room floor so I wouldn't get hurt. She almost made it to the front door, when, *crack!*—a dinner plate bounced off the back of my head. Freddy tore down the street with me flopping in her arms like a rag doll. She didn't dare return until it got dark and she knew Mom had headed into her room for the night.

Freddy moved out almost immediately after that. A little while later, she met and married Rasheed. Whenever they showed up, it was a lot of fun. She'd take Grant and Victor and me out to play ball in the field or climb the monkey bars at the school. Grant and I knew the rules—no speaking to an adult unless you were spoken to—but Freddy was different. She asked us questions and paid attention to what we had to say. Rasheed was awesome too. He'd hold his arm out and bend his elbow and I'd do chin-ups on his biceps.

Freddy converted to Islam. She was already very interested in leaders like Malcolm X, and it was only six years since Cassius Clay had changed his name to Muhammad Ali. She was also very active in the Black community. She volunteered with underprivileged kids, taking them on field trips and to sporting events. She said she liked the value system Islam offered. To her, it provided security and consistency. She became a Muslim and started calling herself Na'ema, although she was fine with us still calling her Freddy. Harold wasn't thrilled about it. He shook his head and told her, "What's the next step, the Black Panthers?" But Mom was actually pretty open to it.

On Christmas and different occasions, we'd all sit around the large, oval wooden dining table, having dinner and playing cards. It felt wrong because it made it seem like we were a family.

Freddy noticed that Mom was getting even more unpredictable. We had a good-sized lawn and one day Freddy was playing football with some of the neighbours, as well as Victor, Grant and me. I was little, four or five, and Freddy noticed all the older kids were calling Victor "she." She found this very upsetting. She asked Grant about it. He told her, "Mom always calls him 'her' and 'she.'"

Freddy went into the house and found Mom. "Jeanne, why is everybody calling Victor 'she'?"

Mom said, "'Cause that's my little girl."

Freddy said, "That's ridiculous!" She had no idea why Mom would do something like that. He didn't look like a girl. He was about five years older than me, tall for his age and had the big hair. Freddy didn't see him as effeminate in any way.

Mom went on to sign Victor up for figure skating. In fact, he ended up being a pretty good skater. He didn't train enough to become an Olympian or anything, but he would often place in competitions. I'm not sure why she messed with his identity, but she did.

One morning when Mom didn't show up for breakfast, Freddy went to see what was wrong. She knocked on Mom's door and then opened it up to say good morning. Mom was lying in bed, her forearm flung over her eyes, and she was moaning, "I can't do it, I can't get up!"

Freddy walked over to the bed, concerned. "Why can't you get up, Jeanne? What's wrong?"

Mom moved her head from side to side. "I can't walk!"

Freddy moved closer. "Oh no. Why can't you walk?"

Mom sat up suddenly and glared at Freddy. "Because you pushed me down the stairs!"

Freddy said, "W-what do you mean?"

Mom narrowed her eyes. "I know it was you."

A few days later, Harold woke Freddy up at midnight and asked her to take Mom to the hospital. He said, "She's havin' a lot of pain. And she needs some pain medication and the doctor won't give her any unless he sees her." Freddy loaded Mom in the car and drove into Newmarket, but by the time they arrived, Mom was unresponsive.

Freddy ran into the emergency entrance, looking for help. She found the admitting nurse and said, "I have somebody in the car. I was supposed to bring her here to get some pain medication, but she's in the car unconscious!"

The next morning, when Freddy drove back to the hospital to bring her home, she was directed to Mom's bed. When Mom saw her, she started screaming, "They won't give me any more pain medication! Get me out of here! They won't help me! They're bad people! They're not helping me!"

The doctor pulled Freddy aside and told her they were not going to prescribe any more meds because she had overdosed the night before. Freddy looked at him, and suddenly it all began to make sense—the up-and-down moods, her temper and her erratic behaviour. Jeanne Joseph was a drug addict.

CHAPTER 4

Pretending to Be Curtis Joseph

I WAS SIX years old but small for my age. I stood on my tiptoes in front of the bathroom mirror over the sink and took a long look at the kid looking back. Long hair down to my shoulders. There was no regularity to haircuts. I might go a year without one and then, on a whim, Jeanne or Harold would take me to the barber. I couldn't argue because that meant the back of a hand to the face. Even though I never talked back, she might decide to whack me anyway. But I had good reflexes, so I learned to duck out of the way quick.

I remember sitting on the bus after a trip to the barber. Kids were pointing. "Look at your short hair, hahaha!" I turned my head to the window. I didn't want them to see me wiping away the tears.

Standing in front of the mirror, I'd open my mouth to try to see down the hole at the back of my throat. I'd wiggle my eyebrows, raising one up high and pushing the other one down, like Superman. I'd bow my head, keeping my chin down and looking up, staring at the kid staring back.

I could see blue eyes, but I could never find myself. It was confusing, like looking at someone else. I'd make a few more faces, and then, moving closer to the glass, I'd scrunch up my nose and clamp my teeth together. I'd never been to a dentist, but I had no cavities, probably because I didn't eat or drink anything with sugar—no candy, no pop, no dessert. No breakfast cereal, that's for sure. Nothing but milk until lunch, which was a peanut butter or Cheez Whiz sandwich. We had supper only if Mom managed to get up. I stood back and pulled off my shirt. The good thing about being so skinny was that you could sure see my muscles.

I was shy. Always quiet and watching. I stayed out of sight most of the time. But you know what? I thought a lot of myself. Not in a bad way, but in the way little kids do. I had an inner confidence. I don't remember Mom telling me this, but I knew I was adopted before I even knew what "adopted" meant. And I would recommend that to anybody who has an adopted child that you let them know as early as you can. Don't spring it on them when they're older. That's the one thing that was done well. I was told when I was very young, which for me, was a good thing.

In my heart, I knew I was the son of somebody very special. I thought my parents must live in a kingdom. That meant I was a prince from a faraway land. Someday my real parents, the king and queen, would come and take me back to the palace. I was pretty sure my real mother was pretty and blonde and wore one of those queen outfits the colour of roses with a royal blue cape, like Sleeping Beauty's mother on the cover of an old book I found kicking around the house.

My father was working as a knight, fighting off some giants and trying to save the kingdom. I figured they had stashed me with Harold and Mom to keep me safe. That's why nobody knew who I really was. Mom and Harold probably did, but we didn't talk about it because the enemies of my real parents might find out where I was, and that would be dangerous.

I didn't feel any sense of abandonment. I didn't. I never felt sad about it either. I knew that everything would be explained and that I would be with my parents again someday. Every night before I closed my eyes, I thought about them and wondered when that day would come. Until then, I would go along and pretend to be Curtis Joseph, Grade 1 student at Whitchurch Highlands Public School in Gormley, Ontario.

CHAPTER 5

Topsies and Knockdowns

SCHOOL WAS WONDERFUL. Whitchurch Elementary was one of the first schools in the area to implement team teaching. Mrs. Simms and later on Mrs. Sarr were our homeroom teachers. They were nice ladies. Our music teacher, Mr. Burrows, who was also our science teacher, was nice too. He taught us to play "O Canada" on the recorder. But my favourite teacher was Mr. Bucholtz. He was friendly and athletic—a larger-than-life kind of guy. Sometimes he'd bring his good friend Mike Kitchen to school to talk to us about hockey and character. Mr. Kitchen had won a Memorial Cup with the Toronto Marlboros and was currently playing defence for the Colorado Rockies in the NHL under coach Don Cherry. Don had coached Bobby Orr in Boston for a couple of years.

Two of my best friends were Mike Hinton and Harvey Libby. Mike and Harvey and I, we loved all sports. We lived for our O-Pee-Chee hockey cards. Bobby Clarke, Guy Lafleur, Bobby Orr, Wayne Gretzky, Darryl Sittler, Mike Bossy, Denis Potvin, Bryan Trottier, Larry Robinson and all the Toronto Maple Leafs. To us, those cards were as good as money. A big stack of them made you feel like one of the richest guys in the world. We didn't trade them, we gambled for them—playing Topsies and Knockdowns. At the start of Grade 2, my older brother Grant gave me a handful, and by the end of the year I had piles and piles.

The boys' bathroom was our casino. From Grades 1 to 4, I spent an incredible amount of time in there. If I close my eyes today, I can still smell the industrial cleaner mixed with dirty mop and see the slick, speckled concrete floor.

Knockdowns required good hand-eye coordination. We'd stake out a spot up against the blue square tiles under the sinks, and each of us would lean cards up against the wall. The more cards you lined up, the more chances you had to win. When it was your turn, you'd back up about ten feet and, using your index and middle fingers, you'd flick another hockey card towards the target cards on the wall. You kept all the cards you were able to butterfly down.

For Topsies, we'd all lay cards on the floor and take turns chucking more cards at them. Whenever one of your cards landed on another card, you'd get to keep it. Some guys would go into the bathroom with a huge stack and come out with only a few. It was like Vegas.

At school, we did a lot of track and baseball thanks to Mr. Bucholtz. I was good at track for two reasons: I had this spaghetti-like body and I had help from my older brother Grant. He built a long-jump pit in our garden and taught me how to run and touch and take off. In Grade 2, by the time the other kids were being introduced to it, I was already distancing nine feet. I had a big advantage. Grant also taught me the Fosbury Flop. Remember that? Named after Dick Fosbury, the American who won the Olympic gold medal in high jump in 1968. Grant found some old mattresses and set them up under a high-jump bar he constructed out of some scrap lumber and an old broomstick. He taught me how to run at it diagonally and then, just before the bar, pivot, lean back and jump up backward. You lead with your head, arch your back as your shoulders clear the bar, then flip your legs up at the end. You go over a bit like the letter *S*.

Grant should have been jealous of me because when I came along, Mom kind of pushed him aside. I was the shiny new object. She liked taking care of little, helpless things, like babies and dogs and cats. She often carried around a tiny poodle named Bojack. We had another poodle, a grey Standard named Bear that barked and barked and barked. Freddy's kids were scared of him.

I was a small baby and a pint-sized kid. That bought me some time in Mom's favour, but the shine was off the apple when any kid hit ten years old. It must have been hard for Grant, but he was a good brother when I was younger. By the time he was a teen, there was no supervision and he was able to get out of the house a lot, so that's what he did. But I don't blame him.

I wanted to play ice hockey with my friends, but I knew that was never going to happen. Mom said it was too dangerous and it cost too much money. Instead, I played road hockey all the time—before school, after school and all through recess. I always carried a stick. Anything could be a hockey net—a church pew, cement parking blocks, doorways. If a puck could hit it, I shot at it.

For me, there were only two seasons—baseball season and hockey season. And in Gormley, the weather was perfect for both.

Our school grounds had all this space that you could run on. There was a nice track, a baseball diamond and monkey bars for tag (when you fell off and hit the ground, you were out). Winters were way snowier than they are today. I remember snowbanks three or four feet high after the plow came by. Perfect height to contain the puck. Mother Nature's boards.

An hour after the morning school bell rang each day, my brain stopped being able to listen to Mrs. Simms. It wasn't her fault. I just couldn't concentrate for very long. I liked being near a window. There were woods next to the school. Three hundred yards deep along the whole width of the schoolyard. And it was full of pine trees. On a windy day, the branches would blow back and forth and grab the sun, making it look like a forest full of silver. We'd play soccer out there and make forts and use sticks for sword fights with the boys a grade older. In the spring, Mr. Burrows would take us out there for science class to look for larvae.

Every day, I'd sit at my desk and daydream about playing in the woods or winning hockey cards or sliding across the parking-lot ice and scoring goals. And then the bell would ring and I'd jump up and run out the door and do it all for real.

At Whitchurch, we were in pods, open-concept "classrooms," named after planets—Venus, Jupiter, Mars and Saturn. It was kind of like the USS *Enterprise*. State of the art. You had to shove your way through the older kids down a long, angled hallway out to the back where the pavement was. In the fall, we'd have races around the school, but by December it was cold and windy. Most guys would grab their coats, toques, mittens and boots and bundle right up. I didn't bundle up as much as most. I rarely had a winter coat, so I'd layer up with sweatshirts and pajama pants under my cords.

I was afraid of Mom. There was no love, no back and forth. I never asked for anything. I don't remember ever having boots. I don't have big feet—even today, I'm a size 9½. You know how they used to bind the feet of Chinese girls so they wouldn't grow? Well, I'd wear the same shoes for a year and a half, long past the time my feet had outgrown them. There'd be holes where my toes had worn through the leather. But I was lucky enough to get Adidas. Maybe Mom would go to the same store or something, but thank goodness she did, because I loved those white Adidas Rom runners.

It's funny how the body gets used to things. Yeah, it was cold outside in the winter, but I don't remember feeling it. Maybe it's because I never stopped moving. We'd grab our sticks, which we'd have left leaning up against the brick exterior of the school, and then run to the far end of the parking lot, where we'd make a circle and throw our sticks in the middle to pick teams. I remember how fun it was when you'd be running along and catch a patch of ice, and then use it to let the shot go and watch it rocket through the goal.

My upbringing, the fact I never had any money, made me a pretty reserved spender. I'm happy to buy things for others, but I have trouble when I need anything for myself. I was the same when I made generous amounts in the NHL. I'm not one of those impulse buyers. I'll look at a car or a set of golf clubs, or even boots or shoes, and I'll go away and think about it, and then come back and maybe go away again, thinking, "Do I really need this?" And then, eventually, I'll pull the trigger. Unless it's a steal. Unless it's a great deal, and then I might pull out the plastic.

Mike Hinton and I rode the bus together, and every once in a while, I'd be invited over to his place. Mike lived on a ten-acre parcel. I remember his three dogs. They were always running around and coming back covered in porcupine quills. I remember his mom. She was nice. She'd ask me how I was doing, things like that. And she always made great snacks. Hot chocolate and cut-up buttered toast sprinkled with sugar and cinnamon.

I'd sleep over at Harvey Libby's place too. The Libbys lived on a twenty-three-acre piece of land in Stouffville, pretty close to the school. Oh man, I loved going over there. Harvey's dad, Harry Libby, owned a print shop. They had a nice place. A big house, two storeys on a little bit of a hill with a walk-out basement, a big TV room, a pool table and an outdoor swimming pool. But as nice as it was on the outside, it was even better inside—around the kitchen table. Their family was tight-knit. Harvey had two older sisters, Cathy and Colleen. They'd laugh and talk about their day, everybody would be teasing and interrupting each other, and his mom, Irene, was friendly and happy, always buzzing around.

Mrs. Libby would make us grilled cheese sandwiches, and then Harvey and I would run outside and tear around the property. I was fascinated by the whole family and I used to wonder if my real mother, like Mrs. Libby, was also from "Nordern" Ireland and said things like, "Ach! You poor wee thing, didya hurt yourself now?"

At night, we'd sleep head to foot in his wooden Sears captain's bed, warm under his navy blue sleeping bag. We'd talk until his dad came in and turned off his wagon-wheel bedside lamp. We'd wake up to the delicious smell of bacon and his dad calling up the stairs, "Toad in the hole, boys!" which meant fried toast with an egg in the middle. I wasn't as big as most of my friends, almost half a foot shorter than most—probably due to the fact we just never had much to eat at home.

When I got a little older, there was another family I hung out with, the Weilers. I was there a lot. They all played sports and were very good at them. Martin Harding and Joe Weiler and I, we'd play road hockey after school at the end of Patterson Street in Newmarket. And sometimes there was this little kid who kind of hung out with us bigger kids. His name was Bruce Gardiner. That little kid went on to play in the NHL. Six seasons, mostly with the Senators.

Jean Weiler, Joe's mom, was great. Quiet and kind. Nice to us kids. She used to work at Granny's Tarts. She'd bring home muffins and tarts—apple, blueberry—and these little chocolate-chip cookies that were always our favourite.

The Weilers lived in a duplex attached. Modest, but to me it was the best. They laughed, they played games, they'd argue a little bit—but not much. There were two girls and two boys. Twins Jeannette and Joe were my age, and then there was Robbie and Carol. Their dad was Bill.

I started going there after school almost every day. We were always outside. We played tons of road hockey. Our little gang of guys, we actually used to play against other streets. There was also baseball at the park. And down at the end of their street, we'd go into the forest and play hide-and-seek. If one of us was spotted, Joe and I would switch clothes and keep playing. It was pretty funny.

I started sleeping there fairly often too. The boys had the entire basement. There were a couple of beds down there, and we took turns sleeping on couch cushions on the floor. I loved hanging out there and playing hallway hockey on our hands and knees with a tennis ball.

Jean taught me how to drive. She had a big, blue four-door Chevy with a white top—the Big Boat. Bill was a plumber in the days before plumbers made much money. They probably lived paycheque to paycheque, but they fed me often. Pork chops, Kraft Dinner, beans and wieners, hot dogs.

I thought at the time that all these families were rich. Maybe they were, maybe they weren't, but to me, all my friends were extremely wealthy. I think the most valuable thing I learned by hanging with my buddies at their homes was seeing what normal was. When I stayed with the Hintons, the Libbys and the Weilers, I filled up on their food and their love.

CHAPTER 6

My Very Own Cuckoo's Nest

Now, let me tell you what it was like growing up in a home for the mentally ill.

When I was ten years old and in Grade 5, my life changed big time. Mom's husband, Harold, was fired. He'd worked at Sterling Drug in Aurora as a production planner. He was a very good worker. Got promotions and all that. Then, all of a sudden, he got his walking papers. It was a puzzlement to everyone at the time, but looking back, it makes sense. He was probably stealing drugs for Mom and got caught.

Harold was out of a job, so Mom started doing home care for the inmates at Martin Acres. She liked it there. She was in charge of handing out the medications. The men took all kinds of pills. The owners, Al Martin and his wife, were getting older and were talking about retiring, but they had no succession plan. Mom went to them and offered them a deal. Harold owned an eleven-room house in Aurora. How would the Martins like to trade Harold's house for the business of running the rehabilitation centre? The Martins agreed on the condition that they kept ownership of the land and building. All Mom and Harold had to do was pay for the utilities. Mom and Harold jumped on it, and Harold signed over the house he and his first wife, Rose, had worked tremendously hard for.

I had no idea we were moving. I found out one day after school. There was no conversation about it, just "Get in the station wagon." We pulled up past a sign that said MARTIN ACRES and onto the driveway that ran in front of the house. Harold told me to hop out and unload my stuff. That wasn't hard because I had only a few shirts, a couple of pairs of underwear and three pairs of socks, two sweatshirts, one pair of blue jeans, a pair of cords and my hockey cards. My whole world in one suitcase.

I followed Harold through the front door, then through another door, up the stairs to the right, above the garage. There were four bedrooms up there. He pointed to the first room on the right. "This is yours," he said. The other doors were all opened a crack and I could feel several pairs of eyes watching.

I found out later that my room was with the men who were on the calm side. The other side was a little more dangerous.

Wellington was a pedophile, for sure. He was a big, meaty Black guy, sweaty and bald. He didn't talk a lot and he had a strange way of looking at you. Karen told me later that all the men were on some sort of castration medication, but Wellington would follow me down to the potato cellar and flash me. When I was down there, I'd hear a creak on the top step and I'd fill the bag as fast as I could and then hide. But he'd stand at the bottom of the stairs and wait for me to come out. I did my best to avoid him. Any time I had to go anywhere on the property where there was a possibility he could corner me, I kept my head on a swivel.

I finally told Harold about Wellington's habit. It was the first of two times I saw Harold get really mad. The other time resulted in a violent fight with my brother Grant. The memory of that fight still bothers me to this day. I'll get to it later.

Harold found Wellington and threatened to beat the ever-livin' tar out of him. No swearing—Harold wouldn't swear. I felt good about Harold sticking up for me, but it didn't change anything until the day Wellington tried it with Mom. There was a laundry room downstairs near the dining hall. Mom was in there, ironing, and he came up beside her and exposed himself. Mom didn't hesitate. She lifted the hot iron and tapped it on the tip of his penis. Wellington stayed out of the laundry room after that.

Tony was an Italian guy in his mid- to late thirties. He was about five foot ten and roly-poly, with dark eyes and olive skin. He was probably the youngest and best-looking guy at Martin Acres. Tony wasn't all there upstairs, but he took care of himself. You could see the comb marks running in neat rows through his thick black hair. He wore it long on top and slicked back.

Tony obsessed about his "thirteen imperfections." If you went anywhere near him, he'd tell you, "I have thirteen imperfections." And then he'd show you a freckle or mole. We were all told not to go out behind the barn because Tony might be lying in the sun, stark naked, out there. Sometimes he'd sit by a window in the commons room, take his shirt off and suntan. I guess it was his way of trying to get rid of his thirteen imperfections.

The patients rarely had visitors. I mean, nobody visited these people. Tony was one of the few guys whose family came by. They saw him a couple of times a year and they dressed well and drove nice cars. I never thought about what I didn't have or what I did without, but they seemed rich to me.

Little George would sit in the same worn leather chair in the vestibule, at a table for two, every day. He was a short, portly Jewish guy. He had blue eyes and a big smile, although he was ornery a lot of the time. He complained a lot—he wasn't getting enough food, he needed more cigarettes. "Where's my medication?" Stuff like that.

His job was to empty the wastepaper basket. He'd been a lawyer, but one day, crossing the street in Toronto to get a *Globe and Mail* newspaper, he didn't see a truck coming at him from around the corner. It rolled over him and the back of his coat got caught in the undercarriage and he was dragged. His cranium bouncing off the pavement for a fair distance caused brain damage. If you put garbage in the wastebasket he'd say, "Whoop! Whoop! Garbage, garbage, garbage," grab the wastebasket and off he'd go to Harold's big burn barrel out back. He was like Charlie Chaplin in the way he moved—really fast, but with a wiggle because he took such short little steps.

Karen came by a fair bit to help wash walls or take care of the patients whenever Mom and Harold went away. She'd rip a page out of a newspaper, ball it up, walk past George and drop it in the wastebasket. "Whoop! Whoop! Garbage, garbage, garbage!" And off Little George would go to the burn barrel. It seemed to make him happy.

Little George was a midnight raider. When people were sleeping, he'd sneak into their rooms and collect their socks and combs. In the morning, Rose, the lady who helped clean up for the men, would gather whatever he stole during the night and put it all back.

Little George's son would come visit every month or so, and when he came, he brought chocolate bars for all the men. Little George lived at Martin Acres for the rest of his life. He died long after we left. He wandered off unnoticed and walked in front of a train only two miles from the house. It was shocking because I'd known him for ten years. Brilliant lawyer at one time, from what I was told.

Big George—there was a Big George and a Little George—was a nice soul, a great soul. We knew him the best. He was the closest to us, like part of the family. He was tall, very tall—probably six foot three— and he stunk of BO. It was bad. He would have been in his fifties. He had white hair with a thinning comb-over and was kind of funny-looking because of his big features—big ears, big nose. Big George talked to himself a lot.

Big George's parents were good friends with the original owners, Al Martin and his wife. When he was eleven, there was a car accident and both parents were killed. George sustained a head injury that resulted in brain damage. It halted his intellectual and emotional growth. No matter how old he got, he was forever eleven years old.

Big George liked to do dishes and odd jobs. He would always ask, "Can I do somethin'? Can I do somethin'?" And Harold would give him little tasks to do. He was friendly, quiet, congenial and curious. He was always lurking around the corner whenever adults had a conversation. If he was doing dishes and Harold and Mom were talking, George would stop washing the dishes, drop his hands in the water and just stand there, listening.

Harold would tell him, "Okay, George, come on, finish up the dishes there."

George would nod. "Okay, Harold."

Big George didn't like it if Grant and I fought, even if it was a play fight. We'd tease him by pretending to wrestle and that would make him lose his mind. Every time. Like clockwork. His tongue would come out of his mouth and his eyes would pop open wide and his face would start twitching. I know it sounds mean, but honest to God, it was funny.

Ding Wong was a slender Chinese guy. Very skinny. Early forties, maybe. He had long nails and fingers yellowed with nicotine. Most of the inmates were like that because they smoked so much. Ding walked and walked and walked and walked. He'd leave the commons room, walk through the vestibule and out the door. He did this day after day, and eventually he wore a path all the way around the building.

While he was walking, he would just lose it and start screaming at the top of his lungs in Chinese, like he was being bombed in the middle of a war. And then he'd pivot and start walking fast around the house in the other direction.

When Karen came to visit, she sometimes wore this soft, fuzzy, colourful pullover sweater—red, yellow and blue stripes like the rainbow. Ding would come up to her and run his hand up and down the sleeve and say, "Nice, nice, nice. Like! Like! Nice, nice. Like!" He was absolutely in love with this sweater. One day, she gave it to him. He put it on and wore it all the time after that. Mom used to argue with him about it because he wouldn't let her wash it.

There was also a Big Albert and a Little Albert. Little Albert was short but wide. Harold did all the cooking for the men, but Little

Albert helped in the kitchen. Now, he didn't do meat, and he didn't do all of the cooking, but he helped make the soup of the day. That meant chopping up all the potatoes, carrots, turnips, vegetables . . . that kind of stuff. Little Albert mostly kept to himself, but he was nice. Always had a kind smile. He came to a sad end. Years after we moved out and the home was taken over by someone else, Albert went out the side fire-escape door for a smoke and stood on the stairs. Somehow, he fell through, broke his neck and died.

Big Albert was a monster of a man. Huge. Over six feet and about 350 to 380 pounds. He was bald on the top but had hair around the sides like Friar Tuck.

I was told he'd been a professional wrestler, kind of a violent guy. The story goes that he lost his cool and killed somebody. That's why they sent him to Nine Ninety-Nine and gave him a frontal lobotomy, which made him gentle as a lamb.

Once they saw he had been rendered harmless, he came to live at Martin Acres. He was strong as an ox. I remember him helping Harold move his big Wurlitzer organ through to the living room. It wasn't like the digital organs you see now. It was a big, walnut-cased, two-keyboard reed organ with pedals and it took up a lot of space in our apartment inside the house. Big George lifted his end up like it was a box of oranges. But when they got to the doorway and Big Albert went to shove the instrument through it widthwise, Harold had to stop him and tell him to turn it lengthwise. Because of the lobotomy, Big Albert had lost his ability to figure that out himself.

Big Albert would lie in his bed every night, repeating over and over, "I'm dead. I'm in the morgue. I'm dead. I'm in the morgue." One time, Karen was sleeping in the room below and it was driving her crazy. She hopped out of bed, ran up the stairs and gave him a little pinch on his arm.

He said, "Ow!"

She said, "Did you feel that?"

"Yes," he said. "That hurt!"

"Well, then, you're not dead in the morgue. Now stop it and go to sleep."

We had an architect living there. I don't remember his name. Maybe because he was nonverbal. Tall, slim, salt-and-pepper blondish hair, blue eyes. Good-looking guy. German, I think. Mom and Harold had to guard all the pencils because if he got hold of one, he wrote all over the walls in tiny, tiny, tiny print. Not random drawings—numbers. Measurements. He didn't have a tape measure or anything like that. He wrote down what was in his head—widths, heights and lengths.

He had a bit of a phobia about kitchens. When Mom gave out medication, she'd leave his little glass of juice and his pills on the kitchen table and call him to the door. He would come to the doorway and not move until she stepped up the small stairway into the dining room. She'd watch him come up to the table, pull out the chair, sit down, take his pills, shoot back the juice, turn around, open his mouth, lift his tongue to show her that they were all gone and walk out of the room.

This happened only in the kitchen. He'd sit in the commons room and eat with the others in the dining room. But there was no way he was coming into that kitchen while anybody else was there.

There was another guy—Dave. I didn't know much about him, but he came with long hair, really scraggly. He was brain-damaged from drugs, for sure. He looked like what you might think a heroin addict would look like. Absolutely fried.

He'd been a drummer in a band, took too much of something and burned his brains out. Harold played the organ all the time—the same Wurlitzer Big George helped him move. Church music—"How Great Thou Art" is one of the songs that still rolls around in my head. As a fellow musician, I think Harold felt for Dave.

Dave didn't say much. Life was a lot different for him than when he was in the band. He went from giving the finger to the establishment to being institutionalized. Harold cut his hair, like he did with all the men, because they couldn't risk lice, and he was issued government clothing. Pretty demoralizing for a guy like Dave. He'd sit in a chair across from Little George at the table for two in the vestibule, chain-smoking and staring at the floor. I think Harold worried that Dave was depressed.

He hadn't been with us very long when Harold spotted a full set of second-hand drums in the classifieds. He decided to buy them for Dave. He didn't check with Mom, so he caught hell for it later, but it was worth seeing Dave's face light up when he led him out to the barn where they were all set up. And, as much as Dave's mind was gone, he could really play those drums. He'd sit out there for hours, banging out songs like Iron Butterfly's "In-a-Gadda-da-Vida" or "100,000 Years" like Kiss's drummer, Peter Criss.

Like I said, Harold was a very kind and compassionate person. But he wasn't my dad. He wasn't interested in being fatherly to me. When I think of Harold, I think of him more as—a guardian, you know? I can't remember him ever giving me advice or anything like that. Mostly "Go water the garden, go weed the garden." The garden was his thing. I picture him in a straw hat, riding on his mower through this magnificent vegetable garden with stalks of corn and tall, fluttery sunflowers. Looking back, it taught us about hard work, because the garden was huge. Massive. It was half an acre.

I spent a lot of time with Harold in the car because he drove me to and from school. We moved to Martin Acres in Sharon while I was still at Whitchurch Highlands. They didn't make me change schools. Harold would drive me from Sharon to the school-bus stop, and then coming home I'd take the bus from school to the same stop— the bus didn't stop anywhere near our place. The plan was that I'd wait outside a gas station a few miles from Martin Acres for Harold to come and get me. Trouble was, Harold had narcolepsy. He would actually fall asleep while playing the organ. That meant I might wait until all hours of the night for my ride. Eight, nine, ten o'clock. From Grade 5 to Grade 8. Three or four times a week. He'd rarely be on time. But I'd have a hockey stick with me, and a ball. I'd spend most of that time shooting it against a tall propane tank shaped like a rocketship. Sometimes it got extremely cold and my fingers froze up, which meant I couldn't hold the stick. I remember jumping up and down, just shivering. I was too shy to ask the attendant to use the bathroom. There were occasions when I'd pee my pants, but in the end, waiting for Harold was a great thing because I used the time to learn to handle the puck.

CHAPTER 7

Processed Cheese

As HARD AS Mom and Harold worked to take care of the men, Victor, Grant and I were left to fend for ourselves. Today, I'm a big hugger. I hug all my kids and they hug me all the time, but I grew up with almost zero physical contact. No pats on the head, no kisses, no hugs. Um, check that—the Grade 7 dance was a highlight. Mike Hinton brought along the album of the night, a classic. Michael Jackson's *Off the Wall*. Actually, it was the only record he owned, but it was a great one. The boys were on one side, leaning up against the wall, and the girls were on the other, just like that scene in *Footloose*.

The girls spent most of the time pretending they didn't care if we asked them to dance, and we spent most of the night working up the courage. Laurie Shaw, Linda Addison, Alison Staley and Lynne Missingham—really nice, pretty girls with the shiny hair that smelled like shampoo, the rosy cheeks and the cherry lip gloss. Mike called them "hot ladies."

They would leave notes for Mike and me, telling us to meet them behind the school at recess. We'd go and they'd lean us up against the brick wall and kiss us. Alison Staley was Mike's all-time favourite crush. Mike stuttered a bit. And when he got uptight or nervous, it was tougher for him, so he slowed down.

One time, Alison caught him in the hallway by the lockers and she said, "Do you want a kiss on the lips or on the cheek?" He swallowed and, very carefully, without stuttering, replied, "Cheek, please." But those girls . . . I remember getting a kiss and then going back into class just on cloud nine. Just like Tim McGraw's song, "The heart don't forget somethin' like that."

When we first moved to Martin Acres, I shared a room with Victor. Grant was on the other side. Victor and I had two dirty mattresses on the floor. No sheets or anything, just some smelly blankets.

Mom had two cats. One was Siamese and one was a Burmese named Burmy. I don't remember the name of the Siamese. Those damn cats. They'd pee and shit everywhere, on our bedroom floor, all over our mattresses. We'd come home and have to shove the crap off the mattress and find a dry spot to curl up on to sleep. It seemed like Mom just didn't want to be a parent anymore, because she stopped doing anything for us.

Harold did all the work at Martin Acres, with help from a German lady named Rose. She was a nice lady. Very slight with a thick German accent. Rose was daytime staff. She did the patients' laundry, changed their beds and cleaned the rooms. Mom basically stayed in her room and read and slept. She wasn't very present. She'd come out to the dining room at lunchtime and eat the food Harold or Rose prepared, and then back she'd go. But Harold had married her for better or for worse. It was Harold who cut the men's hair, cooked for them and helped with the twice-a-week baths.

We never celebrated birthdays. They just came and went. I remember getting a card in the mail one time. It was from Metropolitan Life, a generic card that said, "Happy Birthday." Friends' birthday parties were a sore spot. I was the only kid who didn't bring a gift. Stuff like that would remind me that my life wasn't normal. But my friends were cool about it. They didn't even seem to notice.

I was pretty good in school—As and Bs—but never had any help with homework. As I got older, I found math pretty tough. Not only did my parents never help, but they never even seemed to care. I think I went after good grades purely out of peer pressure. There was zero pressure from my parents. Zero interest.

After we left Gormley and moved to Martin Acres, we stopped eating together as a family. At Martin Acres, all the food came in huge, white, industrial, government-issue boxes. It was all supplied. The men ate downstairs. They had their own kitchen. Harold always made sure that was running smoothly, but we never had family dinners. When I was about ten years old, I started making dinner for myself. I'd just grab food out of the fridge. I'm a terrible snacker now. I love to graze.

Processed cheese was my main staple. It came in a package the size of a two-by-four piece of lumber and you'd cut it into slabs. The hamburgers were the same. They came in a huge box, all frozen, and you'd peel them apart. I told you about the filthy old barbecue outside the kitchen door. I'd fire it up and throw a couple of burgers on the grill. They were the quality of sawdust.

Harold would put this rusted-out old steamer on the stove with a little water in the bottom and fill it with chopped-up vegetables. It would sit there for the week. If you wanted any vegetables, you just turned on the stove. It was best to kind of hold your breath if you came near it, because it stank.

I was always burning calories. I ran cross-country for the school, played road hockey, played baseball, all on fumes. I'd made my own lunch since kindergarten—two pieces of bread, a piece of cheese and some stale industrial cookies that didn't smell too good. We had this huge roll of Saran Wrap, and I used it to wrap up my lunch every day. No juice boxes or anything. I drank from the water fountain at school.

At home, there was milk. Bags of it. I'd always be cutting the corners with scissors and pouring myself glass after glass. I grew up to be five foot eleven. I should be bigger. I should be taller. No question, it was the lack of food. My kids are all like . . . big. My daughter's five-ten, Taylor's six foot one, Tristan's almost six-three—just under. Luke's six foot one, and he's sixteen, still growing.

Rose used to bring me clothes in garbage bags from the Salvation Army. I remember going through them. She had a heart of gold, and this sounds awful, but I remember pulling out those clothes and not being able to find anything to wear. There was just nothing. It's bad of me to say, but I'd go through the bag and think, "Oh man, I don't like anything!"

Mom would buy me the odd thing, like the Adidas. I remember getting a pair of Pony low-tops one time, and I was devastated. They were uncool. I was like, "I can't wear these." And she got me a Montreal Canadiens jacket. The Habs? Are you kidding? Everybody was a Leafs fan. You couldn't wear anything Canadiens! I was horrified. It was the most embarrassing thing. Of course, I couldn't say anything. I had to wear that stupid jacket for three years because there was nothing else. Believe me, I was constantly punched in the arm until I was black and blue.

Victor was a sweet talker. I wasn't built that way, hadn't learned that skill, but Victor, he could make Mom smile, and even laugh, at his stories. As a result, he got a car, a Walkman, nice clothes, the Lacoste shirts and stuff. I feel bad about admitting this, but I would sometimes take them out of our shared bedroom closet, wear them to school and sneak them back after school. When I walked into class wearing one of Victor's shirts, I felt like a million bucks.

Victor and I shared a bedroom for a couple of years. We drew lines on the floor. "This is your half and this is mine." He was nice to me, but neither of us talked to each other much. It must have been just awful for him. He starts out with this nice mom and dad and sisters and a happy family, and he ends up with us.

CHAPTER 8

Keep Your Eye on the Ball

I LIVED FOR the accolades of sport. That's how I got my attention and praise. And that's where I found some self-esteem. So, when I was nine, in Grade 4, and finally got the opportunity to play hockey, it was like winning the lottery.

All my friends played hockey, but I'd never even had a pair of skates. I knew better than to ask. Meanwhile, Karen had signed up her son, Mark, to play hockey on a house-league team in King City. The green team. But they were moving to Peterborough and weren't going to be able to make it for any more games. She took me over to the rink and said, "How would you like to take Mark's place on the team?"

Karen said my eyebrows shot up right off my forehead. "Yeah!" I said. "Yeah!"

I borrowed Mark's gear, stepped onto the ice for my first game and . . . I couldn't skate. I basically fell all over the ice. At that moment, I would be the last kid in the universe you'd pick to make it to the NHL.

Didn't matter. I loved it. The next game, the coach put me in net, because that's what you did with the kids who couldn't skate. We were a last-place team anyway. What could it hurt?

I played the last four or five games of the season and then playoffs. First place played fourth place and second place played third place.

Winners played each other. We ended up taking the championship. I couldn't skate, but I could stop pucks. That's how it all started.

Honestly, to play house league? It was twenty-five bucks, max. What a pittance. AAA hockey today? It's $5,000 now, which is a lot of cash, and it's not transferrable. I don't understand why I couldn't have played earlier. It doesn't seem money was the obstacle. But I believe Jeanne could be talked into things by sweet talkers, and Karen spent a lot of time sweet-talking her into letting me play.

Remember I told you about Topsies and Knockdowns? I have good hand-eye coordination. We were maybe eleven or twelve, playing road hockey over at one of the public schools in Holland Landing. Somehow, somebody took a shot and the tennis ball ended up on top of a hill in the schoolyard. I ran after it and teed it up with my hockey stick and it sailed forever.

When I was older, we played flag football, and the guy that we had as our quarterback was a Canadian university football player. A good quarterback named Jimmy Tierney. His son plays for the San Jose Sharks right now. Jimmy was an excellent athlete, a great guy, a super-nice man. He could throw the ball like nobody else, had an arm like a cannon, which made it tough to handle. He used me as his receiver. "Okay, just run, Curt. Run as fast as you can, get downfield and I'll hit you." Then he'd throw the ball and I'd always make the catch.

I talked to a guy who explained to me why I was good at sports. Bijan Pesaran, a professor of neural science at New York University, watched a few of my saves. He said I'm athletic thanks to a trifecta of systems in my brain, starting with coordination. Coordination comes from how you're moving in response to what you're seeing. It starts in the eyes. The periphery of the retina is where you detect movement. "What is going on? Is it changing? Where is it?" A pro athlete has a faster ability to quickly detect and respond, a faster speed of processing. Bijan says you aren't born with it. It is something you develop.

The next part is your motor system, which depends on where you're looking. If you are riding a bike and you're worried about a bump or a pothole and you look at it, you're going to hit it. You can't steer away from that location. It's like a magnet. You're entering your body in line with that location and you inevitably head towards it. But you can learn to orient where you're looking in order to improve your accuracy. The old expression "Keep your eye on the ball" works. They have measured the eyes of USA Ping Pong champions, using super-slo-mo cameras. Those guys are able to look at the ball right up to the time that they hit it. They see the ball, not their opponent.

And of course, everything depends on doing things at the right time. Watch a kid try to catch a ball. They're always too late—up to a certain age, that is, around five. And then they learn to predict where the ball will be. Our sensory systems are tied to our brains through wires and it takes time—twenty milliseconds, maybe thirty or forty—for that information to enter the brain. And then it needs to be processed by the brain, and *then*—this is the important part—it has to be sent out, like a command, along another set of wires, into your arms and your legs. And that takes another fifty to one hundred milliseconds. Believe it or not, that's a significant fraction of time. All told, about two hundred milliseconds before you can do something about it. By that time, the world has moved on.

A top athlete short-circuits that loop. We do not rely solely on seeing the ball to decide what to do. We predict where the ball's going to be and respond to that prediction accurately. The brain runs a simulation of what is going to happen. Ha! Perfect for me. I never read instructions, just tried to get from A to B and get there fast.

As a goalie, it breaks down to how well you can perceive and detect small movements. How a shooter is setting his stick, for example. What's he aiming at? Which direction is he skating? It's situational awareness and the ability to adjust where your head and body are pointing. Getting into position is more than half the battle.

Same story in tennis. The game's about footwork. Get your body to a place where your arms can extend to swing through the ball. The same in golf. The backswing puts your club in a place where your body can bring your arms back through the ball with the most speed and accuracy. When you're a goalie, it's all about reading and reacting. Not just making the save, but *preparing* to make the save. You learn it through trial and error, by facing thousands and thousands of shots.

Another thing I had going for me was my competitiveness. I had that competitive fire. I *had* to win. When I first played goal, I didn't play pretty, but there was no way anybody was going to score on me. I channelled my whole being into stopping the puck. Winning was everything. When you get to the NHL, virtually everybody has that. It's about the most competitive place on the planet.

CHAPTER 9

"Take a Knee"

THE YEAR I went into Grade 5, we moved to Martin Acres. Because of the location, I enrolled in East Gwillimbury minor hockey. The arena we played in was known as the Sharon Arena, because Sharon was the name of the hamlet within the town of East Gwillimbury. Grant drove me to the arena to try out for Atom B, and I made the team. I was ten and the only goalie, so I got to play every game. It was fun to be part of a team.

Our coach, Paul Torkoff, was a pistol. I mean, he was old-school. It was his first year of coaching and he was hard. Or you could call it emotional—that's a good word for him. It wouldn't be unusual for Paul to break a stick over the crossbar or against the ice or boards in practice to get his point across.

In January 2018, Calgary Flames head coach Glen Gulutzan stopped practice when he got mad, broke a stick and threw it into the stands. TV crews caught it and played it on the evening sports highlights. Some people were remarking that he wasn't showing respect. And setting a bad example for kids. I don't see it that way. I think Paul was showing us respect. He was treating us like hockey players, not children. Anyway, that was Paul. If he wanted to get his point across, he got his point across. And he could be very loud. He'd yell, scream—he'd kick a garbage can, break a stick. He was good for it all.

The first time he broke a stick, let's just say he had our attention right away. We were all at one end of the ice, lined up at the blue line, facing him, in front of the net. We'd been doing skating drills and he started in. He yelled, "knee," and we all went down while he gave it to us. We weren't putting in enough effort. Weren't trying hard enough. He expected 110 per cent even in a skating drill, and if you weren't going to try hard in practice, then he said that would reflect your effort in a game. Suddenly, he skated out to the end of the crease, turned and cracked his stick right over the top of the net. Broke it in half.

Everybody's eyes flew open wide and you could hear a pin drop. And in no way, shape or form was anybody about to give him any kind of backtalk. It shocked and scared us. The kind of scared that runs down into your throat like a handful of steel beads. Your whole body gets a bit of a tremor, and you think, "Does he mean *me*? Was it me who wasn't giving the effort?" True, he's giving it to the entire team, but you can't help but wonder. Again, we were ten and eleven years old. As an adult, you might be like, "No, you're wrong, because I know the effort I gave." But at that age, it's "What did I do wrong?" and then "Okay, I guess we're digging in harder here, then." That's all it was. You tried a lot harder. You gave more of an effort or you moved on—or he moved you on. That's all there was to it. Nobody quit. Not that you'd want to, but quitting wasn't an option in those days.

Another thing that Paul did, and it was quite a treat, was to invite us over to his house to show us Howie Meeker videos. We practised together once a week and played our games together, but I still went to Whitchurch Highlands Public School. I didn't go to school with my teammates, so we didn't know each other all that well.

I remember going down to Paul's basement. It was a palace. Wood panelling on the walls and a thick shag carpet in a deep, dark brown. We all gathered on the floor, sitting there on our knees or butts, just watching. There was an unlimited supply of Eddie Shack's Pop Shoppe pop, bowls full of buttered popcorn and Humpty Dumpty Ripple chips. Talk about a great way to get players to bond. Just a great, great day.

The other teams we played were Stouffville, Unionville, New-market, Aurora, King City, Bradford and Bolton. Little towns all around our area. Jeanne and Harold had no interest in hockey, so I'd have to find rides. Paul or my buddy Tim Francis and his dad, or the parents of another good friend, Martin Harding, or the Weilers stepped up. The Weilers used to pick me up and take me to hockey or baseball. They'd drive up and I'd be waiting on the driveway. They took me to a lot of games. The oldest brother, Joe, was on the team.

I was lucky that so many people looked out for me. You know the phrase "It takes a village to raise a child"? Yeah, well, East Gwillimbury did that for me.

CHAPTER 10

A Girl on the Team

I DIDN'T KNOW about this until fairly recently, and I am glad because I probably would have been crushed at the time, but it will give you an idea of how small I was. Around February, we went to my very first tournament ever. It was in Oak Ridges, about twenty minutes from Newmarket. We were doing pretty well, winning most of our games, when just before the final, an official from the OHA found Coach Torkoff and said, "I understand you have a girl on your team."

Paul said, "A girl?" This was in the day when it was absolutely taboo to have a girl on your team. It meant the coach could be suspended. "No, I don't have any girl on the team."

The man showed Paul his credentials and said, "Well, I'm going to have to go into the dressing room and check things out."

Paul said, "What? Who are you concerned about?"

"Your goalie."

"My goalie? Curtis? He's got long hair, but he's not a girl."

The guy said, "Yeah, we'll see. Let's go." They came into the dressing room while we were putting on our gear. Neither of them said anything, but when they came back out, the guy said to Paul, "Okay, no problem. Everything's good."

A little later, we went to a tournament in Stayner, Ontario. This time, we got to stay overnight at the motel there. I couldn't get over the luxury of it—from the stiff, clean sheets to the folded towels and free shower caps to the soaps tightly wrapped in waxy paper. We lost our very first game, which took us into the consolation round, but from there we started winning, and by the end I was named the most valuable player of the tournament. It was my first taste of real success. Everybody was happy for me. I felt good about myself. I took the trophy home and went to show it to Mom, but she was in one of her Sunday moods.

When she was like that, you'd get blamed for things that you never did—taking something, or moving something. Everybody got in trouble for things they didn't do. As soon as she saw me walk through the door, she narrowed her eyes and snapped, "Before you went gallivanting all over the place, where did you hide my extension cord?" Now, I was far too scared of her to even think about touching her stuff. I looked down, shook my head, and in a quiet voice I said, "I never took it."

I remember the look in her eyes. She was wild with anger. She started yelling. I was an ungrateful, lying little thief. She yanked me up by the arm, dragged me into the bathroom, sat down on the closed toilet, whipped down my pants, threw me over her knee and went to town with a hairbrush. She was out of control. It was terrible. It hurt, obviously, but I was ten. Having my pants down across her knee was awful—just so embarrassing. I shoved the trophy under my bed and forgot about it.

Apparently, the Peewee A team had been watching me progress. The next year, I moved up a level. And that's when I met some guys who would become my friends forever. I played two years of minor and major peewee for a man by the name of Jerry Campsall. He was a firm guy—well, not firm compared to Mr. Torkoff. But Mr. Campsall was with the RCMP and he was a real gentleman. I was always looking for role models on how to be a man. Mr. Campsall taught us a lot of that through example, like how to carry yourself at the arena. Just with his mannerisms on the bench. Very professional. He stood up straight.

He stood tall. He wasn't at attention, but he had a presence. He said please and thank you, and he was well groomed. Very soft-spoken— no yelling, nothing unexpected. He was very clear and concise in what he expected from you, and he was a man who expected effort.

And then, for two years in bantam, we played under a gentleman by the name of Warren Ruscoe. He was an RCMP officer too. Mr. Ruscoe didn't sugar-coat anything. You knew what he wanted and expected, but he got that point across in a mild-mannered kind of way.

You know the old expression "Always a bridesmaid, never a bride"? We were bridesmaids for those two bantam years. You want to be called champions of the Ontario Minor Hockey Association—the OMHAs, or the All-Ontarios, is the title that everybody played for. Teams in Ontario still do. We didn't get there, but I remember we reached the final four in both years.

Mr. Ruscoe taught us a lot about hockey, there's no doubt about it. Playing for him, that's when I started to really develop. He taught systems. More than just the power play and penalty kill. Instead, he focused on where to be without the puck. That helped me, because when you are in goal, it's not just about your position or responsibilities. You have to read every position, the whole game.

Then in midget, Tim's dad, Mr. Francis, applied to coach the team. Reuben. Ruby. Rube. He knew how to recognize people's strengths and weaknesses. Not everybody is Wayne Gretzky or Mario Lemieux. It takes a vast combination of players to make a great team, right? Mr. Francis was able to accentuate the positives in everybody. And again, he was another guy who was very clear about what he wanted from you, what you were expected to do. A disciplinarian as well. I mean, you know—there are rules, and everybody has a role, and everybody's expected to fulfill their role.

He was a Newfoundlander who worked on the line for North York Hydro, climbing the poles during storms when the power went out, connecting the wires, keeping the lights on. Tim does the same thing Rube did today. It's a dangerous job.

Mr. Francis got respect from us. He was always there, always on time, and he was dedicated to the team. That team-first attitude. He showed a lot of support for the team and for each individual player if you needed something, but he wasn't afraid to call you out on what you were doing wrong either. He would point out what you'd done right, but he would also tell you what you'd done wrong. Mr. Francis taught us to own up to our mistakes and move on. No time for sitting back and wallowing or whatever. If I let one in, it just meant I had to stop the next one.

Mr. Francis never played anything but street hockey, but he loved the game and he made himself better as a coach by taking courses that were available through the OMHA and reading books on practices and playmaking, and whatever he learned, he taught us. Most of our drills revolved around getting me shots. I was always being worked in practice. It was great.

We lost out in the quarter-finals in the first year, and then in the second year, our major midget year, we won the OMHA championship. The final was a best-of-seven series, and we were playing Niagara-on-the-Lake. In the first game, we got blown out 10–1. I hate getting scored on, and I remember thinking, "Oh no, what are we in for here?" You're in a provincial final and the first game you play, you lose 10–1? But we tightened up and played a bit better and won the next two games. Game Four we got blown out again, 10–4. Horrible. Between the second and third periods, I remember sitting in the dressing room with my head down, just steamed. I was so mad, I wanted to kick over garbage cans. More than that, I was humiliated. It was the haircut-on-the-bus scenario. I didn't cry or anything like that. First of all, you never want to show weakness or your team will lose confidence. And secondly, if the other team gets a whiff that you are uncertain, you are done for.

I lifted my head and looked around the room at the sweaty heads and downcast eyes. "That's it," I said out loud. "That's it. No more. No more. That's it."

We won the next two games. The final game, Game Six, we won at home. It was huge, especially for us in small-town Ontario. The arena was just an orange barn. No foyer or anything. Just this big A-frame, all orange. That arena was packed deep. There wasn't even standing room. A lot of fans, a lot of friends and a lot of scouts from junior hockey were there too. A lot of people from our high school, Huron Heights, came to watch. People in the community, people from all around. It was crazy. When the game ended, there was a monster pile-on. Everybody was excited. They jumped off the bench and automatically rushed me.

I crawled out from under the pile, and it was loud. I remember that. Jubilation all around me. For us, for the town, that was the biggest hockey win we'd ever had. Rube was standing there with his arms crossed. Proud. He was the strong, silent type, but you could see the tears in his eyes.

CHAPTER 11

Barenaked Lady

ONCE I STARTED playing hockey, my whole life changed. Mike Hinton and I would run out and shovel his pond and pull out an old wooden hockey net they kept at the back of the house. We'd take turns in the net, playing Showdown—like the skills competition that used to air between periods on *Hockey Night in Canada*. I was the French Connection—the Buffalo Sabres' big line of Gilbert Perreault, Rick Martin and René Robert—and he was Rick Vaive, the Toronto Maple Leafs' first fifty-goal-scorer, or sometimes Mike Bossy, because Mike had an Islanders jersey. If he was taking shots on me, I'd be Don Edwards, and then I'd say, "Your turn" because I didn't like being in net.

We both had wicked curves on our sticks. I always seemed to get one of those gas-station sticks for Christmas, but they would break within the first few days. Didn't matter. I'd find a way to get a bright yellow Cosom floor-hockey stick from the school gym. And then I'd shove a wooden shaft through the hollow middle and use inter-changeable fibreglass blades that I'd keep in place with a screw. At Mike's place, we'd turn up an element on the stove, grab a tea towel and heat up both sides of our blades, roasting them like marshmal-lows. Next, we'd wrap a towel around the hot blade, lay our sticks on the ground, kneel on them, and then grab the blades and bend them into a gnarly hook. The bigger, the better. Those curves were pretty aggressive.

I rode the bus to school—this is before they finished connecting Highway 404 to Newmarket and places farther north. We'd take Woodbine Avenue past the cornfields and horses and cows that didn't even bother to lift their heads as we drove by. I'd stare out the window without seeing the long driveways that curled up to the farmhouses and I'd daydream about hockey. I'd think about the next game and who we were playing. I used to keep all the stats. I'd have a schedule and all the scores taped up on the trim around my bedroom door and I'd calculate my goals-against average and my save percentage, all that stuff. Every time I walked by, I'd look at it. There were no computers back then. I didn't even have a calculator. I did it all in my head. Long division.

Because we lived out near Sharon, the high school I went to was Huron Heights. My Whitchurch friends didn't go there. That was tough for me because I was painfully shy. But I met a kid named Tyler Stewart who would become a lifelong friend. In fact, we ended up together on the ice at the 2002 Olympics. I was there with the Canadian men's hockey team, and he's a drummer, so he was performing with his band, the Barenaked Ladies.

———

I LOVED BASEBALL. I think if I had been born in the U.S. and had some luck, I might have ended up playing pro baseball. I'm like a dog—throw the ball, I'll go get it. I can't help it.

Tyler loved baseball too, but he was the wildest pitcher I ever played against. Tyler's pitching strategy was to throw the ball as hard as he could. He used to throw hard and fast, it was like a missile, but you were never sure whether it was going to hit you in the head, sail over the screen or land in the strike zone. Standing in the batter's box when he was on the mound, you were taking your life in your hands.

The first time I ever laid eyes on him was at Park Avenue Public School in Holland Landing, Ontario, at a school tournament. We were both in Grade 7. I played for Park Avenue and he played for Meadowbrook Public School. The rivalry was fierce.

Tyler had this giant Afro. Under a baseball cap it bushed out on the sides. If you look on Google for a photo of major-league designated hitter Oscar Gamble in 1975, you'll see what I mean.

We played underarm fastball. He had the intense windup, the big windmill. And then he fired it in there. Not many guys were hitting that day. Later, Tyler told me that when he saw me, he thought I was incredibly skinny. Just a scrawny little guy. He said his coach told him, "The kid can hit. He's got the most home runs in the school league."

And as much as he'd been warned about me being a hitter, our coach had warned us he was a madman on the mound. Coach called Tyler a headhunter.

I came up to bat, and because Tyler had it in his head that I was a guy who could hit, he threw me a pitch a bit to the outside, but I stepped into it and connected for a home run, and it was 1–0 Park Avenue.

When I came up again, he tried to back me up a bit by throwing a wild pitch. He grazed my head a little bit and he mixed it up with a couple that were outside. But the last one came right over the plate. Another home run. Next inning it happened again, and it was 3–0 Park Avenue.

Tyler and I ended up going to the same high school, Huron Heights. Alan Frew from Glass Tiger went there before us, and NHL winger Steve Downie came after. That area around Newmarket was good for hockey and hockey culture. It's probably doubled in size since I lived there, because Newmarket and Aurora are growing like crazy. If you follow Yonge Street northbound out of Toronto, Thornhill is on the south side of Highway 407. And then, on the north side, you've got Richmond Hill, Oak Ridges—which is a tiny, little place— Aurora and Newmarket. Newmarket's the big town in York Region. It's more blue-collar, and Aurora is more affluent. Aurora is kind of like Oakville.

Tyler and I played baseball together on the same team. Tyler was always outgoing and funny. I gravitated towards guys like that because I could never be like them. I was just too shy. I loved being around him—opposites attract.

He was such a great storyteller, complete with sound effects. He still makes me laugh. When we get together, I'll be like, "Tell me about the time . . . ," and he'll give me the Jim Carrey version.

Everybody liked Tyler. He was even friends with the teachers, which impressed me because I didn't talk to my parents, let alone an authority figure like a teacher. And the baseball coach liked him too. He made them laugh, and—oh my gosh, he was great. In high school, he played third base and I played shortstop. We played on the same side of the infield. I remember him just breaking me up out there.

Tyler was really good at sports, and he was also in the music program at school. He played bugle and he was in the drum corps. We were in classes together and we spent time in the library playing euchre or in the cafeteria, just joking around. I think what might have even bonded us closer was that he was struggling with his racial identity. I was older and had dropped the king-and-queen idea, but I knew I wasn't who everybody thought I was. I figured my father was some sort of amazing athlete. Probably an Olympian. The details of that situation weren't perfectly clear, and I didn't dwell on them, but I figured that's why I was pretty good at sports.

Right around the time Tyler and I first met, he found out his biological father was Black. He'd always wondered about it. He was this little brown kid with curly hair and his sister Melanie was a blond-haired, blue-eyed white girl, his mom was white and his dad was white. He was also getting it from other kids. Mild racism. Guys on other teams skating past and calling him the N-word. And then one day, he looked at his Grade 8 graduation photo, in which he's standing next to Melanie, and that *Sesame Street* song came into his head—"*One of these things is not like the others . . .*"

He asked his mom. "Why do I look so different? Why?" And she laid it all out for him. The man he had called Dad all his life was actually his stepdad, and his biological father was a Black man. A gay Black man.

It took Tyler a long time to forgive her for not telling him sooner. She had good intentions, but he felt like it was some sort of dirty secret as opposed to celebrating half of who he was. You would think that that discovery might make him shy or rebellious, but Tyler was a total extrovert. President of the student council, played on all the teams—football, hockey, baseball—performed in all the high school musicals, played marching drums in the Ambassadors Drum and Bugle Corps.

And then he became a drummer in a basement rock band that went on to worldwide success.

Maybe that's why guys like Tyler and me succeed—because we weren't sure of how we fit into the world. Here he was, this brown kid living with a white family, and there I was, a white kid living with a Black man. We laughed at that over the years, kind of like, "Maybe we're actually long-lost brothers or something." I remember Tyler joking, "Maybe we should just trade families. You come live with Bob and Sandy and I'll move in with Harold and Jeanne."

I could count on one hand the number of times that any of my friends ever came over to our house. Ty came by to pick me up one time. Rose let him in, and as he stood in the vestibule, he was freaked out by the institutional smell and the vibe. I appeared out of the blue and said, "Hey, man, how's it going?"

"It's going," he said. "This is where you live?"

"Oh yeah," and we walked outside. Big George was skulking around the corner, and the presence of a stranger kind of upset him. He came to me, babbling a bit, and I calmed him down. "That's okay, George. Don't worry about it, man. Harold will come out for you in a minute."

We got into Ty's car and he looked at me. "What is this place?" he said.

I just shrugged. "It's a group home." And nothing more was ever said about it.

We all wanted to play football in Grade 10, so we went out for the team—the Warriors. I was a wide receiver and liked it. Ty played inside linebacker.

The next year, Grade 11, we both had a chance to play for the junior squad again, and our team looked like it was going to be pretty good. We thought we might even win it all. But then Mr. Francis found out I was on the team. He was like, "You can't be playing football. You're our only goalie. You'll get hurt! You'll get killed!" I had to step out of football that year.

It didn't break my heart—I was small and had a bad heel and could barely walk. I was glad he said, "No football." So I found another sport. My buddy, Dan Parsons, was lean and tall. He played doubles badminton. He was looking for a partner, and we were a good match. I was quick and he had the wingspan. It was fun. We actually made regionals.

CHAPTER 12

"How's This Going to Work?"

WHEN I WAS thirteen, Grant moved out of Martin Acres after a big fight with Harold and I moved into his room over on the dangerous side of the house. All that stood between me and the men on my floor was a fifty-cent hook-and-eye latch screwed into the door jamb.

Harold always stuck up for Mom, even though she belittled him in front of everybody with falsehoods like "You're cheating on me! I know you're seeing someone behind my back. You're a cheating liar!" We all knew Harold was doing nothing but working all the time. I always thought her accusations were unfair.

Grant was more confrontational with Mom. Maybe because he had a different story—he was blood-related. When she was unreasonable with him, he would speak his mind. When he got older, he was becoming more independent, thanks to a car and a driver's licence. And this night, he'd had enough. Harold was at the organ and Grant and I were sitting on one of those plastic runners that covered our crappy red carpet, watching television.

Mom yelled something at Grant and he said something back, and then she lit into Harold for not defending her and stormed into her room, slamming the door. Suddenly, something just seemed to break in Harold. He stood up, tipping over the stool he'd been sitting on, and told Grant to shut his mouth. Grant challenged him, and they started swinging at each other. I was mortified. I had never seen them have a confrontation before.

They were about the same size and they were just hammering each other—in the head, in the shoulders, punching as hard as they could. I could hear the blows land as they connected. And Grant's face . . . there were veins standing out on his neck and his eyes were wet with fury. Harold looked like a bear caught in a leg trap. His teeth were bared, his head was back and his eyes were wide open and glaring down at Grant. The whole scene was sickening and traumatic. Two people I cared for, fighting over somebody who wasn't worth it. For years afterward, I would have to go for a run or a workout to shake the picture of that fight out of my head.

Three years later, when I was sixteen, Mom and Harold moved. Just like that. They decided to retire in Nova Scotia, where he came from. There was little conversation about it. I was left thinking, "How's this going to work?"

I met my first girlfriend in Grade 10 at Huron Heights and ended up marrying her just a few years later. I never dated anyone else. She was the first person who actually loved me. She had a sister a few years older, Sandy. Sandy was married to a carpenter named Guy. They were nice people. I hung out with her family a lot, and Sandy could see that the last thing I wanted was to move to Nova Scotia. She sat me down and said, "What if you lived with us?"

They met with Mom and Harold, who said it was fine with them.

Guy asked, "What about guardianship?"

Mom asked, "What do you mean?"

"Well, if Curtis gets hurt, we need the right to get him medical help."

Mom said, "I'll have to get back to you on that." And then they agreed that Mom and Harold would pay them $200 a month for room and board. Mom said the government would pay for me until I was eighteen. I thought it was strange at the time but figured it was just the way adoption worked.

Mom and Harold sold the business, packed up and moved to a place near Port Wade, taking Big George with them. I never saw Mom again.

Sandy and Guy were good to me. They were nice. They had a little bungalow, and they gave me my own bedroom. I did my own thing but didn't get into much trouble. Guy drove me to most of my games and bought me skates and a catcher. The $200 a month Mom and Harold sent didn't begin to cover what they spent on me. I stayed out of trouble, but Guy was a little frustrated with my nonchalant attitude. At the time, he thought I was as lazy as Bob's dog.

The thing was, I hadn't learned to count on anyone or anything and thanks to Mom, I avoided confrontation at any cost. I just rolled with the tide. When anyone asked me to do something, I'd say, "Yeah, yeah, sure," figuring everything would work out, without thinking it through.

Being punctual wasn't one of my strengths either. Guy got mad at me once when I missed a game. He had to work that night, so my girlfriend's brother picked me up and I didn't know where the hell we were playing.

I was usually the only goalie on my team, and you can't play without a goalie. But I was used to being picked up and driven around and never having to give much thought about where the games were. We didn't know where we were going that night, and we got lost. When we got home, Guy was waiting. He'd heard I hadn't shown up to play. He said, "I'm disappointed because this is what you say you want, but you don't seem to care about it." I felt terrible. It didn't turn me around completely, but I made sure to always take a good look at the team schedule after that.

CHAPTER 13

Wild Nights

ONE OF THE best things about living with Sandy and Guy was the food. I'd make sandwiches all the time, because that's what I was used to eating. After a game, I might come home and eat a whole loaf of bread and drink a jug of milk. They had regular food from a grocery store, but I didn't want to put them out. I had rarely been in a grocery store. Today, I love going to the grocery store. And every time I go, I take my time and walk up and down the aisles, marvelling at the food.

In 1984–85, my first year out of midget, I played Junior B for the King City Dukes. A big step up from single-A hockey, especially as a seventeen-year-old, to junior, with players as old as twenty. Adam Graves, who went on to score over three hundred goals in the NHL, was on our team. It was stacked, but we lost in the first round of the playoffs.

That year I also played two games with the Junior A Newmarket Flyers under coach Terry O'Brien. The Flyers had more goalies than they needed, so they let me go. In 1985–86, I went over to their biggest rival, the Richmond Hill Dynes, coached by one of my first coaches, Paul Torkoff.

Terry and Paul were always competing for the same players. Toronto got most of the best players because everybody wanted to play for Wexford, St. Mike's or North York. Those clubs were everyone's first choice.

Paul had completed his Level 4 Canadian Amateur Hockey Association coaching certification. It was mandatory to take Level 1, but he was eager to learn as much as he could. He read a lot of books as well. He was a big fan of coaches like Dave King and Roger Neilson and went to a lot of seminars at places like York University to tap into their knowledge.

Both King and Neilson had studied coaches like Viktor Tikhonov in Russia. Tikhonov's system had everybody moving at the same time as a single unit. Paul tried to teach us to play like the Russians. We'd break out with the puck and throw it to the centreman. The centre would loop back and a winger would loop over, lots of criss-crossing. You didn't shoot until you had a clear look at the net. That's what he tried to instill in us, and it wasn't that we couldn't grasp it, I don't think we wanted to grasp it. Our guys were creatures of habit. They had their lane and they went up and down their lane. The centre went into the corner and the D ventured no farther than the hash marks. Old-school Canadian hockey. That was it.

The teams we faced were doing the same thing, so Paul wanted to find a way of gaining an edge. And when we weren't doing something right, he'd fly off the handle. Look, it was good of Paul to try to teach us, but it was just too new. In the end, he settled for teaching us to switch up, which would sometimes at least confuse our competitors.

Hockey back then wasn't anything like hockey now. You would get a two-hander across the ribs, you'd get speared, you'd get slew-footed, you'd get sucker-punched in the back of the head. Rock 'em, sock 'em. As soon as it happened to you, it was your turn to go out and do the same thing to them. And then a whole melee would start up. Most of the instigators were the twenty-year-olds, and they'd take out the sixteen- and seventeen-year-olds, the young guys.

Fighting in hockey can serve a purpose, but the stuff we did at the junior level in those days was extreme. It was about intimidation. It was about control of the ice.

Terry O'Brien loved a good hockey fight. We were playing in Newmarket one night, and during the pre-game warm-up his whole team came out, gloves off, ready to scrap. Newmarket had an affiliation with the Kitchener Rangers of the Ontario Hockey League back in those days, and he would bring in tough guys from Kitchener. We had a big brawl before the game even started. It seemed they just picked a guy and started fighting. The first guys they went after were our skilled centre, Scotty Wingrove, and Randy LeBrasseur, our right winger. And me.

One of our players, Ray Buchan, got injured in that fight, and that was the end of his career. He got punched in the eye and he couldn't see out of it for the rest of the season. I look at that now and think, "Hell of a price to pay." But back then, it was part of the game.

Hockey Night in Canada's Ron MacLean reffed that game. He had just moved out from the West and it was one of his first junior games in Ontario. He wrote about it in his memoir, *Cornered.*

Everybody came to see the game. There was a full house . . . Six players were ejected for fighting in the second period. In the third period, with twelve minutes to go, a brawl broke out between the fans and the players. I looked up and saw fans spilling into the players' bench, fists flying. Jamie Macoun's dad, Charlie, a director and general manager of the Newmarket franchise, was standing behind the glass . . . I went over and said, "Charlie, I'm going to have to call this game because it looks like deep trouble. In fact, we've got to bring in the police." . . . People were getting hurt, so I called the game and called the police, who showed up but said they were not in the business of policing hockey games. The crowd was in shock. Calling a game was unheard of. Later, the OHA said, "Ron, what the hell were you doing? You can't call a game. It's a black mark for hockey." I wrote a letter back explaining that you have to have security at the benches if you're going to have those kinds of wild nights.

During those fights, the other team would put two or three guys on top of our tough guys, Kari Leivo or Marv MacNeil, to hold them back. Kari was only six foot one and 173 pounds, but he was fierce and wiry. He was very skinny and had quick hands. He could throw more punches and didn't get as tired as a big guy. He'd say, "You just throw. You don't stop. You don't stop, you just keep on throwing and throwing and throwing and throwing. If you hit the referee—oh well, that's his problem, not mine."

Kari's son Josh was a third-round draft pick of the Toronto Maple Leafs in 2011 and has played some games with the team. Kari never liked fighting and never encouraged Josh to fight. Never. He taught him how to protect himself, and how to drop the gloves if he had to, but he focused on making sure Josh was a good goal scorer and good puckhandler instead.

When Kari joined the team, it was made clear to him what his role was—even when he was trying out for the Dynes. At a Junior A tournament, in a game against Windsor, Kari took on Bob Probert in order to prove himself. Probert was already a phenom as a fighter. Absolutely feared through the league. Kari said he basically hung on for dear life. Paul Torkoff's teams were . . . let's just say they were very feisty.

Intensity works for some guys. I can't play angry. I'm calm, confident, cerebral, not scatterbrained. I don't need someone beating me over the head. I was tough enough on myself. If we won, I was happy-go-lucky. But if we lost, this terrible anger would just well up inside me and eat my insides out, and I think Paul sensed that, because he was good to me. Playing for the Dynes, I'd see fifty to sixty shots a night. It was a great way to improve my game.

Paul worked with all of us, even the goalies, on how to use our edges for balance. His thinking was that if you learn how to use your edges, it will be harder for opponents to knock you off your feet. We'd do a lot of "shoot the duck," where you'd squat down, stick one leg out in front of you and continue coasting from one end of the ice to the other end—on just one skate.

By the time the playoffs began, we knew we were out. But there was talk about a big trade between us and Orillia. It looked like they might make it to the Centennial Cup that year. Wingrove, LeBrasseur, Kari and I were supposed to all go up there and help out, but Paul wouldn't pull the trigger. A couple of the guys were a little sour. They thought Paul was saying, "You guys are being a bunch of jerks and so you can forget it." But Paul's feeling was that Orillia had nothing to trade. In the end, it didn't matter. Orillia went all the way to the semifinals of the Centennial Cup that year without us.

Chapter 14

A Tough Way to Go

ON NEW YEAR'S DAY 1987, a few months before my twentieth birthday, I got word that Mom had died.

Mom and Harold lived in a place so small I'd hardly even call it a village. Annapolis Royal is on the southwest coast of Nova Scotia, about a two-hour drive from Halifax. It's beautiful there, though, and it has a ton of history. At one time, it was the gateway to the New World. In fact, in 1605 it became North America's first permanent European settlement north of Florida.

Harold wanted to live there because it's where he was born. Harold's grandfather, Robert Joseph, was a slave in Britain who came over to Canada from England to fight in the War of 1812. Afterward, he defected to Nova Scotia, where the Mi'kmaq community took him in.

Mom and Harold lived right where the Annapolis River meets the Bay of Fundy. Their house had a little sun porch hallway leading to a small library. There were windows on either side, with daybeds under each. Mom, like one of her cats, would lounge in the sun, reading. On January 1, 1987, she was lying there, eating a grapefruit—peeling it like an orange and pulling out the sections. Now, the wall, or inside membrane, of a grapefruit is much thicker and tougher than the wall of an orange. She started to choke on it. Big George was in the kitchen, washing dishes. He heard her thumping around and ran in to see what was wrong.

Harold was out back behind their garage, splitting logs for the stove that heated the house. Working in the cold was exhausting, especially for a man his age. There was record snowfall that year in the Maritimes. That same month, Moncton, New Brunswick, just two hours from Mom and Harold's house, got over twenty inches (fifty-two centimetres)—almost two feet—of snow in one night. Harold had just finished stacking the wood onto a tarpaulin and was getting ready to drag it back across the yard to the house when he saw Big George running towards him in the snow—in his socks with no coat on. Big George was panicked the way he used to get back in the day when Grant and I would wrestle. Harold told him to calm down and then asked, "What is it, George?"

George told him that Mom was "making noises and funny faces."

"I don't know what she wants. You'd better come in and find out."

Harold said, "What are you talking about, George?"

Big George said, "She . . . she was holding her . . . her neck and, and then she closed her eyes and turned all blue. I poked her, but she won't wake up."

Suddenly, Harold understood. He ran like hell into the house and called 911. But because of the weather, it took over an hour for the ambulance to come, and by the time they got there, she was gone.

Her autopsy showed she'd had a heart attack, so we're not sure of the order of things. Did she choke on the grapefruit, which caused the heart attack? Or did she have a heart attack, which caused her to choke on the grapefruit? Either way, it's a tough way to go.

Guy called me. I was kind of in disbelief. He offered to buy me a plane ticket to Nova Scotia. I had never flown before. I couldn't be excited about it because of the circumstances, but I remember looking out the window as we took off and being amazed.

Victor wasn't there. I don't think Grant was there. Karen wasn't there. But I went because I thought it was my duty to go. I didn't feel anything at the little church service. In fact, I don't remember it very well. But that night, I sat on the side of the bed and started gulping air. I remember a feeling of loss filling me up. My head dropped, I covered my eyes and warm tears started falling on my fingers. It was the end of something and the beginning of something else.

CHAPTER 15

Drilled

BOTH GUY AND Coach Torkoff were calling all over, trying to get me a scholarship to a U.S. college. Schools in the States were allowed to pay the full freight for guys to play NCAA hockey: tuition, room and board and new equipment. My second year with the Richmond Hill Dynes, I was named the most valuable player in the Ontario Provincial Junior Hockey League. But still no bites.

Paul Saunders, who drove a delivery truck for Vince's Fruit Market in Sharon, became one of those guardian angels you sometimes meet. I'm not sure why, but he was a huge supporter. Paul paid for me to go to Johnny Bower's goalie school. I had never had any goalie instruction, and just to be there with all the other goalies was incredible. I was a little out of my element because I was very shy and embarrassed about not having my own equipment like the other guys. I was lucky because I was able to use the East Gwillimbury Minor Hockey Association's equipment. Everything—gloves, catcher and shoulder pads. At the rink in Sharon, I'd jump over the wire fence into the equipment room and then climb up on top of the Zamboni in the dark and stick my arms into the dusty open plywood shelf near the ceiling, and I'd feel around, trying to find the best pair of pads. The chest pads were so thin that in reality each was just a quilted jacket. I was always covered in bruises, fresh and healing—red, yellow, green, blue and purple.

But Paul Saunders signed me up for camp and paid my fees, which was incredibly nice. I remember dreading the thought of telling the grumpy farmer I'd worked for all that summer that I would have to take my final week off. I worked for him five days a week, all summer—for $5.50 an hour. I told him and was shocked because he was fantastic about it. He said, "Yeah, good plan. It will help improve your game. In fact, it'll be great for you." I thought, "Okay, that was easier than I expected."

Working on the farm was like advanced fitness training today, thanks to the hay bales. They were heavy—forty to fifty pounds each. When they got wet, they weighed more. You use your legs, like you do with deadlifts and the clean and jerk. Turn and push up—medicine ball throws—to stack them up on the trailer bed. It's all explosive movement.

That's how Bobby Hull got so strong. Every summer, he threw hay bales around while the other guys in the league basically took the summer off. He was in just as good shape at training camp as he was at the end of the season. That's what kept his career going into his forties. He wasn't just good, he was great because he was fitter and stronger than everybody else.

Being a goalie is more of an anaerobic position than aerobic. But I had strong legs. I was blessed with great knees. No concussions—lots of fluid around my brain. And a strong back. My only weakness was my shoulder. I had a dislocating shoulder.

When I was sixteen, in midget hockey, I got hit. I was freezing a puck when somebody came around the net and drilled me with their knee right in the back of my shoulder. It popped out and eventually popped back in. I didn't know what a dislocated shoulder or anything like that was, but it hurt for about a month. I was in severe pain. Never went to a doctor or to the hospital, though. Never did anything. It was brutal. That injury lingered for the next five or six years.

IN THE SUMMER of 1987, I was twenty and still hadn't received any scholarship offers. Paul Saunders had a son who went to Notre Dame College in Wilcox, Saskatchewan. Rod Brind'Amour was on the hockey team there.

Roddy was from Campbell River, British Columbia. He was a super-talented, ambitious kid who worked harder than anyone else on and off the ice. Roddy's mom was a school secretary and his dad was a pipefitter. He told Roddy, "If you don't wanna end up in a job like mine, you better do something different than the other kids." Every kid wanted to make it to the NHL, but Roddy decided his edge would be to train harder than anyone else. He never wanted to look back and say, "I didn't give it enough."

Roddy's folks didn't want him moving away from home and playing junior, but another player from his hometown, a kid named Terry Perkins who was a few years older, went to Notre Dame and spoke highly of the school. Roddy decided to take that route.

I cannot say enough about Roddy Brind'Amour. As I said, his parents were hard-working people. His going to Notre Dame represented quite a financial sacrifice for them. One time, they sent him a card in the mail for some occasion, and there was a $20 bill in it. Roddy exchanged the bill for two tens. He kept one and sent the other back. That's the kind of guy he is.

CHAPTER 16

"What Do You Have to Lose?"

EVERYONE KNEW THAT Roddy Brind'Amour was one of the top players on NHL scouts' radar. The *Regina Leader Post* printed an article on him in 1985, when he was fifteen, calling him a blue-chip prospect for the 1988 NHL draft and predicting he would be a first-rounder—three years before he was eligible. That meant a lot of college recruiters would be flying into Regina and then making the thirty-mile drive south to Wilcox.

Between 1970 and 1976, the Notre Dame Hounds were a Junior A team playing in the Saskatchewan Junior Hockey League, but the school didn't have much money and the travel was just too expensive, so they opted out of the league. In 1980, one of their players, defenceman James Patrick (who ended up playing 1,280 regular-season games in the NHL), finished Grade 11 and could no longer play for Notre Dame because he was too old. There was no real elite league. James, who would have come back for Grade 12, ended up going to play Junior A with Prince Albert. There were a lot of kids like him.

In 1986–87, the Hounds had a phenomenal team, led by Brind'Amour, who was one of the best seventeen-year-olds in the country. Their Midget AAA team had made it all the way to the Air Canada Cup final before losing to the Riverains du Richelieu from

Sorel, Quebec. The next season, Martin Kenney, the president of Notre Dame College, and Barry MacKenzie, the school's principal as well as coach of the Hounds, decided to apply to get back into Junior A. Barry said, "We might not win a game, because we are so young. On the other hand, we might be pretty good."

Back in Ontario, Paul Saunders made a couple of calls—first to Kenney, and then to MacKenzie, who had to be talked into letting me come and try out. He said, "No, no, we've got a goalie. We don't need another goalie." He had Willie Mitchell, who had backed them all the way to the national Midget AAA finals that year. But Paul persevered and even got Johnny Bower to write a letter on my behalf. Finally, Barry told him, "Look, you can send your goalie out, and I'll take a look, but I'll only guarantee him one thing. I'll guarantee him a ride home."

Paul asked me if I'd be interested in heading west to try out for the team. I told him I would have to think about it. I couldn't afford the tuition and had no skills other than goaltending.

I went back and forth about going out there. I spoke to two of the people I trusted, Guy and Paul Torkoff. Guy said, "Curtis, what do you have to lose?" When I asked Coach Torkoff, he said, "Well, Curtis, you know what? It takes care of all your financial problems. You're going to get your education, and you're going to play for a high-quality team. Why wouldn't you?"

Why wouldn't I leave my friends and the only life I knew? Because it was safe. I was MVP of the league. People knew me. Where I lived, they knew me as a goaltender—knew me as a *top-notch* goaltender. I was going to leave all that and go out west, where I didn't know anyone?

I remember getting to Wilcox and standing in the middle of the street in front of Notre Dame. People were talking to me, and a tumbleweed went by. This big old tumbleweed. I'd never seen one in person before. I swore I heard that theme from the Clint Eastwood movie *The Good, the Bad and the Ugly*—*woo-ee-oo-ee-oo, wah-wah-wah, woo-ee-oo-ee-oo*. I looked around and thought, "Where are the trees?" And then I looked down the street—or rather, the dirt road. It went on forever. There was no end.

I didn't realize it then, but going to Saskatchewan was the best decision I've ever made.

I was a twenty-year-old walk-on, wearing the scabbiest equipment ever. Starting with the old, dark-brown Cooper pads that doubled in weight by the end of the game because they absorbed all the sweat and melted water from the ice surface. I once told a reporter, "My old catching glove was as soft as the tie I'm wearing now." It went with a beat-up blocker. I looked like a gnarly old-school goalie from the '60s.

I think that's what stood out about me originally. To a man, the players all said, "Who *is* this guy?" But I hated getting scored on, even in practice. I wouldn't let them see me lose my temper, but I would get visibly choked when I was getting scored on. I tried on every shot. Never took any time off. The more often you do something right, the better you get at it. When they started shooting on me, they were like, "How did this guy drop through the cracks?"

Students at the college usually supplied their own equipment. In my case, that wasn't possible. Martin Kenney, who was known for his deal-making skills, headed into Regina to meet with the owner of Kyle Sporting Goods—Montreal Canadiens legend Bill Hicke. Knowing that Hicke had a soft spot for hockey players, Kenney told him, "Look after this guy. He's going to take us far. The lad doesn't have the money, but you know us—we'll find it somehow. Set him up with the best equipment you've got." Hicke sold the equipment to Kenney at less than cost.

There is no smell in the world as wonderful as the smell of new leather pads—except maybe raw lumber in a new house. When our manager, Jacques Gauvin, handed them to me in the dressing room, it was like stepping into a dream. They were Heaton pads, no less. Gorgeous. Amazing. They really were. And the colour scheme— white down the middle with red on the sides and black bands across the shins. I'd never had colour on my pads—it was always old brown leather. This new equipment was not only new and improved but colourful and stylish too! I never had any money, but I always liked to look good, right from the time I "borrowed" clothes out of Victor's closet. And my glove was huge! I was used to something the size of an old baseball catcher's mitt, but this thing, it could stop a freight train. And my blocker—it was a beauty too. All white with stiff curves. It would not only protect me but let me deflect the puck into the corners. I remember looking at my stuff and thinking, "Wow! What did I ever do to deserve all this?" And when I stepped out on the ice in that new gear, which weighed half of what I was used to and yet provided better protection, I didn't let anything by. I would wear those pads right into college, and they made me look good because they became covered in black puck marks. Puck marks are good. Puck marks mean you are stopping pucks.

The food at Notre Dame was amazing. They had a school cafeteria where you could line up and eat as much as you wanted. Meat loaf with plenty of ketchup! Pork chops and gravy! Mashed potatoes! Salad! Buns! Dessert and unlimited glasses of milk! Breakfast was eggs and bacon, with toast and porridge sticky with brown sugar. Oh my God, so good. On top of that, there were Crock-Pots going in the trailer I shared with a few teammates and in all the dorms. We'd make "Krafti-ichi" and cheese on a regular basis. All you needed was water, Kraft Dinner and ichiban noodles. Absolutely delicious.

We played ninety games that season. That's a monster schedule, more games than an NHL regular season. Most players found it hard to keep the weight on, but in my case, I left a couple of inches taller, and heavier, with more muscle. Being on the ice every day and eating good food turned me into a horse, strong and durable. The farm work had given me big legs for my size, and they became even stronger.

That little kid half the size of everyone else in my high school basketball team picture? He just couldn't compete. He was too weak—no legs. In baseball, I remember running as hard as I could to get to first. My head was almost exploding with the effort, but I had no power. My legs were under there somewhere. They just needed food. I came to Notre Dame wearing shirts with a 15½-inch neck. When I left, I wore a size 17.

CHAPTER 17

The Hounds

MY FIRST GAME as a Hound was a pre-season game down in Minot, North Dakota. We took the bus down, about a four-hour trip. None of my teams had ever had a real bus. We'd just travelled in school buses where we threw all the equipment in the back. But this one, even though it was old and rickety, even had some sleepers in it. We played cards and listened to music, and some of the boys studied. Over half the guys were still in high school, and a few went to Regina for classes.

I stepped onto the ice in my new equipment and stopped twenty shots in the first period, and in between the first and second periods the University of North Dakota offered me a scholarship on the spot. At the end of the game, the University of Wisconsin came up to me and did the same. I went from no one interested to two scholarship offers. Barry pulled me aside afterward and told me, "Curtis, you are going to have your pick of a lot of colleges by the end of the season."

On the bus on the way home, a couple of the guys looked a little worried and asked me if I was going to leave the team. I told them, "You know what? I think I'll stick it out with you guys for the rest of the year."

———

BACK IN THE day, Notre Dame had the "old boy, new boy" system. It was a lot harsher environment than today. The old boys ran the school when teachers weren't around. For the young guys coming in, it was a little bit of a survival-of-the-fittest kind of thing. There was no mom or dad around to go to if things weren't working. You just had to figure it out. And I think that's what made that place special.

I mean, times have changed and the school has had to adapt. I doubt that system exists anymore, but if an old boy came into a new boy's room and said, "Here's a toothbrush—go clean the shitter, and it better be *clean*," the new boy would do it. And if he didn't, he'd have ten old boys on top of him, giving him shots to the arm. It sounds rough, but the guys on the team had all come up through the system, and so, by the time they were seventeen, they'd become tougher and hardened up enough to be able to play like men.

I was a new boy but probably one of the oldest new boys in the history of the school, and I wasn't living in the dorm. I didn't have that same experience. In fact, I lived in a trailer on the property with five other junior players, all guys who had already graduated high school. It was your typical single-wide 1970s trailer. A vintage tin trailer in the middle of the Prairies. It was split into two halves, with a couch and TV in the middle. The back half had bunk beds where four of us slept. We used the top bunks as our closets—we just piled our clothes and stuff all over them.

The trailer was great. People who came from a great house and a great life and had had everything handed to them might look at it and go, "*Pfft*, I'm not staying here. Live in a trailer with a bunch of guys?" But I loved it. A trailer full of guys who played hockey? It was awesome.

The six guys in the trailer were Guy Sanderson, Tom O'Rourke, Darrin MacKay, Rob Schriner, me and our other goalie, Willie Mitchell. The "maintenance crew." We did various jobs at the school—shovelled snow, mowed grass, hauled garbage and did odd jobs around the community.

Guy Sanderson was the only guy I know who could give himself a nickname and everybody would start using it. And he gave himself a new one every month or so. He was hilarious. He called himself "Wolfie." He called himself "Amadeus." He called himself "The Bod" in jest, because we had Rod Brind'Amour, and so he was teasing him a bit. He was hilarious, that kid.

He had fun in the game, but that doesn't mean he let up on the ice. He was still effective. He'd played two years for Barry, but Barry's as old-school as they come and you didn't fool around. At the start of the season, Barry told Guy, "You won't be able to play for me. You don't work hard enough. No sense in coming back, because you're not going to make the team."

Guy said, "Can I show you?"

"If you want to, but you've got a strike against you because I watched you play. You've got talent, you've got a lot of skill, but you just don't have a work ethic that is going to sit with me."

Guy dialed down his antics in front of Barry and he ended up back on the team.

He has one of the driest senses of humour of anyone I know. I saw competitors in the faceoff circle thrown off when he'd start talking about his sexual frustrations with his girlfriend. It's hard to win a faceoff when you're laughing. He always had a quip. Some of them not exactly appropriate. His younger brother, Geoff, played for years in the NHL, but when Guy decided to apply himself, he was as talented as anyone.

Darrin MacKay—that guy could talk a dog off a meat wagon. He lives in Calgary now, working in oil and gas. His nickname is Wiz. He got it in Grade 10 after his first practice at Notre Dame. Nobody knew him, but he could skate so darn fast. Faster than anybody on our team, that's for sure. We called him the Wizard or Wiz. Tommy O'Rourke gave the nickname to him.

Wiz is from Saltcoats, just outside Yorkton. He has that small-town Saskatchewan sense of humour. You know—"That guy's equipment smells so bad, it'd knock a buzzard off a shit wagon at forty paces." Stuff like that. Constantly. "Hey, nice haircut. You get a free bowl of soup with that?" God, he was funny.

Rob Schriner was the best third-line centre you could ask for because he was punishing as a player. Schrinny never stopped hounding the puck. But off the ice, he was one of those real quiet guys, a small-town Prairie boy from Colonsay. He had a humility about him, but he could be quietly sarcastic. I don't know what it was, but we had a lot of guys who didn't say a ton, but when they did, it was super funny. And I think Rob showed great leadership. He could've been our captain as well.

Willie Mitchell, our other goalie, was from Windsor, Ontario. Best-looking guy on the team. He's the one the ladies always flocked to, for sure. Willie was the Hounds' star goalie in midget. When I showed up at camp, Willie was their guy. It was obvious the guys had a lot of respect for him. I admired Willie because he never showed any resentment to being my backup. Never. In fact, we became good friends. Of course he wanted to play, but he stepped back and gave me total support. Class all the way.

Tom O'Rourke was tough. Tommy and I spent a lot of time together. He was like a little brother. I was twenty and he was seventeen, but we hit it off. Tom and a lot of the younger guys sort of looked up to Rod and me, Rod because he was captain and me maybe because I was older. That was a first for me, feeling sure enough about my own strength to help other guys like that.

Remember, Wilcox was very small—no McDonald's, no 7-Elevens. There was nothing to do but practise, train, play, eat and sleep. All we had was each other. And that made us incredibly close.

At night, we'd sit in the trailer and listen to the local radio station talk about the Saskatchewan Junior Hockey League. Tommy and some of the other guys would prank-call the station, giving us props.

"This Curtis Joseph guy? I think he's just great!" "Rod Brind'Amour, what round do you think he's gonna go in? First, right?" "What do you think about this team at Notre Dame? I think they are the best in the country." It was hilarious.

In October, at the start of the season, a few of us were driving around in this three-ton truck, a farm truck with the big sides on it. We were picking up mattresses in Wilcox for one of the dorms. As we were driving down Main Street, Tommy and I started wrestling on the mattresses in the back of the truck. We hit a bump and I bounced up and over the tailgate, onto the road. Darrin MacKay was driving, and he slammed on the brakes and jumped out. Everybody's heart just kind of stopped. But when I hit the ground, I just kind of automatically did a drop and roll. When I stood up, they all started breathing again, and we were able to laugh about it. I'm not sure whether Barry ever found out about that one. I know he wouldn't have been impressed.

We did other stupid things, of course, like the Chinese fire drill. I don't like that expression now, but that's what we used to call it. We'd drive around a field and the passenger would jump out the window, run around the truck—while it was moving—and hop into the driver's seat, while the driver would slide over to the passenger side, hop out through the window and then jump through the window into the back seat. And if you lived in Saskatchewan back in the day, you would "bumper shine"—hang on to the back bumper while the driver would drive in circles on icy roads, trying to shake you off. Yeah, I know. Real smart.

Tommy had tremendous parents, Barb and Dennis. They'd drive down from Edmonton to come to our games and bring food, not just for him but for all of us. Barb and Tom's sister Shelly would clean up the trailer and cook. They'd even drive Tom and me into Regina to go shopping. If they bought Tom a new winter coat, they bought me one too. Barb still sends me Christmas cards.

Just like the Weilers, Tom's mom and dad treated me like one of their own. I remember thinking, "Wow, what a great family." When

I saw tight, loving families like that, I'd feel a bit of a pang. Not of jealousy—I was happy for my friends—but I'd get this feeling and think, "I hope I will be loved like that someday."

CHAPTER 18

The Bear

BARRY MACKENZIE—"THE BEAR"—was one of the best hockey coaches at any level. He never let you let up, and he demanded the best out of us. That helped me as I moved on. He had tremendous hockey knowledge, and he just hammered it into us. I owe a lot to him.

We were a very good team that year. Our record was 53–5–2. That's a lot of wins. But win or lose, if MacKenzie didn't think we played well or didn't play up to the standard that he expected, then "Hurricane Bear" came out to coach. Barry used to tell the team that no matter which stage of the game we were in, we could always learn something—prepare for the future. And there's always something you can learn. There was a game against Estevan where we won. Blew them out without a ton of effort. About halfway in, guys started dumping set responsibilities and rushing the puck, and they started forgetting about backchecking. Letting up.

He pulled us in during the second period. "You're not listening," he said, and told us to stick to our plan. A little while later he pulled us in again and said, "You're not listening." And then, partway through the third period, he pulled us in a final time and said, "You're not listening, so I'm not talking."

We won. We beat the team by about five goals. We came in the room all happy, and Barry walked in after us and said, "Keep your gear on. You missed out on about thirty minutes of where we could have learned something different. We are going to make it up now." He didn't like the way we won. He didn't think we played well enough or hard enough. All I remember is going back out on the ice and looking at the players from Estevan carrying their bags out of the rink, and here we were getting bag-skated because we won 7–2. I think at that point, Estevan realized there wasn't much chance of beating us the rest of the year.

We skated hard for the next half-hour. Multiple players used the garbage cans he had lined up against the boards. Yeah, we'd won by a big margin, but in his mind we weren't going to win a championship playing the way we played that day. That lesson stuck with us. You have to be able to do it right all the time, no matter what, and that's what he drove home to all his players.

You know, when I first got there, I had this cheesy 'stache that I shaved off right away because, when I saw the guys with their baby faces and mullets, I thought, "Aw geez, they're all so young. I gotta fit in." But then you start playing together and you forget about age.

Tim Green was all heart. He'd take shots off the ankle, soak his foot in a five-gallon pail of ice between periods, and then put his skate back on and go back at it. He'd throw his body in front of the puck at any given time. A real team guy, Tim was.

David Stevens. "Haah!" That's what we called him. I don't even know how to spell it, and I have no idea why. It just kind of stuck. A 140-pound guy, and he held his own on the ice. Full of skill, he finished third in scoring on the team that year. Very quiet, but every once in a while he'd throw out quiet barbs that would double you over. Didn't command a lot of attention, but man, when he made one of those observational comments, it was gold.

1 | Putting up a tent with Harold. He loved the outdoors. COURTESY JEANETTE TURNER AND FREDERICA JOSEPH

2 | I remember being worried about drowning because I couldn't swim. My cautious nature continued into adulthood (although I surprise myself from time to time). COURTESY JEANETTE TURNER AND FREDERICA JOSEPH

3 | With my big brothers, Victor and Grant. I'm the shrimp in the middle. COURTESY JEANETTE TURNER AND FREDERICA JOSEPH

Victor looking fly at Canada's Wonderland amusement park in Vaughan, Ontario. He used to sneak me in through the workers' entrance. COURTESY JEANETTE TURNER AND FREDERICA JOSEPH

A rare photo of me with my mother, Jeanne. She never joked around, and I was afraid of her at the time. COURTESY JEANETTE TURNER AND FREDERICA JOSEPH

The house at Martin Acres. We took this photo when I went back in 2018, for the first time in thirty years. The trip brought a lot of raw feelings to the surface. COURTESY KIRSTIE MCLELLAN DAY

Playing for Sharon when I was ten, with borrowed equipment. Can you believe I used that same Titan goalie stick for four years?

Playing for Sharon at an Atom B tournament. Beside me is Ed Harding, who drove me to hockey and baseball most of the time. He really looked out for me. COURTESY PAUL TORKOFF

My biological father, Curtis Nickle, and my biological mother, Wendy Munro, close to the ages they were when I was born. PHOTO OF WENDY MUNRO COURTESY WENDY GRAVES

A photo of me next to one of my biological father, Curtis Nickle. There is a strong family resemblance. He was just a teenager when I was born, so I never really got to know him. Photo of Curtis Joseph Courtesy Kirstie McLellan Day

A school picture taken when I was in Grade 10. I never had short hair until my teammates in junior chopped it off with scissors during rookie initiation.

Man, I loved to play baseball. I played sports all day, powered by a morning glass of milk and a cheese sandwich for lunch.

My high school basketball team. I'm in the first row, second from the left. Looks like there was no minimum height requirement!

Here I'm wearing what is obviously a jacket borrowed from Victor's closet—unbeknownst to him.

Here I am back in 1986, when I played with the Dynes. I had some serious eyebrows back then, including the one over my lip.

As a twenty-year-old, playing in the Saskatchewan Junior Hockey League All-Star Game. That equipment propelled me all the way to the NHL.

With long-time friend Tyler Stewart, drummer for the Barenaked Ladies, at Doug Gilmour's charity event, Dougieball!

Left to right: Shane Doan, Taylor Joseph, me, Luke Joseph and Sean Hill. It's a good day when your boys are old enough to play with these two warriors!

Brett Hull is either singing a song from the '60s in his head or imagining how good he'd be if he only had someone to play with (this was pre–Adam Oates). COURTESY SUN MEDIA

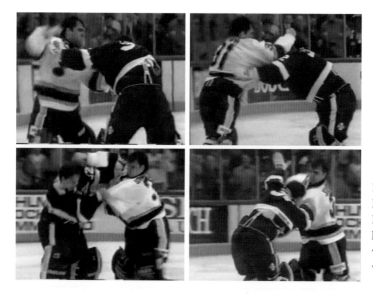

In a 1993 goalie fight with Detroit's Tim Cheveldae. I went in thinking, "Just keep throwing!" COURTESY THE NATION NETWORK/ WWW.HOCKEYFIGHTS.COM

Joby Messier was a local guy from Wilcox. He was a serious guy and a fierce competitor. No matter the size or reputation, he was ready to go. When he turned it on, he turned it on. Strong as an ox. He bounced on a trampoline for years as a kid, and his thighs were like tree trunks. He's some kind of cousin to Mark Messier, but I never heard him mention it. Joby was his own man and he still is. He didn't count on anybody, that guy.

Jeff Kerr had curly hair with these chubby cheeks and a round face. His nickname was Fatty. He and Jeff Batters were good buds because they both grew up in B.C. Jeff's from just outside Campbell River, the same town as Rod Brind'Amour. They played bantam hockey together. Jeff was an amazing bantam hockey prospect. He was as good as there was in Canada. He came to Notre Dame as a big name—bigger than Rod, initially. He'd wind up for a slapshot and the opposition goalie would almost move out of the net. He had a heck of a wrist shot too. What a joy to have around. He'd bring a lot of levity to the room.

Scott Pellerin is one of the nicest guys I know. Just such a fierce competitor, but humble. He was so good and yet the last one to take any credit. He always deflected the glory onto others. What a classy, classy guy. Solid, willing to take the body, good offensively, good on the power play. He wasn't the tallest guy, but boy, could he hit. He'd take down guys twice his size with his big barrel chest. He just ran them over. Scott was probably one of the main reasons we went all the way. He was a Hobey Baker Award winner at the University of Maine. He played over five hundred games in the NHL, but if he'd been drafted by any team other than the New Jersey Devils, he could've easily played eight hundred or a thousand games. Scott spent a long time in the minors because the Devils were winning Cups at the time and they probably didn't feel the need to make too many roster changes.

Greg Beaucage was a solid third- and fourth-line guy. What I liked about Boker is he became kind of a role player for our team. He was a bit of a scrapper, even though he was pretty undersized. But he had game. He sacrificed a few teeth hitting guys, fighting, killing penalties. Fearless.

Jason Herter was only sixteen years old. And yet, he might have been the guy with the most talent on that team in '87–88, and we had some good players, as you've probably guessed. Great shot, great passer, great skater. For the level we were playing at there, he was probably one of the best defencemen in Canada. He was a player at that age, that's for sure. He was so skilled. He had the size, he had all the tools. He was a first-round pick by the Vancouver Canucks, but injuries got in the way of his career.

Llew Ncwana was, and still is, a guy that you think of and you just chuckle. He was a friend to everyone. Llewie's from Ottawa, and his dad, Ezra, was a giant of a man who spoke with an African accent. When he came to visit, it was, "Lleeeweee Ncwaaaannna, come here and give your fadder a beeeg hog!" Llew was such a talented two-way player. Llew was very, very gifted. He played defence when guys were hurt and then back up to forward heading into the playoffs. But the most easygoing guy. Darrin MacKay used to say that you could pee on his snow cone and Llew would still be in a good mood. Super easygoing and didn't love the off-season workout regimen much. There were times when Barry tried to light a fire under him.

Derek Hopko—Hopper. If there was a guy who had a propensity for trouble, it was Hops. Or he was probably the one who got caught the most, let's put it that way. Hopko was a mischievous soul, and he would pull Llewie into all sorts of shenanigans. Hops, Ncwana and Guy Sanderson, the Three Amigos, used to hang out together all the time. Those three were inseparable and a lot of fun to be around. We were all amazed when somehow Derek ended up with a PhD in psychology. When I heard about it, I was like, "Really? Hops did *that*?"

Moving up from Midget AAA, the Hounds had a very young team. We had a bunch of seventeen-year-olds. Barry knew they were going to have to stand up to the other teams, who had many players aged eighteen, nineteen and twenty. At one of our first practices, Barry locked the doors to the rink and we worked on fighting. He knew that all the other teams would be looking at us, going, "Well, if we can't beat them on the scoreboard, we'd better beat them up." He had the guys pair up with somebody the same size and taught them how to keep their balance while throwing punches. It's not like they were a bunch of choir boys at that point, but this was the era of no full face shields or visors. Barry also realized we'd need an older protector for the playoffs. He brought in Sandor Fizli about halfway through the year.

Every once in a while between games, Sandor, Hopko and Llewie would head to the bars in Regina. One night, on their way home, they went through the McDonald's drive-thru on Albert Street for cheeseburgers. Up the road about fifteen minutes later, they all got out to water their horses and Hops and Llewie accidently drove away without Sandor.

Sandor watched them take off and started running after the car, whistling and yelling. They'd just made it over a little hill when they finally heard him. The boys put the car in reverse and started backing up, but he was on the highway and so they ran over him! Thank God they just knocked him down. They brought him back to Notre Dame and threw him in his bunk, where he passed out. The next day in practice, Sandor was like, "Geezus, why do my ribs hurt this bad?" He had no idea he'd been hit by a car.

Dwayne Norris—we called him "Newfie." Newfie was a guy who was very, very gifted on the right wing. I loved having him on our team because he could score and he was fast. He could shoot hard for a relatively small guy. He was from St. John's and had that Newfoundland accent that we all loved. You could tease Newfie all you wanted and he took it with a smile. He worked hard, and not just in hockey. On the bus, he'd be asking the guys, "I'm on this chemistry question here. I need to know something. Let's pull out the books." Very humble too. He had multiple scholarship offers, yet he kept that to himself. You never heard him gloating.

Eric Schoefield was a guy who was in and out of the lineup all year. If there was an injury, he'd come in, but what a testament to his character that Schoey just worked and worked every practice. I don't know how many games he played that year, but he was there when we needed him—he was that type of guy. He had to embrace that role because he knew he wasn't going be in the lineup every night, and when he was, he was kind of a fourth-liner. All the guys liked him because of that.

Todd Clark had a twin brother, Trevor. They played the year before on the team that reached the Air Canada Cup final. Toddy was a fun guy. Like Beaucage, he was in and out once in a while on the fourth line. A super guy.

Stephane Gauvin was the son of our manager, Jacques, who was a sweetheart to me. Steph was our team's conscience. Our team's moral compass. He's probably the nicest guy you'll ever meet. Smart, funny, generous, a leader. Always dependable. Worked his ass off. Super, super kid. Best friends with everybody. We always thought he'd be the guy who would run Notre Dame someday. That's how highly everyone thought of him. He's a teacher. Maybe he hasn't closed that chapter yet, but I think Moose Jaw, Saskatchewan, has a special hold on him. He was a teammate to the end. The best kid on that team. We had a lot of smart guys on our team, and between Steph and Roddy, it was like they were in competition to outdo each other academically. Both of them had an average better than 95 per cent. Steph ended up playing in the Ivy League, at Cornell.

Finally, there was Batts. Jeff Batters was sixteen. A fun-loving kid, always smiling. Didn't care what other people thought about him. You never caught Batts in a bad mood, except when he was on the ice. There, he could get kind of ornery. But he was jovial at all other times. He was a stay-at-home defenceman for the most part. Tough to beat one on one, would always make good passes. A bread-and-butter guy. One of those guys you can always rely on, and he stayed healthy all year. He got better as he got older, that kid. Sadly, he's the only guy not with us anymore. Super kid. Had a big future ahead of him too. When he was in his mid-twenties, he was teaching at a hockey school in Banff. Around 3 a.m., he and a bunch of guys were heading to Canmore from Banff when they decided to take a shortcut through a ditch, crossing the oncoming lanes to get up an on-ramp. The pickup truck slid, a wheel caught the edge of the pavement, and it rolled over, killing Jeff and a passenger named Sherri Kacan. Joby's brothers Mitch and Marcus were also seriously injured.

Batts was such a good kid. He was just getting his break. He played in college in Alaska and had played sixteen games over two seasons in the NHL with the Blues when it happened. In fact, he stayed at my place down in St. Louis for a while. It was hard to hear that he died. Really sad.

━━━

WE BATTLED FOR number one spot with the Humboldt Broncos all year, and in the next-to-last game we beat them at home, clinching the top spot. After that big win, some of the guys were like, "Hey, we should celebrate with some brewskis!" I walked down the road to the bar, the South 40—not far, the distance of one stop sign—and bought a case of beer. The drinking age in Saskatchewan at the time was nineteen, but I thought nothing of it. I've never been a big drinker, but a few of us sat around the trailer and had a little party with a few laughs while we finished the case.

Of course, it's a town of two hundred people. There are no secrets at Notre Dame. The next day, Barry called me into his office. "Students can't be drinking underage! And here you are, you idiot, pulling beer for them!" He was getting madder and madder until he was shouting. I was kind of horrified to see he was that upset.

Remember, he was the principal as well as the hockey coach. He could kick you out of school *and* limit your playing time. He held all the cards. Barry never had to say much, though. All he'd have to do is come into the room and say, "You guys are pissin' me off," and then he'd walk out. The funny thing about him was you didn't want to disappoint him. I think that's partially why we played hard. We all wanted to make him proud of us.

So I was honestly shocked at his reaction. I hadn't been in trouble very often in my life, so for me this was a big one.

A couple of years ago, we had a team reunion out at Predator Ridge in Vernon, B.C. I got there, walked through the kitchen and picked up a beer, and then went outside to the patio where Barry was sitting. I smiled at him and held up my beer. "This okay with you, Bear?"

———

WHAT BARRY HAD said after that pre-season game was right—a lot of colleges had started to take an interest in me. Three of us—Rod Brind'Amour, Steve Widmeyer, who was also a big prospect back then, and I—went on a recruiting trip to Wisconsin. I knew I wanted to go to the University of Wisconsin because it's a big school and they needed a goalie. Their goalie, a senior, was graduating.

Anyway, a couple of players took us out one night to the Kollege Klub—it's known as the KK—and I drank too much. As I said, I wasn't a drinker at all, but they were buying. I still had to watch my shoulder. It would dislocate while playing basketball or volleyball—it was always coming out—and I would pop it back in myself. It must have come out a dozen times since high school. It was weird. It wouldn't come out all year, and then it would happen on a weekly basis.

I was really drunk when I got back to the dorm. I guess I rolled over on my shoulder while I was sleeping, and it just slipped out. I woke up and I was like, "*Ugggh! Ow!* My shoulder is out!" It's the worst feeling in the world. I got up and went downstairs. I don't know how I got a cab—I was *that* inebriated. I made it to a hospital close to the university, and the emergency room doctor asked, "Have you been drinking tonight, son?"

I woke up on a gurney in a hallway with no idea of how long I'd been there. My shoulder was back in place, so I swung myself off the gurney and slipped out the door. Gone. Like I was never there.

Rod called me at 6 a.m. Rod was such a focused guy. You'd roll out of bed at seven in the morning, look over at the other side and he'd be on his hundredth push-up. In bantam, he'd be on the road for a tournament and he'd be doing curls on the living-room chairs at the billet's. He was all gung ho that morning. "All right, Curtis! Are you ready? We gotta do a campus tour."

I croaked, "Roddy, I'm deathly ill. I popped my shoulder out. I'm not doing it."

He couldn't believe it, because that wasn't like me. We went back to Notre Dame later that evening and my shoulder felt fine. I think I was so drunk that my muscles were relaxed, and that meant I didn't put up any resistance. It allowed my shoulder to easily slide in and out, and as a result, I wasn't sore. I played our next game. And the shoulder stayed in place the rest of the year.

CHAPTER 19

A Season Nobody Expected

ON APRIL 6, 2018, I was writing this part, about the rivalry between the Hounds and the Humboldt Broncos in the '80s, when I heard about the Broncos' bus crash. The Broncos were on their way to Nipawin, Saskatchewan, for a playoff game when a semi collided with their bus, killing sixteen people and injuring thirteen. It was a devastating loss.

I think everybody in the hockey world felt the same way. Guys around the league were almost too beat up to talk about it.

It hit home for me because I know those roads. I travelled those roads and sat in those same bus seats.

A friend of mine, ex–NHL defenceman Chris Joseph, lost his boy Jaxon. Chris is around my age, so we often played each other. We'd always kid about having the same last name. It would confuse people to see C. JOSEPH on both rosters.

Losing a child . . . I cannot imagine what that does to a family. I prayed that God would place His hand on Chris's shoulder and help him and the other families heal and carry on.

Back in 1988, Humboldt knew our team from Notre Dame wasn't going to give up. It was going to be a battle right to the end, so they tried to retool and even brought in a bunch of guys from the Western Hockey League. And when they didn't win the league regular-season championship, they fired their coach, Bernie Lynch. Lynch had coached Humboldt to the league championship and the Centennial Cup final in the previous season.

Lynch's firing was a big deal to us because we had expected to face Humboldt in the playoff final. Now they were in disarray. They won their first-round series, but then lost to the Yorkton Terriers in the semifinals. That meant we faced Yorkton in the final, a team that had come in a distant third in the regular season.

It was still a tough series, but we won in six. Yorkton wasn't Humboldt. I remember Willie played in that series and played really well for us. I closed it out, but Willie played a couple of the important games. Dennis Polonich was the Terriers' coach, and they came after us hard. They were a little bit bigger and a little bit older. They tried to dig into us. We didn't have a lot of enforcers except for Sandor, but both Tommy O'Rourke and Steve Widmeyer were tough enough.

After we beat Yorkton, we had about two weeks off until the Anavet Cup against the champions of the Manitoba Junior Hockey League. We weren't sure who that was going to be because the Manitoba guys were still playing. Barry told us to go away for three or four days and relax. I went with Sanderson and Hopko and a few others to Edmonton, just to get away. And when I got back and we practised, it was like, "Holy—I don't think I've been on skates for a month!"

We took the next week to get back in shape and then went up against the Winnipeg South Blues, beating them twice at Notre Dame, and then beating them 3–1 in a ten-minute, non-sudden-death overtime in the third game in Winnipeg. Their goalie was Duane Derksen, who was also headed to Wisconsin on a scholarship.

Tommy O'Rourke was always in my corner. After the game, the *Winnipeg Free Press* asked him, "What do you think of the goaltending tonight?" He said, "Well, I know they're both going to Wisconsin, but I think the best goalie won."

The night before Game Four, we were having a team meal in one of the hospitality suites at our hotel, and some former Notre Dame students wandered in to say hi and "Hey, I went to school with you"—that sort of thing. I remember Barry walking over to them and saying, "You know what? This isn't your time right now. Beat it." He was very protective of what we were trying to accomplish, and he didn't want any outside distractions. Barry kept us focused and we swept the series.

Next up for us was the Abbott Cup series against the champions of the Alberta Junior Hockey League, the Calgary Canucks. Of all our playoff series, this was the most memorable, for sure. They were the next-best team in the country and they had a great scorer, Dean Larson, along with a couple of guys who had gone to Notre Dame. They won fifty-one games that season, including a twenty-one-game winning streak. It could have gone either way. A coin toss. In Game Three, we were back at Notre Dame and our fans, our school, were going crazy. And we were down 2–0 in the series.

Don Phelps was the coach of the Canucks. He had a long career with them, including five provincial championships and a Centennial Cup. When he retired, he had more wins than any Junior A coach in Canada, more than a thousand. But our fans weren't impressed with him or the Canucks. They were all over Calgary, and the Canucks didn't like it. In fact, one of their goalies, Buddy Brazier (the other was Corey Hirsch) got into a stick-swinging battle with the fans. It was an absolute nuthouse. We won that game but lost the next one and were down 3–1.

Barry was worried. He'd heard that the feeling from some on the team was "If we lose this game, we don't have a chance. We have to go back to Calgary, and the chances of beating Calgary three games in a row with two in their rink are not good." He lay awake that night, thinking about what to say to us.

The next morning, before Game Five, Barry called a meeting. We didn't have a pre-game skate because there were too many teams competing and not enough ice time. We were all sitting at our lockers when he came into the room. He only weighed about 175, but years of playing the game like a 220-pounder had given him a bit of a hobble when he walked. He had scars all over his face, a bent nose—it had been broken multiple times—and his voice was a raspy growl. But we all knew there was a huge heart underneath his red sweatsuit and team logo—a big white greyhound running across the ND lettering.

Like always, his greying hair was perfectly parted and neatly combed in place. He had our attention right away. "You know what? We're not playing to win the championship. We're playing to win every game. It's a commitment that we make to ourselves and to one another that we're not going to take anything for granted and we're just going to play one game at a time. For many of you, this is going to be the best team you ever play on. You guys have had a season that nobody would've expected, and if you lose tonight, you're still gonna be heroes. You will still have accomplished more than anyone would've thought possible.

"But why would you stop now? Why would we stop now, when we have that opportunity? You've got a chance now to be on one of the best teams ever. In twenty-five years, you want to be able to have a reunion and say, 'Yeah, that was the best team we ever played on.' So, let's just go and give it all we've got for tonight."

On his way out, he passed a sign that Terry McGarry had written up and hung up on the wall for us. Terry did maintenance at the school, but he was also a local poet. On the sign, there was a quote from Father (Père) Athol Murray, the founder of Notre Dame College. THERE WAS A VISION IN HIS MIND UNDIMMED THROUGH ALL ADVERSITY. I know it inspired me, and I think a lot of the other guys too.

I have always remembered that sign and Barry's speech as being responsible for our turnaround. We won that night. And won again. And forced Game Seven.

In the dressing room, we were nervous and pumped up because it was Game Seven—and partly because, even though it was an away game, the building was full of Hounds. This was thanks to our president, Martin Kenney. He'd hired a fleet of buses to bring in dozens of Hounds from Wilcox to Calgary to fill the stands. It's an eight-hour drive—a long one. Didn't matter. The kids were insane with excitement.

The dressing rooms at the Max Bell Arena in north Calgary are underneath the concrete stands, but when our students arrived, I thought I could feel the building shaking. It was powerful, the energy they brought with them. The fans were going bananas just before game time, and we could feel it. It was unbelievable. I'll never forget that. We skated out, and the place erupted. The kids were screaming the national anthem at the top of their lungs.

The Canucks played hard. They were trying to get under my skin, absolutely they were. Their top scorer, Dean Larson, spit in my face. I think that was an indication of how much was on the line. You know, make it as hard on the goalie as you can. But they were very skilled too. They probably thought they had it in the bag, and if I were them, I would have felt the same way.

We always had a prayer that was said between the second and third periods. Generations of Notre Dame students before us had said it, as would generations after. The football team said it while huddled around Père Murray's gravesite—right outside the football field— before the finals in Saskatchewan, and basketball teams said it in the gym before their games. Boys' teams, girls' teams. It wasn't so much a religious thing as it was a team-bonding exercise. I'd call it a mantra more than a prayer, an oath of allegiance to each other. We pulled on it when we needed it, and we needed it in that game.

Tommy O'Rourke said, "Let's do the prayer," and we all took a knee. "O Heavenly Father, help us to play hard within the rules, to never lose heart, to struggle and emerge, for Père, for Notre Dame, for the team and for Hounds and Houndettes everywhere. Let's go!" And then off we went for the third period.

With just seconds left in the third period, we were up 3–2. The Canucks were trying everything, just peppering us with one shot attempt after another. The puck landed in our crease and popped loose with two seconds to go. Batts saw this and knocked our net off its horns. The ref blew the whistle—penalty shot. The crowd lost its mind. All the Notre Dame kids started chanting, "Be there Père!" The noise was deafening.

Of course they picked their best player, Dean Larson, to take the penalty shot. Same guy who had spit at me. I was glad it was him, because there was no way I was going to let him score on me. I'd played a lot of games before, and I played a lot of games after, and I've had nerves when certain guys have come in on me, but I was never more confident about making a save in my life. Dean made a nice move and deked, but I spread out and blocked the puck with my pad and sealed it for us.

The realization that we'd won was just unadulterated joy, and our fans were jumping up and down on the boards, hanging over the glass, pounding it, shaking it, shrieking. We skated around the Max Bell Arena, high-fiving everyone in sight. The boys gave me a lot of credit, but we wouldn't have won the game without Barry's coaching and the effort of each and every guy on that team. And all those fans bringing all that energy. It was magic.

I'll always remember the Canucks players as they sat on the bench after the buzzer. How utterly dejected they looked. I didn't know it then, but that same look was in my future. It's in every NHLer's future, even the greatest players, like Wayne Gretzky.

———

WE SHOWED UP for the Centennial Cup tournament in Pembroke, Ontario, and they had a big banquet to kick things off. I looked around the room at the guys from the other three teams. Virtually every player in the room had a playoff beard—except for the guys on our team. It wasn't for lack of trying. There were only maybe four of us who could grow one. And there were beers on every table, but not on ours. Our guys were drinking full glasses of milk. It was pretty funny. You could see the other teams looking at one another, going, "Who the hell are these kids?"

The host team, the Pembroke Lumber Kings, was highly favoured to win the tournament. We were a little concerned about them. After beating the Halifax Lions 6–5 and the Thunder Bay Flyers 9–7 to open the round robin, we lost 4–3 to Pembroke in triple overtime. That meant we had to play them again in the semifinal. It was kind of a tense game. They had a rink full of their supporters, and they were good. But we won 7–3 and moved on to face Halifax in the final.

We'd beaten Halifax in the round robin, but they'd beaten Pembroke and Thunder Bay by two goals each, so their goal differential earned them a bye into the final. We were down 2–1 going into the third period, and Barry MacKenzie again came into the room, looked around and said, "You know what, guys? I look good in silver, but I look way better in gold." Then he turned and walked out.

We went out and got a couple of big goals. Rob Schriner scored, and then Dwayne Norris got the game-winner on an assist from Roddy Brind'Amour, who was tournament MVP. To this day, I can't tell you how much I owe Roddy. Team leader, great season, national championship, and most of all, wonderful friend.

I remember returning from Pembroke, and it was great. We celebrated that night with a little bonfire, thanks to the wooden fence around the trailers. But then you go back to regular life. The guys like me, who were no longer in school, went home after a couple of days and I remember feeling kind of sad that the ride was over. We had just won the Centennial Cup, the biggest win of my life to that point, and yet I was a little bummed out, as odd as that sounds. I knew I was going to miss it all. The team, the spirit at the school, the guys. I didn't know if I'd ever experience anything like it again.

That year at Notre Dame was a whirlwind for me. I guess it was just nine months, but it was the most important nine months of my hockey life. I don't think there's been a team since that had that many kids earn college scholarships. Nineteen altogether, fifteen to schools in Division I, which is the top tier.

In the NHL, you develop a brotherhood because you go through a lot together, but that Hounds team . . . what a special group it was to be around. I think that was a big reason for our success. We had such a good group of human beings and we all got along so well. There was not one selfish player. Every guy looked out for the others. Still do to this day.

CHAPTER 20

Donnie

THE UNIVERSITY OF Wisconsin Badgers were losing Dean Anderson, their goalie. As a senior, he was due to graduate. To replace him, they would be going with two freshmen goalies. Because of that episode with my shoulder, I had missed my chance to learn about the academic aspect, but coach Jeff Sauer and assistant coach Mike Kemp had shown us around and we'd been to a game. I loved the rink, the school, the atmosphere and the fact that I would have a chance to play a fair bit.

At that time, the NCAA rules limited you to four recruiting trips. Besides Wisconsin, I visited North Dakota, Maine and Michigan State. All had big arenas and great programs. Jacques Gauvin from Notre Dame played a big part in helping me decide. He was instrumental with all the guys because he was the liaison with the colleges. He'd research the schools, talk to representatives of all the teams, and find out who needed a forward, who needed a goalie. The recruiters would come in and he'd say, "Well look at this guy. He'd fit perfectly with you guys." He pushed for every player on that 1987–88 Hounds team to get a scholarship.

Michigan State came in late with an offer, and it was an attractive one because I knew three guys who were going there—Joby Messier, Dwayne Norris and Rod Brind'Amour. Roddy could probably have gone to an Ivy League school, but he was really good friends with Joby and his family, and Joby's older brother, Mitch, went to Michigan State. Roddy was destined to go to Michigan State through those connections alone.

But the University of Wisconsin was the school I fell in love with first so that's where I committed. Also, I wanted to go into business, and they had a great program. Pete Johnson, son of the legendary UW coach Badger Bob Johnson (who coached Pittsburgh to a Stanley Cup championship in 1991), was the other assistant coach. Good guy.

We played forty-six games in 1988–89, and I appeared in thirty-eight. They gave me every chance to take the starting job and run with it. I ended up with a record of 21–11–5, very decent. In conference play, we went 17–13–5, good for a third-place tie with North Dakota in the eight-team Western Collegiate Hockey Association. In the conference playoffs, we beat Michigan Tech in the first round but lost 4–2 to Northern Michigan in the semis. Then we beat the Minnesota Golden Gophers 4–3 in the third-place game. We were invited to play in that year's NCAA tournament, where the Gophers eliminated us in the quarter-finals.

I don't remember specifically thinking, "Boy, I am doing well" that season, whereas there would be times in the NHL when I could say I was very good. Even though I don't think I dominated, I won the WCHA's Freshman of the Year and Most Valuable Player awards, something no first-year player had ever done. And I was a Second Team All-American. The year before, Robb Stauber had won the Hobey Baker Award as the top college hockey player in the country— that's the best college player, hockey's version of football's Heisman Trophy. That's what I was up against. I remember Bruce Hoffort being very good too. Bruce was named top college goalie in the nation. He was more polished than I was in college.

I was on a full-boat scholarship and loved the college, but I was at a different point in my life than most of my classmates. I was coming off my freshman year but was at least as old as most seniors. My girlfriend and I were talking about getting married and having a family, while most of the others were only eighteen and had just left home for the first time. So, the fit there was not great.

I'd always dreamed of playing in the NHL, and after my year at Wisconsin, the dream seemed close to coming true. At the same time, I can't say I was aware that many teams were interested in signing me. A couple of scouts had contacted me by mail, but the only one who ever spoke to me directly was David McNab of the Hartford Whalers, and he only did it because I already knew him. He'd played at Wisconsin—he was their third-string goalie in the late 1970s, including 1977, when they won the NCAA championship. He's got a ring. Wonderful guy.

Most scouts are on the periphery. They don't talk to you. They take notes, and then they leave. David was different. He was a hands-on guy. He was the guy who told agent Donnie Meehan, "You've got to see this goalie. I watched him at Notre Dame."

Dave started contacting me long before I even had a whiff of the NHL. I would run to the mailbox at Notre Dame, and there'd be a little package shoved in there. I'd open it and find a Whalers hat or T-shirt, along with handwritten letters from him. I'd think, "Oh my gosh, look at this NHL stuff!" I would never wear them, of course. That would be braggadocious. But I don't think he realized what it meant to me. It was such a motivator. It kept me going, kept me focused.

I may not have been hearing from scouts, but a couple of top agents, Meehan and Bob Goodenow, came to Madison to sit down with me. Thanks to my upbringing, I knew nothing about anything. I was completely wide-eyed. There was no parent to talk to or get advice from. And there was no social media, no Google, so you couldn't even find out for yourself. I was totally uninformed. I felt like I did when I was back in the equipment locker in East Gwillimbury, just feeling around in the dark for my pads.

Bob was great—well informed and professional. He represented Brett Hull. Very, very smart man. Three years later, he was head of the NHL Players' Association. But I liked Donnie's personality and approach—everything about him. He was easy to talk to. He laid it all out. "You're a free agent. This is how it works. This is what could happen." He went through various possible scenarios.

I hadn't been drafted, so I was free to sign with anybody who made me an offer. But before I met Donnie, I had no idea what that meant. He told me it meant I was a very attractive commodity.

Donnie was indispensable throughout my career. He weighed in on all the major decisions I made. Our relationship was great. Fantastic. He was a total professional in the way he conducted business. I didn't make a financial decision or even a purchase without consulting him. I started to think of him as a father figure. He didn't know all about my history, how I didn't have a father, nobody to turn to, or why I looked to him for all the answers. But I leaned on him for everything. We talked all the time. If he wasn't available, I'd talk to his associate, Pat Morris, or somebody else in the office.

Pat helped me buy my first car. He said, "Hey, we have a client whose parents have a Toyota dealership." I bought a white Supra. I know what you're thinking—a Toyota doesn't sound very enticing—but the Supra was a sports car. Other guys were buying the Camaro Z28, or a Corvette. I got something fairly responsible, and I loved it. And bonus, it was a stick shift. When I drove it, I felt like a million bucks.

Once you start making money, you need good advice. Lots of guys sign their first contract and then spend like crazy, and when the ride is over, they end up broke. Donnie and Pat had connections for everything. Donnie would tell me which investors his company used. I put my trust in him, and he didn't fail me. In fact, Donnie is the big reason I still have money.

I was one of Donnie's top clients for a number of years. I never changed agents. I'm a loyal person, by nature. He represented me from 1989 right though. My last few years in the league, I was a backup goalie, which meant I wasn't signing big contracts. I think my last contract was for $700,000 for a year, but it was with the Leafs, which was great. Donnie has a lot of influence in the game and I thank him for that.

Before I got my first cheque, Donnie said, "Repeat after me: 'I'd like to invest in your project, but my money is all tied up with my agent.'" I ended up using that line for years. First of all, it was true, and secondly, I had no choice. A lot of people are looking for investors. A lot of people target athletes making good money. But I would tell them, "Oh, you know what, it's tied up—I've got it in this, I've got it in that," and that became my out. Today, I'm fifty-one years old, and when I think of all the horror stories I've heard, you know, I've gotta thank Donnie for all the terrible investments I *didn't* make.

Chapter 21

Once-in-a-Lifetime Deal

DONNIE TOLD ME that ten NHL teams had expressed an interest in signing me. There were twenty-one teams in the league at that time. Those ten teams got narrowed down to four serious contenders—Dave McNab's Hartford Whalers, the New York Islanders, the Edmonton Oilers and the St. Louis Blues. All four were in the same range moneywise and the bids kept going up and up. Half a million, three-quarters of a million, and then a million! It was crazy. It finally came down to "$1.1 million for four years and the team will pay for your schooling if you don't work out."

I loved Wisconsin, and the Badgers seemed poised to have a good season. But my thinking was that if I went back to school and hurt my knee, an NHL career might be gone forever. With this kind of money on the table, I had to take the deal and try. As I told Donnie, "I cannot pass up this once-in-a-lifetime deal." It wasn't like they were putting fifty or seventy-five thousand in front of me. Back then, a million dollars could have set me up for the rest of my life. Staying in school and risking getting injured wasn't an option.

There was another goalie, Bruce Hoffort. He grew up in North Battleford, Saskatchewan. He went to Lake Superior State, and they won the NCAA championship—the Frozen Four—in 1988. He was named the tournament's MVP and the player of the year in his conference. Bruce hadn't been drafted, and he got the exact same offer as I did—$1.1 million—from the Philadelphia Flyers. But it didn't work out the same. He played a few games and then went into a slump. He bounced around the minors and never regained his footing.

That's what happens. When you get that kind of money, they give you every opportunity to fail. You're like a first-round pick now.

The first team I went to meet was Hartford, and I got to meet Gordie Howe, who was working in the front office. That was incredible. He'd been retired for nine years. He must have been a little older than sixty. But he still looked powerful. Soft-spoken, very nice. And Hartford, that's where David McNab worked—the scout who believed in me, right? I felt an affinity to him, but the Hartford Whalers weren't the Chicago Blackhawks or the Toronto Maple Leafs. They weren't an "Original Six" franchise. And they had never been close to a Stanley Cup.

Next, I went to the Island, where I met with Bill Torrey, the famous architect of one of the greatest dynasties of all time—Denis Potvin, Bryan Trottier, Mike Bossy, Clark Gillies. Four Cups in a row. The only team to win nineteen straight playoff series. The Islanders might not have had that Original Six heritage, but what a history. Torrey was an interesting guy—famous for always wearing a bow tie. The thing is, they had Kelly Hrudey, and I didn't see him going anywhere, which meant I'd be sitting on the bench, watching him play. (As it turned out, he was traded that summer to the Kings.)

The closest I'd ever been to Edmonton was Calgary, that time we played the Canucks. I didn't know anything about the place, except that they were pretty well set in goal with Bill Ranford and the people in Calgary seemed to harbour an extreme dislike for the Oilers.

So I decided on St. Louis, for a couple of reasons. Yeah, they were an expansion team, but as Wayne Gretzky says in his book *99: Stories of the Game*, "They were in so many Stanley Cup finals in the late '60s and early '70s that they almost didn't seem like an expansion team."

Roddy Brind'Amour had signed with St. Louis after his freshman season and they called him up for the playoffs. St. Louis flew me in after the season was over, and they brought Roddy back to drive around with me in a limo and to sell me on joining the team.

Another big factor in my decision to go there was that I liked Brian Sutter, the coach. He brought me to his house to have dinner with him and his wife, Judy. He was the only coach who did that. He introduced me to his family. I also considered the fact that Greg Millen, the Blues' number one goaltender, was a little bit older, at thirty-two. In the NHL back then, that was older. So I got a good feeling there. It looked like I'd have a chance to play.

I've always felt a little bit bad about that decision because Dave was the first guy to see any kind of future in the NHL for me. I felt a loyalty to him. But St. Louis just seemed more promising than Hartford.

Chapter 22

"Coojoe, Stend Up!"

At my first training camp, in the fall of 1989, I tweaked my knee. My MCL. It was ugly. I went into a butterfly, and *"Eeeee-owww-wowww!"* Nicked the inside of the ligament. My fault. I wasn't prepared for practice. Sure, I stretched, but now that I am older and look back at my younger self, I say to myself, "Oh man, why didn't you take better care of your body?" I'd show up to practice not having eaten breakfast, then I'd do a quick little stretch, grab my stuff and rush out on the ice.

My injury was like a sprained knee. I couldn't put any weight on the inside of it. While I rehabbed, I was sent down to the minors, to the Peoria Rivermen. And who did I blame? The coaches.

Brian Sutter and assistant coach Bob Berry sat me down to explain that I'd be spending a good part of my first season in Peoria. "You're as good as the other goalies," they said, "but most guys play junior or university for three or four years. You've played just one year in the NCAA, and in a sense, that puts you a step behind. Every young guy's gotta learn to adjust to the pro level. The NHL has the best players in the world. With your work ethic and mentality, and your character, we believe you could be a special goalie. This is gonna be really good for you. You'll go down and play with Wayne Thomas, your coach in Peoria."

I'd just signed this big contract, thinking that there was no way I'd be sent down, so when Brian told me I was going, I was very, very upset about it. I remember talking to Roddy Brind'Amour. We were pretty close because we'd been teammates at Notre Dame, and besides, I didn't know anyone else on the team. I was just raw emotion. You know how it goes—"Those effing pricks just brought me here and now they're sending me down to the effing minors." I realize now that I was mad because I took it as a rejection. I didn't get it. To me, it was like being cut from Junior A. "Ugh, I didn't make the team!"

I think the fact I hurt my knee in training camp told Brian what an immature human being I was. I wasn't ready for wins, losses, NHL workouts, all that stuff. The kids who come in now, they're much better prepared before they turn pro. Auston Matthews, Connor McDavid . . . they're honed, they check out everything on YouTube, and as a result they know a whole lot more about the game. I knew nothing, and looking back, I definitely needed to go to the minors to figure it out. And that's the thing about being a goalie. If you're in the NHL and not playing, what good are you? You're sure not getting better. You need to be playing as many games as possible.

None of that crossed my mind at the time. Donnie Meehan and I discussed it, but he didn't like to talk negatively. When something happened, he'd console or explain, which of course was his job. But it would have been great if I'd had a dad to lay it all out for me. Now that I'm a dad, I understand what needs to be said. "Listen, these are the pitfalls. It's a tough league. You think you're going to waltz in there and make the team? Forget it. It's a business. The guys there are all professional goalies—something you are not. Yet."

I wasn't buying what the coaches were telling me at the time, but they were right. Wayne, who'd played with the Montreal Canadiens, Toronto Maple Leafs and New York Rangers in the 1970s and early '80s, became my goaltending guru. He's a real quiet, soft-spoken guy. You had to listen hard. But he was a very intelligent, knowledgeable coach. He was quiet, but he got his message across, and he had a calming influence on me.

Goaltending coaching back then was way less technical than today, because the goalies were different. Most played a stand-up style. Wayne Thomas played that way. Patrick Roy, who was a couple of years older than me, was the first of my generation to go down into the butterfly.

I developed a hybrid style, using a bit of both. When the play moved in close, I liked to go into the paddle-down position—pads out, stick down and catching glove raised. Eighty per cent of shots go in below the knees, so the paddle-down position meant I could cover the bottom of the whole net. For me, that was effective—especially against wraparounds. I worked on it constantly until I was good at it. It's still a big part of goaltending today.

I was using analytics before they were called analytics. I used my quickness to make a shooter try to go upstairs, which is much harder because, if the puck bobbles at all when you go high, you are going to miss the net. It's sure to go wide or over the crossbar. Playing percentages was a big part of my game. I wasn't six foot five, so I had to be smart. That meant figuring out how to take away whatever part of the net I could, based on the position of the puck relative to the shooter's feet, for instance.

Of course, I'd occasionally get beat on a high shot. And there were still a few old-school players who hated it when their goalie went down. Esa Tikkanen, the Finn who had been a feisty and very effective winger with the Oilers, played with us briefly near the end of my time in St. Louis. I remember him always yelling at me, "Coojoe, Coojoe, stend up! Stend up!"

———

THE KNEE GOT better after a few weeks and I started playing. I look at my statistics and they're not good, but I still felt like I was playing well. I was learning about myself as a goalie. It's like knowing who you are as a person. I became familiar with my raw strengths. I'd read things about myself in the newspaper. An article might say that I had a good glove hand or fast feet. Or they'd be like, "He's good side to side." I'd think, "Yeah, I am good side to side." I would read about how I could anticipate well. "Oh yeah, that's probably true." That feedback made up for my lack of height and technical know-how.

There was just a fantastic group of guys down in Peoria. I will never forget them. Chaser (Kelly Chase), Twister (Tony Twist) and Jimmy Vesey—his son, also named Jimmy, plays for the Rangers now. Great human beings and a lot of fun to be around. From them I learned about what pros do in their downtime on the road. How they prepare for games. They nap, they go somewhere for lunch as a team or in a group. You've got all this free time, so you continue to bond over golf when the weather's nice, you play paintball, you go bowling. It's about forming a brotherhood and becoming a good teammate you can trust. It's also about respect and sharing a lot of laughs.

While I was in Peoria, I also met two awesome goaltending part-ners, Guy Hebert and Pat Jablonski. Wonderful guys. Hebert went on to become an All-Star for the Mighty Ducks and had a ten-year career in the NHL. Jabber played eight seasons in the NHL. But the three of us started out as young bucks, all of us twenty-two years old, in Peoria.

Jabber was one of the best-liked players on the team. He was funny and outgoing and single, so he was always in the mix. I liked Jabber. Most pro goalies are jittery in the crease—wound up and on edge. It gives you super reflexes. If a fly comes by, you can grab it, right? Jabber had that same nervous energy off the ice too. That's unusual. At the same time, he was the guy you cheered for because he was gen-uine. There was nothing hidden. He wore his emotions on his sleeve. It was easy to be his friend.

CHAPTER 23

Sudsy

WHEN I JOINED the Blues, they were an extremely young team. There were some veterans, but the majority of us had yet to make a major impact in the NHL. The exception was Scott Stevens, a big free-agent signing from Washington in the summer of 1990. He'd been a First Team All-Star and runner-up for the Norris Trophy as top defence-man while he was with the Capitals.

Jeff Brown, who'd been acquired from the Quebec Nordiques in a trade that involved Greg Millen, would become one of the league's top puck-moving defencemen. Brett Hull came from the Calgary Flames, a powerhouse team where Brett got limited minutes. He wasn't a star yet. Adam Oates and Paul MacLean came in from Detroit in a trade for Tony McKegney and Bernie Federko. It turned out to be the worst trade in Wings history, but no one knew it at the time. So, we were all in the same boat. We all needed to prove ourselves in the NHL, and our management group and coaching staff, headed up by Brian Sutter, helped us do that.

We called him Sudsy. Brian was a lot like Barry MacKenzie. I haven't seen him in forever, but I'll bet you he's the same as far as intensity goes. He was also a stand-up guy. The best coach I could ever have in my first year in the league. I can sum up the mentality of Brian Sutter in one minute. During my first training camp, a coaches' meeting was called for the first night. We all sat down in a big conference room, about sixty or seventy of us. First three assistant coaches came up and spoke. The meeting started to drag on, which was a bit of a pain because we knew we had to be on the ice at seven o'clock the next morning. Finally, Brian stood and walked up to the front.

"Lads," he said ("lads" was one of his favourite words). "Lads, if you're a goal scorer . . . score goals. If you're a defenceman . . . be a defenceman. If you're a fighter . . . I wanna see you fight. If you're a goaltender, stop the puck. You have a good night."

And that was it. Meeting over. There were no head games with Brian.

He was hard-core too. Because he was my first NHL coach, and I had nobody to compare him to, I figured that's how it was—they must all be like that. Brian didn't let you smile at a morning skate. If you were smiling at a ten o'clock skate for a seven o'clock game, you weren't getting ready. He kept you on your toes. He was similar to Barry that way. It didn't matter if you had a good game—it was always about the next game. And doing it right.

He was hard on a lot of people. It didn't make him the most popular guy in the room, but everyone respected him because we knew what he'd gone through as a player. Brian was a man's man. He would come in the room and punch guys in the arm. That's how he showed his affection. Punching you as hard as he could on the top of your arm. Brett Hull would skate to the bench after scoring a goal and Brian would give him kidney punches! That was his way of telling Brett how he thought he was doing well and how much he appreciated him.

When I first got there, Brian came into the dressing room and caught me on the shoulder. Honest to God, he almost dropped me on my butt. The guys thought it was pretty funny. Thankfully, I was good at anticipating plays. After that first punch, I always positioned myself out of Brian's reach.

As tough as he was with us, Brian was even harder on his brother Richie. He didn't want to show favouritism, and we wouldn't expect anything less. Brian was in the NHL for years before Richie came into the league, and he had been a great player. Richie respected him for that. The Sutters are all tough as nails. Six brothers made the NHL— Darryl, Brian, Brent, Duane, and twins Ronnie and Richie. Now there's a second generation with Brandon and Brody. All made from the same mould.

CHAPTER 24

A Bucket of Sand

KELLY CHASE BECAME a buddy. Kelly is a real humorous guy, very personable. He's at the top of the list of characters I played with. A lot of his antics took place off the ice. Roddy was one of his roommates, but he was only nineteen—he couldn't drink in St. Louis. Kelly was twenty-one and he took full advantage of the fact that he was of legal age to get served in a bar. They'd grab a quick bite after games and Kelly would throw Roddy the keys to his car and go, "Don't worry, I'll get home."

Kelly was a middleweight, but he would take on heavyweights. It's one thing to fight a dude if you've got a fair fight, but Kelly would go toe to toe with anyone. He fought Tony Twist in training camp. It was the craziest thing, because those two were best buddies, but there are only so many spots on a team for that job. So, they'd drop the gloves and start going at it. "I've gotta beat you up to get that job." Neither of them held back. They were trying to kill each other. Afterward, they'd shake hands and work everything out.

You have to admire Chaser's courage, because Twister was a scary man. Super tough guy. He fought on the street. He fought in the arena. He fought in the ring—both boxing and kickboxing. Unlike other tough guys, Tony never broke bones in his hands, yet he split multiple helmets in half. He said that when he was seventeen, one of his "professors" told him, "Son, you're gonna learn real quick that all of this knowledge is useless if you don't have hands to implement it. You need to start now. Training. Training for impact."

He started with a bucket of sand, pounding his hands into it. They'd swell up. He'd wait for the swelling to go down, and then he'd do it again and again and again. Repetition. Tony graduated from sand to wood pallets and from pallets to rocks—round ones, mind you, to protect his skin. From rocks to concrete and then, after a couple of years, he didn't have to do it anymore—he'd made the bones strong enough. Tony always says, "I can tell you one thing. If I hadn't received that piece of valuable information when I was younger, I would never have made it to the NHL."

You didn't want to get on his wrong side, that was for sure. He, like a lot of tough guys, would protect you forever if you were a teammate or his friend. But if you were on the other side, well, be afraid. Be *very* afraid. Chaser was the same way, even though he only weighed a buck-eighty. Like I said, I give Chaser a lot of credit, because he was small compared to the other tough guys in the league. He was a gamer.

Twister liked to tell us he came from the Charlestown Chiefs, that team in the movie *Slap Shot*. He was referring to the major junior hockey he played with the Saskatoon Blades, which was insanely tough. In junior, players range between sixteen and twenty-one, so there's quite a gap in terms of physical development. Each team could have two over-age players (the twenty-one-year-olds). When Tony started out in junior, with the Prince George Kings, he was sixteen. He'd tell us how they would travel up to northern British Columbia and, during warm-ups, there would be five giants on the other team with huge beards. None of them could skate. That meant only one thing—there was going to be a brawl before the game. He said the police used to have to show up and escort his team onto the ice for games because the boys would be backed up in the tunnel after the Zamboni came off, swinging their sticks and chopping at angry fans.

Twister came by his power honestly. His grandmother Ethel is in the B.C. Lacrosse Hall of Fame. She was so competitive, her nickname was "Dirty Andy." Tony used to say she was a wonderful woman, absolutely wonderful. You just didn't want to piss her off.

Ethel's husband, Tony's Grandpa Harry, had a huge heart. Tony called him a "good, honest, extremely well-defined gentleman." Harry Twist (he fought under the name Harry Runcorn) was the 1923 Western Canada welterweight champion. In one bout, he accidentally killed his opponent, Handsome Howard Weldon, in the ring in Toronto.

Harry couldn't deal with Handsome Howard's death. It was devastating. Boxing ring canvases weren't like they are now. Boxing ring floors are composed of plywood boards with a shock-absorbing covering. In the 1920s, the covering was just felt under a layer of canvas—it had less give. Just like when Twister was with Quebec and knocked out Mike Peluso of New Jersey on December 18, 1993, there were two impacts—in Peluso's case, one from the punch and one when his head hit the ice. In Handsome Howard's case, the second impact was with the floor of the ring. That's usually where the real damage is done.

Grandpa Harry quit boxing and moved to Burnaby, British Columbia, where he joined the RCMP. He also opened up a boxing club that became very successful. And then he did something unusual. When he caught young burglars or vagrants on the street, instead of arresting them, he'd say, "You will report to me on these days at my club and train with me. Otherwise I will put you in jail." He changed gangsters into men.

Tony and his grandpa had a great relationship. When Tony was nine or ten, he'd visit his grandparents in the summer. Every morning, they'd get up at 6 a.m. and arrive at the men's spa by seven. I don't know if you're familiar with how that works. Everybody walks around naked, taking a steam, playing cards, grabbing a coffee. It's like a hockey locker room.

When Tony was at his grandparents' place, he would develop huge bruises on his arms, both left and right. You see, Grandpa didn't know how hard he hit. So he'd give Tony the old "Hey, youngster!" punch on the arm. Tony would smile—"Doing good, doing great, Grandpa"—and then stagger into the next room and fall against the wall. "Holy shit, that hurt!" But he never said a word.

One summer, his parents came to pick him up. His mom saw Tony's arms and said, "Son, what happened?"

"I got them playing lacrosse," Tony fibbed.

"No. Lacrosse has been over for two months. Where did you get those bruises?" She narrowed her eyes. "Is Grandpa hitting you in fun?"

Tony nodded. "Yeah, but he didn't mean anything by it."

"Well, why didn't you tell him?"

Tony shook his head. "I'm not gonna tell Grandpa. No way." He thought, "Grandpa's taking me to the spa to be a man. I'm not going to whine about how it hurts."

Later that day, Grandpa came up to Tony and said, "I'm so sorry, youngster, I had no idea!"

Tony said, "Well, I didn't want you to."

They got home and Tony got ready to go back to school. He asked his mom, "What do I tell the principal when he asks me, 'How'd you get those bruises?'"

She said, "Tell him you were playing lacrosse."

CHAPTER 25

No Backing Down

I LOVE TONY. But he was intimidating, even to us. He knew his job and he did it to the max. Nobody wanted to fight Twister because they could get seriously hurt. He threw punches that would knock guys' heads off. I watched him grab a guy in a fight, and when he went to punch him, the other guy ducked and the punch landed on the player behind him, breaking his collarbone. That's how hard Twister punched. Past the point of impact and he breaks another guy's collarbone.

It got so nobody would fight Twister anymore because he had such a reputation. There are guys who are gonna fight you and beat you, and there are guys who are gonna beat you and then kill you, meaning they'll break your jaw or end your career. So, Twister and Chaser cooked up a system.

Pound for pound, Chaser was one of the toughest guys ever, but he was a middleweight. In the NHL, there are middleweights and heavyweights, and tough guys would follow a code—they'd fight within their weight class. Except Chaser would go after a heavyweight. Once challenged, the guy would drop his gloves and then Chaser would back away and Twister would jump in. I'd see the guy's face drop—like, "Oh, shit." But once the gloves were off, there was no backing down. Whenever Twister and Chaser were on the ice at the same time, I would wait for something to happen.

Twister and Chaser fought to set the tone, not just if we got down a goal. God forbid we *should* get down a goal, because it was "Uh-oh, we're gonna change this immediately."

I'd never been protected like that before. They knew that if I was playing well, I could be a key to the team's success that night. It was nice. I didn't take advantage of it, but if somebody ran me, he would regret it. It only had to happen once or twice, and then it never happened again. It was much the same later in my career, in Toronto with Tie Domi. Nobody would mess with me. Tie would kill them. He and Chaser and Twister were all very good at their jobs. They weren't bluffers. They walked the talk.

Chaser and Twister spent summers in Saskatoon, along with another guy named Darin Kimble who joined our team a bit later. Bar patrons would recognize them as NHL tough guys and want to have a go. Kelly still tells the story of being half in the bag and standing on the bar someplace downtown, calling out, "Who's the toughest guy in here?" Someone would always step up and confront him. Kelly would jump down and tell him, "Okay, take over. I'm leaving."

We actually had a ridiculously tough team. We also had Todd Ewen and Robert Dirk. I mean, we had at least four or five guys who could fight. On the way to the game, the boys would be like, "Okay, we're playing Detroit tonight. I've got Kocur." "I've got Probert." "I've got Kaminski." It wasn't a matter of *if* you were getting into a fight, it was a question of *when*. But you were going to fight. And the guys on the other team were thinking the exact same thing.

Glen Featherstone was tough. A real character, just hilarious. He was a big man—six foot four, 215 pounds. We called him Feather. He came up from the OHL at the same time Roddy came out of Michigan State in time for the playoffs. They were roommates. Back then, teams used to have weigh-ins, but Feather liked to have his beers. He'd sit with a six-pack on the dinner table along with a plate of food. He'd look at one, and then the other, and he'd say, "I gotta choose." The beers always won out. We used to say, "Feather, this is not good for you, you gotta eat healthier." He could gain fifteen pounds in three days. An ongoing battle.

Brian Sutter, man, he would ride Feather hard. I remember him being furious with Feather after a three-day All-Star break. Feather was cramping up everywhere. Lying on the floor, writhing in pain, crying, "Ahh! Ahh! Ahh!" Brian stood over him in the dressing room, screaming at him and looking like he wanted to kick him.

Brian was old-school. Roddy saw him jump in the shower—with his suit on—to go after Sergio Momesso in Detroit. Serge had been kicked out for being the third man in on a five-on-five brawl. He was already undressed, and so, when the period ended, he was naked in the shower. Brian ran in to confront him. Serge had just gone toe to toe with Joey Kocur, one of the toughest guys in the league, but Brian was reaming him out because he hadn't gone after *the* toughest guy in the league, Bob Probert. That's how Brian was. All fired up and emotional and intense about doing it right.

Roddy got into some good fights his first five or six years. Brian just loved it. He pulled Roddy into his office and told him, "That's how I need you to play. You're gonna be like Cam Neely!"

Roddy said, "Well, Brian, I think I can do more. I think I can score and make plays."

Brian told him, "I can control whether you play in this league or not. And if you don't, I can send you to the minors."

Roddy fought a couple of tough guys, but he was smart enough to know that if they were *too* tough, he wasn't gonna go toe to toe with anybody. In other words, you have to fight if you are challenged, but you've got a choice of whether or not to stand there swinging. Roddy was so strong, he could just grab on and make sure he wasn't gonna get killed.

His second-last fight in the NHL was in December 2000, late in his career, against Jarome Iginla. They went at it, and Iginla hit Roddy on the forehead and the punch split his helmet. If Iginla's fist had landed two inches lower, Roddy would have been in big trouble. At that point, Roddy thought, "Forget it, I'm too old for this!" He broke his nose nine times, but never in a fight. It was more from the way he played. He was fearless.

Roddy didn't do anything poorly. Whatever you needed done, he could get it done. He could play on the power play. He could kill penalties. He could take faceoffs at key times. He could do it all. And consistent? He never had an off night. He always gave his all.

Roddy ended his career as one of the top ten two-way forwards of all time. He won two Frank J. Selke Awards for best defensive forward, he had a career total of 1,184 points, and in 1996, he captained the Hurricanes to their first and only Stanley Cup championship. He was right—he *could* do more than just be tough. But it was a different time. Everybody had to be tough. There was nobody on our team who wasn't.

CHAPTER 26

Butchy

THE ST. LOUIS Arena was a one-of-a-kind place. It opened in 1929, but not as a hockey arena. It was built as an ice skating rink and for showing cattle. By the late '80s, it certainly wasn't state of the art, but the atmosphere and character of the place were incredible. I loved the fans. They made a lot of noise. Really got into the game, banging on the glass. Truly a Budweiser-and-T-shirt crowd. Fans who wore good suits to the game had to head to the dry cleaner the next day.

We would come in every morning to the familiar reek of spilled Budweiser, rotting wood and stale cigarettes. It was dirty, it was dusty, and there were rats everywhere—along with cats brought in to keep the rat population down. The training facility had a universal gym, if you can remember what those looked like. It was next to the stick room, and it collected a lot of dust, but it was handy for hanging rolls of tape or drying a jock. When games took place during heavy rainstorms, water would drip through the roof, all over the ice. I loved the place.

In most arenas, the wives' room was far away from the dressing room, but not in St. Louis. It was right beside our room. I'd go in there and have a beer with everyone from the coaches' wives to the owners' wives to my own wife. That meant you got to know everybody. We were a tight-knit group.

Our dressing room was a dump. But it was our dump. It was our home and we spent a lot of time hanging out and chatting in the players' lounge. We'd throw on one of assistant coach Bob Berry's old L.A. Kings game tapes and have a good laugh. We'd be yelling at Bobby that he couldn't skate. "How'd you ever play in the NHL?" Bobby was another great character. A good man.

There were no protein shakes, no riding a bike after the game. You got rid of the lactic acid by drinking Bud. If you were worried about fitness, you drank Bud Light. The best part of the dressing room was the sauna. You could fit twelve guys in there. We'd put down towels on the planks and pull in a pail full of Bud, covered in ice. That way, if the coaches came by, someone would shove a hand or a foot in the bucket and give a wave. It wasn't any of their business. Especially when we knew Brian had done the same thing just a few years earlier.

We'd sit there and talk about the game, bitch and moan about the coaches, bitch and moan about the refs, and tell great stories.

On the way out to the car, we'd pass a police station, right inside the arena. Combined, the office and booking area were the size of a large locker room. There was a jail room to the side, all concrete, with a steel-barred door, just like you see on TV. We were all encouraged to go in there and have a beer with the officers. We got to know them and would sit there and have a beer or a coffee with them while the guys inside the cells were napping, waiting to get transported out.

———

GARTH BUTCHER JOINED the team in my second year. Brian brought him in because he respected him. When Brian played, he and Butchy would fight all the time. That's how Brian knew Butchy was a gamer. To this day, Garth is one of the funniest human beings you'll ever meet. And he was an awesome teammate.

He used to get mistaken for me. He'd go out and it'd be, "Hey, Cujo, can I get your autograph?" And he'd sign programs, sweaters, whatever, in my name. Many mornings after Butchy and the boys had gone out and carried on, while I stayed home with my family, Butchy would walk into the dressing room and stop in front of my stall. He'd grab me by the shoulder and look me in the eye and say, "Wow, Cujo, you had a great time last night. You put on a show."

This was not the best news. I was a young guy with a family, and the last thing I wanted anyone to hear was that I was out drinking beer with the boys, breaking curfew, flirting with the ladies, all things I didn't do. So, I'd be like, "Oh no. What'd you guys do? C'mon, tell me."

Butchy would say, "Yep, people thought I was you and I just went with it."

I'd shake my head and think, "Aw, God, no. What am I going to tell my family?"

Garth would really rub it in. He sat directly across from me in our dressing room, and as we'd be getting ready to go on the ice for practice, I remember him bending over to tighten his skates and then looking up and shaking his head as he was remembering what he'd done the night before and saying, "Sorry, bud."

Butchy came to the Blues from Vancouver, along with Dan Quinn, in a March 1991 trade for Geoff Courtnall, Robert Dirk, Sergio Momesso, Cliff Ronning and a fifth-round pick. He and Brett Hull became good friends. The first time Brett met Butchy was in a Vancouver Canucks–Calgary Flames matchup. Brett was with the Flames and Butchy played for Vancouver.

Butchy went up on the wing for the faceoff at centre ice, and Hully was beside him. Butchy stuck his stick between Hully's legs and lifted it up rather aggressively while threatening to kill him and then decapitate him and throw his head into the stands. Brett was just a young guy and not a fighter. He didn't say anything back. Butchy wanted to emphasize his message, so he cranked Brett up a little higher until he had him almost lifted off the ice. Referee Kerry Fraser was about to drop the puck when he looked over and said, "Hey, hey, Butchy! You know he's got some balls under there."

And Butchy shot back, "That's not what I heard."

CHAPTER 27

A Red Necktie

GARTH BUTCHER AND Brett Hull sat at the back of the bus because they were the captains. Rookies sat at the front. That's part of a rookie's rite of passage into the NHL. Don't get on the elevator before the veterans. Don't go to the back of the bus and help yourself to beer—don't even think about it. Show respect. These policies are necessary. You can't have rookies thinking they're too good too early because there are too many ups and downs in the game. Make them pay their dues. No one just has it handed to them. You have to earn it.

Brett was so used to being good that when he played with guys who couldn't do the things he could, he'd get frustrated. And bored. My first three years with the Blues, from 1989–90 to 1991–92, Hully scored 228 goals—an average of seventy-six goals per season. Amazing. In those three seasons, he had several hat tricks but never scored more than three goals in any single game. The most prolific goal scorer I ever saw, and for him not to have a four-goal game seems surprising, especially with eighty-six goals one year. Part of it was that he never got an empty-net goal. By comparison, Wayne Gretzky had fifty-six empty-netters in his career. Nothing against Wayne, but he iced a lot of games that way. But for whatever reason, Brett wouldn't do it. He always passed off to a teammate.

I never saw a harder shot. In practice, he could fire the puck. That release . . . yeah, he was dangerous. But he knew where it was going. He would never hit you in the shoulder or face. When he took a shot, he never missed the net. He either hit the crossbar or the post, or it'd go in. Crazy accuracy.

I loved listening to Hully. He was very smart and hilarious. We were in Los Angeles one time, and it was a treat to play there because they had the Forum Club in their building. It was a great bar. Always full of famous athletes and movie stars. Just a wonderful place to hang out and have a couple beers after the game. At the end of a matchup with the Kings, we'd always move fast to get our gear off and shower and head up there. This one game in particular, we were tied 3–3 with under a minute to go at the end of the third period. Brett had been out for about a minute and a half, and his tongue looked like a red necktie.

There was a faceoff coming up in our zone, right in front of my net, and knowing that Hully—especially in those days—wasn't a defensive stalwart, Brian wanted to get him the hell off the ice. So, he sent Richie Sutter over the boards to take Brett's place.

Richie skated down to the faceoff circle. Hully, who was bent over with his stick on his knees, trying to catch his breath, tilted his head up and said, "Richie, fuck off."

And Richie said, "No, no, Hully. Brian wants me to come on."

"No. Richie. Fuck. Off."

Richie turned and started back towards the bench, but Brian was up on the boards, yelling at him and pointing at him, telling him to get his ass back out there and get Hully off the ice. Richie tried again, but Hully would not come off.

Finally, the ref came over and said, "Look, one of you fuckers has to go!"

Hully said, "Tell Richie to get the fuck off the ice. I ain't leaving!"

The puck dropped and Hully floated up near the blue line, doing absolutely nothing defensively. Meanwhile, the Kings had us trapped in our zone and I was getting spray-painted. And then, all of a sudden, the puck squirted out. Hully picked it up, ripped down the left side and roofed it.

Our guys went crazy! They headed down the ice to congratulate him, but he ignored them all, skated directly to the bench, jumped over the boards, sat himself down, turned his stick upside down and slammed it between his legs. And then he looked back at Brian and said, "Fucking overtime in L.A., Brian? Are you fucking kidding me?"

CHAPTER 28

Hully

HULLY HAD NO filter. None. He was also big on sticks. He'd look at guys' sticks and he'd say, "Look at your fucking stick. No wonder you can't shoot!"

How do you not listen to him? He could shoot. He was the best. My first season, Brett scored 72 goals and 113 points and was making $125,000. Bargain contract doesn't begin to describe it. The Blues let him play it out. They should've bumped it up. But he was a young guy. He turned down their last-minute offer and ended up making $7 million for four years in his next deal.

Like the title of his book said, he came out shooting and smiling. I thought that was funny. Shooting and smiling. He had that big smile and dimples. His teeth were beautiful—white. Huge wrists and strong legs. And he's hockey royalty. He grew up in a rink, listening to his dad, Bobby Hull, who probably had no filter either. Can you imagine all the stories Brett heard over the years?

A front-row seat listening to hockey legends like his dad and Gordie Howe, Stan Mikita—all those guys—talk about the game. No wonder he knew so much. The things he'd say off the cuff were bang on and to the point, whether it hurt or not. You had to be thick-skinned.

Roddy was lying on the table, with the trainer working on him one time, and Hully walked by. "No wonder you can't stickhandle. Look at your arms! You've got too many muscles. You gotta be like me. I don't have any muscles and I'm never hurt. I don't have any muscles to pull." And he was right! Guys with 4 per cent body fat were lying on the table, looking like they were vacuum-sealed, ripples everywhere, and Hully would take it to them.

In six years, the only injury I saw on him was a sore wrist for two weeks. That's it. But great genetics. And he never got hit. That's because he never put himself in a bad situation.

Some of the guys could take what Hully had to say and it was like water off a duck's back. It became something to laugh at a day later. But others had a hard time with it. Twister almost killed him at the start of my first training camp. He was skating down to the net in a drill and Hully put a pass on his tape, but Twister fumbled it. Hully threw his arms in the air. "Who the fuck gave this guy a jersey?"

Twister snapped and went after him. Thank God everybody got in between them, but I remember Twister trying to get at him, yelling, "Fuck you, motherfucker. I'm gonna stick up for the team and you give me that shit?"

When Butchy came in, he'd tell Hully, "Look, if you're going to rip so and so, rip me instead. You can't go there. You're gonna crush him." There were a few times when Hully said something anyway and Butchy gave him a good swat.

Hully was hard on guys, but he loved it when guys succeeded too.

Steve Larmer of Chicago was a great goal scorer, and he seemed to have my number. He would never give anything away with his eyes. You couldn't tell where he was going. He was like the best poker player ever—you could not read him. When a guy comes in on you, you watch the puck, but in your periphery, you also watch his head and where he's looking and where's he catching the puck on his stick. If the puck's far behind him, he's not going to be able to score high, so you immediately drop down low. If the puck's in front of him a little bit, the shot is going high. A player will tell you everything he's going to do with body language, and you make decisions based on that.

Larmer was incredibly crafty. He was always chewing gum with his mouth open on one side, like he was sizing me up. He came down on me with that jaw going and a little half-smile on his face, like it was a walk in the park. Then he ripped a half-slapper over my shoulder, right by my ear. Damn! That's your manhood right there. When a guy shoots it and he scores over your glove, it's the worst feeling in the world. I just hated to get beat there.

I was disgusted with myself and embarrassed. I was a young guy and pissed. I walked into the locker room after the first period and Brett Hull, in front of the whole group, said, "Cujo, is your fucking glove *Velcroed* to your fucking pants?" I know—brutal, right? But he was bang on.

All the guys laughed. Everybody was laughing, and he was laughing with them. He had this chuckle like Johnny Carson's sidekick, Ed McMahon, hee hee hee hee, ho, ho, ho, ho. Today, I tell that story and think, "Oh my God, that's funny." But at the time, I wanted to strangle him and then crawl into a hole and die.

———

BOBBY HULL CAME to our games. Most of the dads didn't have an all-access pass to every arena in the world, but Bobby would just pop in and shake a few hands and sign a few autographs to get past security. We knew that when Bobby was in town, we were certainly going to see him. He would give me a boost of confidence because he was always positive. He went out of his way to say something nice to me. I told you before that I looked to people, Clint Eastwood types, guys you could describe as a man's man, for advice.

Bobby was like that. He had a great energy about him. He was happy and he was proud. In 1991, his son won both of the league's MVP awards—the Hart Memorial Trophy, voted on by hockey writers, and the Lester B. Pearson Award, as chosen by members of the NHL Players' Association. Brett was the talk of the league at that time. It was a good time to be a Blue, and it was a good time to be around the game, because it gave me the opportunity to watch this special father–son interaction.

They both had a wicked sense of humour. I remember one time, Bobby threw three dead Canada geese onto the floor of the dressing room. He'd just gone hunting.

Neither Bobby nor Brett was afraid to be frank. Brett was a little quieter when Bobby was there. Bobby would take the stage and Brett would be respectful and step back. He'd listen to his dad and maybe jump in every once in a while.

In the visitors' locker room in Toronto, there used to be two rooms on two different levels, but the organization took down the wall between them to make it bigger. That made it one room on two levels. Up on the platform, that's where you'd find the defencemen and goalies, because we always sat together. Down on the lower level was where all the forwards sat.

Brian was in the room, giving a pre-game speech, and he was all fire and brimstone. Pointing at us, his face all lit up. "You sons of bitches!" He paced up and down the room and then stormed up the platform, still cursing and giving it with heart. Now, Brian always wore his shirt tucked in, but he was still fit, which meant his pants kept slipping down. In between breaths, he'd stop to yank them up and tuck his shirt back into his waistband with his thumb, and then he'd start up his speech again.

He was up on the platform, taking a breath and tucking. He opened his mouth to continue, when in bounced Bobby Hull. But Bobby, on the lower level, didn't see Brian on the upper level. Bobby had no idea the coach was in the middle of his pre-game speech.

Bobby rubbed his hands together and smiled, "Hey, guys! Here we go!" He picked up a stick and fired a phantom puck down the room. "We're gonna shoot the first one at the goalie's head and the next one along the ice!" Back in the day, Bobby was known for scaring the shit out of goalies by taking one of his patented hundred-mile-an-hour slapshots at their heads. The next time he came down the ice, a goalie would be a little more upright and not so inclined to go down to stop it. This would leave Bobby free to shoot it hard along the ice.

"That's the way I used to do it!" he said. And then he lowered his voice conspiratorially. "You guys are just playing a game. Don't worry about systems and all that shit." He laughed, slapped a few backs and left.

Brian had been standing next to me, frozen in midstep with his mouth still open. But Brian is probably one of the most respectful men you'll ever meet when it comes to players who played before him. Even though it had to eat him up inside, he bit his tongue and let Bobby do what Bobby did. It was hilarious. One of those funny, funny things that you know you're going to laugh your butt off about after the game. You also know you cannot laugh at the time. Brian's momentum was gone. He just turned and quietly walked out.

The room was silent because nobody knew what to say. Finally, I turned to Garth Butcher and said, "Butchy, maybe somebody should tell Bobby that goalies wear masks now."

CHAPTER 29

No Hiding in the Game

I WAS ALWAYS searching for . . . not a father, not a dad, but a role model. Someone who was going to give me advice to make me better, to get me to where I needed to be. Somebody to teach me how to treat people, how to speak to people. When I got to St. Louis, I looked up to all my teammates, all men who set an example and acted like professionals. There were so many solid guys, like Garth Butcher. I was twenty-two and married, but compared to these guys, I felt like a boy.

And yet, here I was, in December of '91, with a family. We named our baby girl Madison. I got her name from the city where I went to college—Madison, Wisconsin. When I first held Madi, she had my heart immediately. She was precious. I loved being around kids anyway. They are so innocent. But the love I felt for her was different. I'd never felt anything like it before. You may know the saying "You think you know how to love until you have a child." It may offend some people, but it's true. I didn't know what love was, or what it was about, until the moment I laid eyes on her.

Madi was an angel. A beautiful blond princess. She made me excited about coming home. And then Taylor came along in January of '94, and wow, nothing prepares you for the feeling of seeing your first son.

I'd just bought our first house. We were building it from plans, a ranch-style home on a cul-de-sac in St. Louis with just five other houses. It cost $250,000, a fortune back then. I remember walking in when it was just framed, before the drywall was up. I stood there, taking in the wonderful smells of fresh lumber, nails and sawdust. I'm a dreamer, and so I was walking around with my hands in my pockets, baseball hat tipped up, looking around wide-eyed.

The general contractor, a gruff middle-aged guy, spotted me and called over. "Hey! Where's your dad?"

I thought, "What's he talking about?"

"I gotta talk to your dad *now*." He punched his fist into his open hand and said, "I gotta make some decisions."

I stared at him blankly. He threw his hands up like he was talking to an idiot. Suddenly, it dawned on me, and I was like, "Ohhhh. No, there's no dad. Just me. I own the house."

He blinked a few times and then said, "I hope you're not friggin' messing with me, son."

———

ON THE BLUES, there were many players who worked hard, like Gino Cavallini and Paul MacLean. MacLean was a veteran who went on to coach the Senators. He knew how to play the game. I was very fortunate to play with those guys in my first year.

At twenty-six, Gino was only four years older than me, but it might as well have been ten. He set an example of how to be accountable. How to put in the work. His dad, Rino, was a great mentor to him right up until he died of pancreatic cancer when he was only fifty-six.

Gino told me that when his dad was eighteen, he immigrated to Canada from Marche, Italy, which is right across the boot from Rome. He did it alone, landing with a $20 bill in his pocket. Rino eventually found work in the marble business.

When Gino was fifteen, he started helping his dad out in the shop. When you are cutting marble, there are no shortcuts. Gino learned that you either do it the right way or the stone is ruined. There is no in-between. Gino took pride in doing everything the right way. He'd say, "There's no hiding in the game."

I would stay out after practice with Gino, and he would pretty much pepper me with shots. I'd be plastered to the net, just like the goalie in the *Mighty Ducks* movie. Gino was a fourth-liner, a third-liner at best. But he wanted to be a better shooter, and here was this young goalie who was willing to try to stop shots.

When I got to St. Louis, I wasn't mature. I wasn't professional. I wore a University of Wisconsin tracksuit to practice every day. A couple of weeks in, Gino pulled me aside and said, "Hey, kid—see how I'm dressed? Nice jeans, collared shirt? We're professionals. You wear that stupid tracksuit every day. Wake up. You're a professional now."

I thought, "Oh man, he's right!" I started to watch how he and the other vets handled themselves. How they tipped at restaurants. I also learned that picking up the tab was always a good idea. If you'd signed a good contract, it was in your best interest to do it.

Gino's role on ice was to be a mucker, and he did it well and enjoyed it. He didn't run away from the job. After a few years in that role, some guys will cave. Not Gino. He fought to the bitter end. He worked to extend his career any way he could. He drank this terrible, awful tasting drink called KM, made by a company called Matol. It was an herbal mineral supplement developed back in the 1920s. Butchy drank it too. Before every game, Gino would down a bottle. I remember Twister asking Gino, "What are you doing?"

"Extend the career. Look at me, look at Butchy."

"Yeah, true. I can't fight you on that one. You've been around for a long time. When did you start drinking that?"

"Last year."

"Jesus, it looks and smells like motor oil."

"Yeah, well," Butchy piped up, "if anyone knows what motor oil tastes like, it's you, Tony."

Gino's younger brother, Paul Cavallini, one of our defencemen, was on the opposite end of the spectrum. Paul was a little more refined. When he made it to the NHL All-Star Game in 1989–90, Paul started carrying himself differently. He assumed the role of the intellectual.

But just like Gino, Paul put a lot of work into his game. The All-Star appearance put him on a pedestal, and he aspired to keep himself there. His career improved because of it. It made him a better hockey player.

It may sound funny to call Peter Zezel a veteran because he was only twenty-four, but he'd been in the NHL for five years. Everybody loved Peter. Always happy in the dressing room. Never came in too serious, but never came in too loose. He was at the pinnacle of his career. Such a solid guy and a good centreman. He was a horse on the ice. We are talking about a guy who was put together. His legs and calves were the size of a football player's. And he had this solid barrel chest. Strong. Not weightlifting strong, but farm strong. He was an anomaly. And man, was he hairy. Biggest, hairiest legs and calves I've ever seen!

I remember he showed up at a golf tournament one time, wearing what looked like soccer shorts, and we all gave him the gears. He was Brett Hull's centreman the year Brett scored seventy-two goals—before Adam Oates arrived. I don't think a lot of people know that.

Peter was kind of the guy who took care of people. He cooked and cleaned up while the guys played Nintendo. Just a super-responsible guy. He was diagnosed with a rare blood disorder when he was in his thirties. He died in 2009 after a ten-year struggle with his health. Peter was only forty-four years old. It was incredibly sad.

Dave Lowry was another veteran presence. He was great. A professional in every sense of the word. He wasn't a great player, but he had a nineteen-year career in the NHL because he was one of those character guys that you want on your team. It's no secret why he's a successful coach. He's very smart. His nickname was Pi—not because he liked to eat pie, but because he was smart like a mathematician. If you met him, I don't think you'd find him very funny or outgoing. But he did have a good sense of humour.

Back then, it was different. I don't know how to explain it, other than there was a lot more joking going around. I've talked to a lot of guys about this. The game's gotten much more serious today. Maybe because guys are younger now. Our veteran players, they'd been around.

CHAPTER 30

Cursing a Lot

IN 1992–93 AND '93–94, we had a pair of fifty-goal scorers on our team—Hully and Brendan Shanahan. If Brett or Shanny didn't score, we were not going to win the game. I loved it when guys on the team would come to me and ask about the other goalie. Shanny always did. He was always grilling me—"Cujo, how do I score on this guy? What do you see?" I loved it, because I'd be like, "Oh, listen. I'll tell you. This is what you do . . ."

We played eight years together. Shanny was a strategist, much like he is now in his role as president and alternate governor for the Toronto Maple Leafs. He liked to know where everybody was going to be on the ice. "You go here, I'll go there, they'll go here, and then we'll come out here . . . and I'll be wide open. Get me the puck and I'll score." Shanny would carry the puck in line with his body, pretending he was just looking. Most guys have to pull the stick back behind them to get enough power behind the blade to propel the puck up or into the net. But Shanny had this tremendous ability to flick it with his wrists without a backswing, and it would sail in between the crossbar and the goalie's glove. He played a lot of lacrosse when he was a kid, and his shooting motion in hockey was very similar to the way you'd shoot a lacrosse ball. What it meant was that a goalie could not read his shot.

Thanks to Patrick Roy, it seemed every goalie in the league was starting to play the butterfly style. The butterfly goalies would often misread Shanny and go down. When you are dropping down, it goes against the grain to raise your glove upward. Shanny would time his release just right. Shooting the puck was a chess match for him.

Later on, when he was an opponent, he knew what I was thinking, so he'd try to do something I couldn't predict. I knew he liked to go high on the glove side, and he knew that I knew, so I was always wondering, "Geez, is he going to go five-hole?"

I was a strategist too, from the other end—the defensive perspective. We'd always talk about players. I'd ask him, "You've played with this guy. Where does he shoot from? Is he going to pass or is he going to shoot the majority of the time? Give me the percentages." And he'd ask me what I saw the other goalie doing. "What can you tell me about him? Where's his weak spot?" Those kinds of conversations.

Brendan was tough too. He could fight. He stuck up for his teammates, even though he barely wore shoulder pads. They were pretty much paper cups on his shoulders.

Like Gino, Brendan worked hard after practice. He shot thousands of pucks as well. Nothing was handed to him. That's why his success later in his career (he was a forty-goal scorer at age thirty-seven, in a much lower-scoring era) came as no surprise.

I only played fifteen games with St. Louis in my rookie season, partly because I was down in the minors and partly because of my knee injury. After Greg Millen got traded to Quebec for Jeff Brown about halfway through the year, Vincent Riendeau became our number one goalie. Vince was my first NHL goalie partner. I loved Vinnie. He was a sweet guy and a good friend. When he joined the team the season before me, he was only twenty-two and had been a top goalie in the American Hockey league.

When you're a goalie, you're an island. It's an individual position in a team sport. You don't interact with the head coaches very often because you aren't on the bench during the game with the coach talking in your ear.

For a goalie, it's all about communication with the defence. It's not about making plays for your linemates or how many points you're going to get that year. It's about saves and wins. That's it. The guy you are usually closest to is your goalie partner. He knows exactly what you're going through, and you confide in him. Today, guys have goalie coaches, but we never had them.

Obviously, I wanted to play more and to prove myself. Vinnie lived fairly close to me and one day he asked me, "Hey, my wife's got to do something. Do you mind picking me up tomorrow?" And part of me was conflicted. I thought, "I'm competing for his job." At that point in my life, I didn't know how to be friends with somebody while at the same time trying to take his job. But Vinnie taught me what a goaltending partnership is all about. How to balance competing for every minute of ice time with becoming close friends.

And then Brian handed me the ball right before the 1990 playoffs. I remember thinking to myself, "Are you ready for this? You're a young guy. How's it gonna go?" We played the Toronto Maple Leafs in the first round and beat them out in five games.

In the third period of Game Five, we were leading when I got knocked into the post and popped my shoulder out. That dreaded shoulder injury that hadn't reared up . . . well, since my college visit to Wisconsin when I was playing at Notre Dame.

It's funny. I can remember cursing a lot. Strange how I can remember these things and not my own mother's funeral. I remember the doctor said the shoulder was out, and I was just cursing like a sailor. Never the N-word. Never the C-word. Not even the Lord's name in vain. More like the F-bomb. And lots of them.

When my shoulder was out, I felt excruciating, never-ending pain. This time, it did not stop. It would not go back in and I was frustrated. That meant the end of my year, and an injury like that can limit your game going forward. It was like an old nemesis coming back and grabbing me again. Playing in the playoffs, beating the Leafs, I was accomplishing everything I wanted to accomplish, and then this. It was terrible.

I was out of the playoffs and we ended up losing the Norris Division final to Chicago in seven games.

CHAPTER 31

Wendy

MY WHOLE LIFE, I was curious about where I came from. As I got older and looked at my strengths, I thought, "In terms of genetics, my parents must be good athletes." And after my first year as a professional hockey player, I didn't cringe inside as much when someone asked me about my past. My confidence was growing. I had this life that I loved. I no longer felt the need to fit in, because I *did* fit in. I had money now. I had a purpose and a direction. It felt great. I was a professional.

On the ice, I was dealing with men like Gino Cavallini and Brian Sutter. These guys were men's men. Practising hard every day made me better and better. I'd learned not to think about how well I was playing. Don't analyze, don't talk about it, just ride the wave.

I didn't want to let anyone down. I had a hockey family and a hockey life. My teammates were my family. Garth Butcher, all my defencemen, these wonderful guys and wonderful coaches who cared so much. We spent more time together than I did with anyone else. The relationships I had with these guys gave me a solid footing.

I'm a dreamer by nature, and an optimist. By 1990, I figured it was time to meet the people I'd fantasized about all my life—my biological parents. I had just finished my first year with St. Louis and was off for the summer when I called Karen and asked her if she knew anything about my birth mother.

Remember how I told you about my first dad, Mom's husband Howard? Turns out he always had it in the back of his mind that I might ask questions someday. "Who are my real parents? Where are they? Can I meet them?" He took it upon himself to keep track of where my birth mother was. He'd met Wendy Munro when she was sixteen and pregnant. She'd been dating my biological father, Curtis Randall Nickle, for a couple of years. But when he found out she was pregnant, they broke up.

When I was little, Wendy would write to Mom asking about me, but Mom would crumple up the letters and throw them in the garbage with the attitude that "he's mine now." I know what my mother was like. I know she would've shut Wendy out.

Howard secretly rescued those letters and hid them. One letter Wendy wrote said that she'd gotten married and that she'd told her husband before she married him about me. Howard knew the name of her husband. In fact, he kept track of her for years after that.

I called Karen and she told me, "Okay, I know her name, but I will have to find her. Call me tomorrow. I want you to think on it and make sure that you really want to know. As far as I know, she was a nice girl, but I don't want to set you up for disappointment. You could be opening Pandora's box. Sleep on it and make sure, and then I'll see what I can do."

I said, "Fair enough."

Karen hung up and called her dad, Howard. "Do you happen to know where Wendy Munro is?"

"I certainly do," he said. "So, the day has come, huh?"

Karen said, "Yep, he wants to meet her."

Howard gave her Wendy's contact information. He even told Karen where Wendy worked. She was a nurse's aide, working in a nursing home in Pottageville, a little town west of Aurora.

Karen phoned the nursing home and asked if there was a Wendy

Munro who worked there. The lady who answered said, "Well, we have a Wendy here, but her last name's not Munro."

Karen explained she needed to speak with Wendy and was given a number. She called it, and Wendy picked up. She happened to be at a patient's home, helping him with dialysis. When Karen introduced herself and told her why she was calling, Wendy was happy but shocked. She told Karen she'd call back and then hung up.

Wendy had a hard time finishing her shift, but when it was over, she went home and told her husband and kids about the call. She had a son named Steven and a daughter, Marlaina. She'd always told her children that she'd had a child she named Curtis before she was married. She prepared them because Steven played hockey and was just two years younger than me. He played in tournaments in Bancroft, Newmarket and Aurora, right around where I lived. There was the possibility we might run into each other. But he never ran into a Curtis Munro because, even though I was Curtis Munro in high school, I stayed with the name Jeanne had given me, Curtis Joseph, throughout my hockey life.

Wendy phoned Karen back and said she wanted to meet me too. She was excited and asked, "Where is he?"

Karen said, "Well, actually, he lives in St. Louis. He plays for the St. Louis Blues in the NHL."

"What?!"

"Yeah, he's a goaltender. Number 31."

Karen arranged a time for us to meet at her place in Aurora. I came in the front door and walked through to the kitchen. Wendy was sitting there, waiting.

She turned, and I saw her reaction. Her face lit up, she was a little nervous, but she looked at me like I was an old friend or someone she missed. The first thing Wendy said to me was, "Oh, you're so handsome!" I don't know if she saw a little boy or my father. Later, she showed me photos and I look so much like him, and I was close to the same age he was when they were dating.

I loved the way she looked. I could tell she was a sweet lady by her face. And she had this gentleness and kindness about her. Even her voice was soft.

I felt protective of her right away. I knew what my childhood had been like. I didn't want to lay it on her and make her feel guilty. I told her, "I'm glad you had me. It was the best decision you ever made."

I learned about her. My biological father, Curtis Nickle, was from Richmond Hill, just north of Toronto. He was the family cowboy, but the rest of them were artsy. There were four boys, Curtis being the oldest. Both of his parents were in the theatre. Lyle Nickle, his dad, wrote poetry. He always dressed in a suit and wore an ascot.

Wendy was the youngest in her family. She had several half brothers and half sisters—thirteen children in all. Wendy was the only child from both parents. Before she was born, her mom, Frieda, had lost her first husband in France, where he was fighting in World War II, and Wendy's dad, Frank, had lost his wife in childbirth.

Frieda was left widowed with four sons. She lived in a farmhouse in Downsview, and Frank, who was a widower with eight children, lived nearby. One night, during a terrible storm, the wind blew the roof off his house. He took his family down the road for shelter, and as the story goes, he never left.

Wendy was sixteen when she found out she was pregnant. She didn't want to have an abortion, and thankfully her mom was very understanding about it. That's the type of person she was. Wendy said her dad was supportive too, but in a man's way. But keeping the baby wasn't an option. Her parents were older. When Wendy was born, her mother, Frieda, was thirty-nine. From Frank and Frieda's point of view, they had already raised thirteen kids. Wendy had lots of married brothers and sisters, but everybody was busy raising their own families.

In those days, unwed mothers didn't stay home while they were pregnant. They were sent away. Frank arranged for Wendy to move to Richmond Hill and work as a nanny for his boss's four children until she had the baby. His boss's wife was very kind and Wendy liked the kids.

Because the Nickle family lived in Richmond Hill, my biological grandmother arranged for Wendy to see their doctor. Some members of the family encouraged her to think about giving the baby up for adoption through the Children's Aid Society, but Wendy didn't want any part of that. She desperately wanted to keep her baby, and would have if she'd had more support. But there was no way. She worked as a nanny for room and board, and her only other means of taking care of herself was a part-time job at a nearby nursing home.

She decided that if she couldn't keep the baby, she would make sure he had a better life. Jeanne Eakins was the charge nurse at the nursing home Wendy worked at. Jeanne had a good job, and when she found out Wendy was looking for a home for her baby, Jeanne was especially kind to her. She told Wendy she could take the baby. Wendy met Jeanne's husband, Howard, and he seemed like a nice guy. Wendy met Grant, another little boy they'd adopted, and he seemed like a nice little guy too. Wendy thought it would be great for her baby to have a big brother.

She thought, "If the Eakinses are my baby's parents, my baby will have a good life. As a nurse and as a mother, Jeanne will know how to look after him." Wendy reasoned that nurses were caring people. And she liked Howard. He seemed thoughtful and gentle. On top of that, they lived in Keswick, which Wendy knew was a nice area with good schools.

Wendy had a few small reservations. Jeanne could be very bossy and overbearing, but because Wendy was painfully shy and unsure of herself, she thought that might be a good thing. Jeanne was a force, someone who could handle things. Wendy thought her baby needed a mother who could handle things.

On April 29, 1967, Wendy went into labour. She took a cab to the hospital. She was there all by herself, frightened and alone. Even though she was just a kid herself, they wouldn't allow anyone but family to be with her. Her parents were away, so she called one of her older sisters who lived in Aurora. This wasn't a sister Wendy was particularly close to, but she was kind and came to look after Wendy. She stayed with her and held her hand.

When Wendy saw me, a rush of emotion came over her. She didn't want to give me up, but what choice did she have? She called the Eakinses.

I weighed only four pounds, ten ounces. The doctors at York Central Hospital in Richmond Hill wanted me to stay longer and gain a little weight, but because Jeanne was an RN and a formidable force, she took me home with her that day.

At this point, Jeanne and Wendy had agreed that Jeanne and Howard could foster me. Wendy didn't want to give me up for adoption. To Wendy, adoption was too final. She didn't want to sever all ties. But when I was less than a month old, Jeanne changed her mind. She called Wendy. The Eakinses wanted to make it legal. They wanted to adopt me.

"No," Wendy said. "I want Curtis to have my name—Munro. It's the only thing I can give him." She promised Jeanne that, although she'd phone and write to see how I was doing, she wouldn't interfere in my life, because she didn't want me to be confused. Jeanne agreed I would have the name Munro, but she wasn't happy about it.

At first, Jeanne kept her promise, but when she split up with Howard, she wrote to Wendy and told her that she and her new boyfriend, Harold, intended to adopt me. Wendy was heartbroken. She wrote back, saying that she'd kept up her part of the bargain and expected Jeanne to do the same. Jeanne destroyed the letter and moved in with Harold without giving Wendy any new contact information. And then Jeanne dropped my last name—Munro—and started calling me Curtis Joseph.

Later in life, this caused a lot of confusion. There was no internet yet. Records were not always checked very thoroughly. Jeanne registered me for school as Curtis Joseph, and I went through elementary with that name. But when I got to high school, they wanted to see a birth certificate. And because my last name was legally still Munro, that's how I was registered. In fact, everyone who knew me in high school knows me as Curtis Munro.

Jeanne told me I had been adopted and that the business about my name was just the result of a mix-up in the paperwork. She told me that my real last name was Joseph. And so, out of respect for Harold, when I graduated high school I switched my name back to Joseph again. I hesitated for a moment while playing for Notre Dame and after going on a couple of college recruiting trips. The college crowds go nuts. They love to jump all over the goalies. I thought, "Maybe I should change my name back to Munro. Because if my name's Joseph, when anyone scores on me, I'll hear, 'Joe-sieve! Joe-sieve! Joe-sieve!'"

Today, I am my own man. Joseph is a name I embrace. It is who I am and it is who my kids are. But I have to admit, had I known the truth, I likely would have chosen Munro. Which means today I might be known as Cumo, instead of Cujo!

After Wendy gave me up, everyone figured she would just carry on with life as usual. But it doesn't work that way. She didn't go back to high school. Instead, her mom arranged for her to go to modelling school in Toronto. Wendy was a very pretty girl with delicate features and gorgeous blond hair. She enrolled in the Eleanor Fulcher Modelling School at the corner of Bloor and Yonge Streets. Every day for a year, she took the bus to and from her parents' home in Oak Ridges, which is located between Aurora and Richmond Hill. A long way to downtown Toronto. In the end, she couldn't handle the city. She was a small-town girl with a broken heart. The whole experience was just too intimidating.

Wendy married and moved to Bancroft, and then she had Steven. He was two years old when one day there was a knock at her door. She opened it up and there stood Jeanne. A child peeked out from behind her—it was me. She knew. She'd recognize my blue eyes anywhere. They were just like my father's.

Jeanne stepped in and I tagged along. I had inherited Wendy's shyness. Jeanne started in. She was still working as a nurse and had been looking after a lady in Richmond Hill who'd just died, and she had a little time on her hands so she came up to visit her daughter, who lived nearby, and thought she'd stop in to see Wendy. Short notice, but she wondered if Wendy had given any more thought to letting her adopt.

Wendy stared at me as I played with blocks. I was small for four, not much bigger than Steven, and why was my hair so long? But a nice little boy. Quiet, well-mannered. Happy.

Wendy was still opposed to the adoption, and when Jeanne realized she wasn't getting what she came for, we left. Wendy closed the door and went over to the window and watched us drive off. She was devastated. It would be almost twenty years before she saw me again.

Chapter 32

Victor

THE SAME SUMMER I met Wendy, I got a call out of the blue from my older brother Victor. I hadn't seen him in years, not since Jeanne and Harold had moved to Nova Scotia. He didn't want anything from me. He just wanted to know if I could come for a visit.

He was living in Toronto. Victor always liked fashion and had studied at Sheridan College and then started working for the John Casablancas modelling agency, recruiting models.

I went over to Victor's apartment in Toronto. It was good to see him. He'd gained a little weight since his figure-skating days. He gave me a hug and it was like hugging an NFL halfback. He was warm and friendly and funny. His usual self.

Victor's place was fairly ornate—yellow and gold with a lot of fancy tables and couches. It was like something out of a magazine. We sat down and his roommate, Shaun, came in. We shook hands and then Shaun sat down beside Victor and grabbed his hand. I thought, "What the . . . ?" And then Victor leaned over and gave the guy a little peck on the cheek. I thought, "Victor's roommate is gay?"

And then it hit me. "Holy crap! Victor is gay!"

I was shocked. Look, today I don't care who's gay and who's not. But this was 1989. Before Ellen came out. Before *Will and Grace*.

Besides, I lived in hockey world. As far as I knew, I'd never met anyone who was gay.

You could have knocked me off Victor's velvet stool. I couldn't believe it. He and Shaun talked about what they were going to do for supper and then they kissed, this time on the lips, and his buddy took off.

Victor and I spent a little more time catching up, and then I left. I'm not sure what we said, because I was still reeling. I do remember he told me he had diabetes.

Knowing what I know now, I wish I had been more accepting. Victor was a sweetheart. Looking back, I'm sure he knew I borrowed his shirts when we were kids and he never said a word. He used to watch out for me too.

When I was fifteen, back at Martin Acres, I played ball hockey with these older guys, they were about twenty. Good guys, but they smoked a lot of marijuana and they had the long hair. Suffice it to say, they looked sketchy. I remember Victor watching out the window when they dropped me off one night, and he overheard one of them say to me, "Hey, man, wanna little something?"

And I said, "Guys, I play goal for you. That's it."

I came in, and Victor looked ready to go beat them up. "You don't hang out with those guys, right?"

Victor went on to a great career. He moved to L.A. and kept an apartment in New York. He became a stylist and a makeup artist. Although Victor was self-taught, he was in demand. He worked on a lot of fashion shoots for famous models and celebrities like Queen Latifah, Faye Dunaway, Shannen Doherty. And he was hired by Saks Fifth Avenue in New York, to do makeup and clothes for a lot of their print ads. In his field, he was a star.

Victor came to a sad end. He loved to vacation in Hawaii and would invite his sisters Jeanette and Freddy, and sometimes their kids, to join him. By 2002, he'd broken up with Shaun and was staying in Hawaii when Freddy received a letter containing $1,000. The letter said that should anything happen to him, he wanted to be cremated.

The next thing they knew, they got a call. Victor was dead. He'd overdosed on his insulin. The girls flew to Hawaii to say their final goodbyes. They cried as they spread his ashes in the Pacific.

I felt terrible when I heard about it.

CHAPTER 33

Positive, Negative and Realistic

THE BIGGEST PROBLEM we had in St. Louis was a lack of continuity. The team was sold in 1991, and general manager Ron Caron was replaced by Mike Keenan in '94. Caron made a lot of player moves, bringing in guys like Brett Hull, Adam Oates, Brendan Shanahan, Scott Stevens and Al MacInnis. It seemed like they were trying to build a Stanley Cup championship team overnight. We made it to the second round in both 1989–90 and 1990–91, but we were nowhere near as good as Chicago, or even the Minnesota North Stars. Teams that were built over a period of years. If they'd kept the core of our team together, I think we could have contended, and maybe even won the Stanley Cup.

Brian Sutter was fired at the end of the 1991–92 season. It was a sad day because I liked Brian. He had been coach of the year a season earlier and we had made it to the second round of the playoffs, and still they let him go. The guys' response was "Ah, it's a business, you know?" Hockey is ruthless if you don't win. Somebody's got to pay the price.

Brian was replaced by Bob Plager, one of the famous Plager brothers who played defence with the Blues in their late-1960s glory days, when they went to the Stanley Cup final in three straight years as an expansion team. Bob quit as our coach after only eleven games and was replaced by our former assistant coach, Bob Berry. I liked him. He had an easier-going personality than Brian, but they'd coached together for a long time, so they had basically the same philosophies. Bob always said, "There's positive, there's negative," and then he'd look at you and say, "and there's realistic." He played me a ton. Sixty-eight games that season, and just twenty-eight losses. It was a good year.

There was bad blood between our team and the Detroit Red Wings. We knew that every time we faced them, there was going to be a brawl. Kelly Chase was going to stir something up, and of course, we had Tony Twist, Bob Bassen and Dave Lowry. They had a bunch of tough guys too, led by Bob Probert, the reigning champ. He was feared throughout the league. Just a great fighter.

January 23, 1993, was one of those nights. It was the second half of a home-and-home—two nights earlier, we'd lost 5–3 in Detroit and it was a rough game. Less than a minute into this one, Chaser hooked Probie, which led to a fight in the corner between Chaser and Jim Cummins. Probie took on both Bob Bassen and Dave Lowry. I was down there in my net, watching it all unfold, when suddenly, Detroit's goalie, Tim Cheveldae, skated out of his crease and jumped Dave Lowry. So, I went after Cheveldae.

I'd had a baseball fight once—minor baseball, town league, and I led with my face. I'd picked a kid who had been in more fights and spent more time in the detention room at school than anyone else. Not a good fight to be in. I wasn't a guy who ever fought, but I slid into him and he tagged me in the face with his glove and then said something. So I turned around and went back and said something back, and he punched me right in the face. Got the jump on me. It wasn't much of a fight. I literally fell down.

After that, I was like, "Wow, you dummy. If you're going to go in and say something, you'd better be able to back it up. That will never happen to me again." I learned to get the early jump and throw fast and throw often. That's what I did with Cheveldae. I got in there, my mask came off, and I threw as fast as I could. It wasn't like I was mad. It was just another athletic contest. Fast and serious. And it worked out pretty well.

We came in fourth in the Norris Division that season, which meant we were up against first-place Chicago in the division semifinals. The Blackhawks were our archnemesis, and they had finished twenty-one points ahead of us in the regular season. They had their share of grinders and tough guys—Bryan Marchment, Stu Grimson and Jocelyn Lemieux, who was Claude Lemieux's brother. He could fly and he could hit. They also had veterans who were maybe a little past their prime but still effective, like Steve Smith, Christian Ruuttu and Dirk Graham. Even their goal scorers were tough: Steve Larmer, Jeremy Roenick, Brent Sutter, Chris Chelios, Michel Goulet and Joe Murphy. They all stepped up when it was called for. Hell, Goulet, who was their third-highest scorer, took on Chaser one time. On top of that, they had Eddie Belfour in goal. A strong, well-oiled team.

But toughness wouldn't sustain them through the playoffs. The NHL had introduced the instigator rule prior to the 1992–93 season and it made a difference in the regular season.

This series would represent my coming out, my first chance to establish myself as a number one goalie in the NHL.

CHAPTER 34

The Hot Spot

CHICAGO STADIUM WAS electrifying. It's not the greatest place to play a hockey game, but it was an incredible experience to win there and it was a devastating place to lose in.

For a visiting team, the place was as intimidating as it got. Coming out of the dressing room, you'd climb a long stairway. Twenty-one steps—guys have counted. The climb was straight up. At the top, you felt like you had come out of this hole like a gladiator in the Roman Colosseum. Raging fans screaming for blood as you are thrown to the lions. The fans were right on top of you, yelling and chucking stuff. No stadium was louder. It was incredible. A tremendous atmosphere.

The Blues and Blackhawks basically hated each other. It's only a four-and-a-half-hour drive from one city to the other, and with that kind of proximity, fans of both teams made the drive, especially in the playoffs. You had to remind yourself that the fans couldn't get to you physically.

We played them in the pre-season three or four times, and then we played them in the regular season seven more. When you see each other that often, guys remember the hits, the bruises, the cheap shots. There are scores to be settled.

I'll never forget the sound of the puck hitting the glass. It was different than in any other rink, a boom like a shotgun that echoed off the boards. The national anthem was so loud that I couldn't hear myself think. I grew up with Harold playing the organ, but this was no home version. This was a Barton pipe organ built in 1929. The greatest organ and the greatest sound in the world with those pipes. It rocked the place like an earthquake. And everybody sang. Just screamed out the words.

I remember after one of the anthems, Chicago started a checking line, which meant they were going to dump it in and then run our defence. It set the tone right away. Jeff Brown came back to me and said, "Cujo, play the puck," because he didn't want to be plastered up against the glass. They had speed and size. Wingers like Jocelyn Lemieux or Jeremy Roenick would rocket in at a hundred miles an hour, ready to clobber anybody near the puck. The strategy was to flatten our D every chance they got, wear them down. The more we got hit, the more likely a turnover might happen, and in the playoffs, you only need one to turn a game around. It worked like a symphony. And they were very good at it.

When they dumped it in, I went after everything. This meant that, instead of turning around and skating back for it, our defenceman would put his stick out and hold up the offensive player for a second and a half, and then let him go. That second was all the time I had to skate around behind the net, stop the shoot-in and pass it off. If one of their forwards hit me, they'd get a penalty.

The first ten minutes of a game were crucial. We had to hold off the attack and the enormous energy they brought. It was "Okay, this is survival. I've got to play the puck around the glass and make sure my D doesn't get hammered. And make sure we don't get scored on early. They can't keep up this intensity for sixty minutes. If we can weather the storm, we're going to be okay." That's what it was like, playing those guys in that building at that time.

After we upset the Hawks 4–3 in Game One, we knew they were going to come after us harder than ever three nights later. It was rough out there. Most of the eleven penalties called in the game were for roughing, charging, high-sticking and even kneeing.

We were competitive because we had traded a lot of toughness for talent. We still had Kelly Chase and Garth Butcher, but mostly we were loaded. Hully would become the fourth-leading goal scorer in the history of the league. Shanahan is a Hall of Famer, and then there was Craig Janney.

Craig was one of the greatest centres ever. He had 106 points that year. He was so smooth, and so underrated, a brilliant hockey player and a super-compassionate man. His game was directly related to his off-ice personality. He was a giver. Terrific at finding the open man. He'd rather pass the puck than put one in. He was reminiscent of Adam Oates, for whom he'd been traded. Don't get me wrong, he scored plenty, but he was generous to a fault. I loved Craig Janney. He'd sit there and smirk and smile and laugh. Always fun, happy and positive.

Bob Bassen was all heart, as were Richie and Ronnie Sutter and Dave Lowry. And then look at our D, led by Jeff Brown and Rick Zombo. Z was integral, but you never heard much about it. He always played against the best of the best. And yet, even at the pinnacle of his career, he was more or less unknown. Shutting down the opposition's best line? That's big. You have to be damn good. But he never got the accolades he deserved. He didn't have points, and his plus/minus was average. That's all a lot of sportswriters see. But as a goalie, I relied on him big time. Just one of a long line of amazing players we had through the early '90s.

As for the Blackhawks, they definitely had talent. Chelios was good—at thirty-one he was so incredibly fit that he was still, effectively, a young player. He'd come down to my end every once in a while and start yelling at me. Oh man, the obscenities—the gist being "We're coming for you! We're coming for you and we're going to kill you!" I was trying to maintain focus and he was trying to get me off balance. But I recognized it as a great compliment to me. I thought, "This is good. It means I'm a factor in this series."

I remember Roenick running around crushing people. For a skilled guy, he could hit. But like I told you before, the one guy I had to really pay attention to was Steve Larmer. He was thirty-two and he hadn't missed a game in eleven years. He was two years from retirement, but he was still dangerous. He seemed unfazed by anything that was happening in the building. He had great patience, great poise, and then, suddenly, he would just rocket that puck into the top corner. I had to know where he was at all times.

That entire week, it felt like I was in a bubble and I was riding a wave. I didn't think about it too much. I just got up, went to the rink and followed my routine. No superstitions, no rituals. I made a conscious decision early on not to hang my game on rituals. I concentrated on one thing. Focus.

Standing in my crease in Game Two, I found myself in a calm spot in the middle of the hectic world around me. The game ended with my first playoff shutout, 2–0. I was in the zone. It starts with the eyes—specifically, the fovea, a small depression at the back of the retina where visual acuity is highest. The fovea only picks up a tiny bit of your field of vision, so if you're looking at something large, you need to move your eyes to take it all in. A lot of adjustments are needed. That's why you see goalies moving and twitching so much. The more experienced goalies get, the quicker we are to get into a "quiet eye" state, meaning we stop shifting our gaze around sooner. We know where to focus our eyes.

Game Three, in St. Louis, was another shutout. It was 3–0 this time. Game Three is always the big game. It's the swing game. Again, I was in the zone, connected to the puck. I could feel it moving along the ice and knew exactly where it was going. Other times, it seemed to be the size of a beach ball and moving in slow motion. When you are a goalie and in the zone like that, the opposing team gets frustrated.

In Game Four, Chicago scored early in the second period, ending my shutout streak at 174 minutes, 18 seconds, during which I had stopped 105 Chicago shots. We were tied 3–3 at the end of regulation, but if you look at the overtime, the Blackhawks knew they were finished. We could smell blood, and that's when we found our stride. We had one scoring chance after another. There was nothing they could do to turn the tide.

Finally, Brett Hull made this wonderful play. A shoot-in sent the puck into their end. Ed Belfour went behind his net to play it, but it bounced over his stick. While Eddie was trying to get back to his crease, Brett took a shortcut, chasing the puck, and Eddie, trying to get back to his crease, bumped into Brett. Meanwhile, Craig Janney, who was such a quick-thinking player, recognized what was happening and slipped a quick wrist shot from the boards towards the net. Eddie, in a panic, dived and took a stab at it but missed. The puck dribbled in. Our guys leaped over the boards to celebrate, and Eddie went nuts—screaming at the refs, whaling his goal stick at the goalposts. He gave it three full Paul Bunyan swings, hard enough to bend the iron, but he couldn't make that stick break.

That was the game, and that was the series.

Eddie was pissed and complained to the ref. Brett yelled at him, "You're an idiot, Eddie! I wasn't doing anything. You tried to hit me!"

The horn blew and Eddie beat up the crossbar and pushed the net over, something I would've done myself. On the way to the dressing room, he knocked over a big coffee urn and a water jug. I will always respect him as a fiery, tremendous competitor. Any time you come out on the winning end as a goalie, after facing a Hall of Fame goalie at the other end, you feel like you've done a good job.

The fans in St. Louis were going absolutely crazy. We were always happy to stick around and sign a few autographs and sticks, but we couldn't get to our cars for three hours after the game. We could not get through the mob who were still waiting and cheering after that Chicago series.

I remember feeling the complete opposite of the way I felt getting that haircut once every two years when I was a kid. I felt proud. I felt great about myself. I felt good about being a good teammate, contributing to the win. And honestly, I can't remember any moment, in all the time I played hockey, that I was a factor like that. When I played at Notre Dame and we won, it wasn't because I dominated in any of the games or anything like that. For the first time in my life, I was a big factor.

CHAPTER 35

I Still Get Mad

WE'D BEEN OFF for eight days when we faced off against Toronto in Game One of the Norris Division final on May 3, 1993. The Leafs had just come off a seventh-game win in Detroit two nights earlier, and they carried that momentum into the series. It was the first time the Leafs had been in the playoffs in three years and everyone back home was going crazy.

The Leafs were tough and they were talented, led by a couple of ex-Blues, Doug Gilmour and Peter Zezel, as well as Wendel Clark and defenceman Jamie Macoun. They came at us with everything they had.

Gilmour was trying everything he could to score. But as I said, I liked to play percentages. Doug was a great player, but he didn't have a great shot—he liked to pass. When he was on, I would play back in the net, giving him the illusion that I was open on one side. I did that because I knew he liked to come in and then pass it for an assist. I'd anticipate and get across and make the save. I played him and Adam Oates the same way.

We were tied 1–1 after eighty minutes. At 3:16 of the second over-time, Garth Butcher held up Mike Foligno in front of the net and they both started to slide. Foligno's leg stuck straight out behind him and his skate caught me in the jaw, cutting me. I didn't know what hit me. My mask flew off and I was bleeding, but that was the least of it. Being on the receiving end of a roundhouse to the face with a skate. Honestly, it was the hardest I've ever been hit in the head.

I could hear the referee, Andy Van Hellemond, shouting, "Get him off the ice!" Honestly, get me off the ice? Get Foligno off the ice. It makes me mad every time I think about it. We saw with Clint Malarchuk what can happen. His throat was slit by a skate in a game in March 1989, but that wasn't even a roundhouse kick. Foligno's skate could have slit everything, basically decapitating me. I was lucky. Foligno should have been suspended for ten games. It was horrible. He didn't even get a penalty.

I had to go to the bench, and Guy Hebert went in for me while they injected me in the jaw. I remember looking up into the stands while they did it. The bleeding stopped and then I went back in net. Guy stopped the only shot he faced. I saved sixty-one out of sixty-three in a 2–1 loss.

I watched that game on YouTube recently and I got pissed off about the Foligno incident all over again.

Nobody was more excited about that series than my baseball buddy back in high school, Tyler Stewart. He's the biggest Leafs fan ever. His band, the Barenaked Ladies, was really taking off, thanks to songs like "If I Had a Million Dollars" and "Brian Wilson." Tyler flew back home to catch the games between concerts and he and I met at Game Two in Toronto during the band's 1993 cross-Canada tour for the *Gordon* album. We would play that album in the dressing room all the time. The Ladies were playing sold-out venues all across the country— seventy-two shows in total, or some crazy number like that. Iqaluit, Charlottetown, Moncton, Edmundston . . . all over.

When we graduated high school, I was doing well at hockey and Tyler was getting into music and the media. He had been accepted at Ryerson Polytechnical Institute (now Ryerson University) in the radio and television arts program. We used to joke that one day, when we were ready to retire from our respective careers as a famous NHLer and as host on a late-night show, we would open a restaurant together. It would have a sports theme with TVs everywhere, and interactive games—kind of like modern sports bars are today. We used to laugh, "I'll see you in fifteen years or so, when we're both famous and blessed with money." I actually wrote that in his yearbook at the time.

It's hilarious. Just teenagers dreaming, right? But lo and behold, if it didn't turn out to be true. Not the restaurant part, that was just a pipe dream, but we each thought the other guy would be famous and do well. It was just teenage pride or hubris, but cut to a few years later— May 5, 1993. Tyler called me. He was coming to Game Two at the Gardens, so we agreed to meet up afterward.

I had a good game. We won 2–1—another one that went to double OT. It was so hard for Tyler. He was conflicted. Happy for me, and yet he couldn't go against his Leafs. We were getting on the bus after the game, and I introduced him to Brendan Shanahan, who was a Barenaked Ladies fan. Shanny was like, "No way! You guys know each other?" And I said, "Yeah, man, of course we do."

Going into Game Seven, I was struggling. There was nothing left and my groin muscles were off the bone, ripped and torn to shreds. I had both of my groin muscles wrapped tightly with Tensor bandages, but even so, I could barely walk, let alone pull my body weight up with them.

In the second period, the score was 5–0 for Toronto. Wendel took a slapshot at my head and launched my mask across the ice. I love Wendel, but that was not one of his finer moments in the game. Tyler called me after and said, "Oh man, I saw Wendel Clark blow your mask off with a slapshot, and I thought, 'My high school buddy inventing himself. The Legend of Cujo was being formed right there. This guy, he's got to be having the time of his life.'"

It gave me a new perspective. Suddenly, the groin troubles and Wendel, even losing the series, weren't so devasting. The Barenaked Ladies had sold a million copies of *Gordon* and won a whole bunch of Juno Awards that year, and I had made it to the second round of the playoffs—playing in Game Seven against the Toronto Maple Leafs. We were both pretty fortunate, considering we were just two local kids from Newmarket who went to high school together.

Chapter 36

Not a Team Guy

WE HAD A solid season in 1993–94 but were swept by the Dallas Stars in the first playoff round, so the organization made another coaching change. They hired Mike Keenan. He was just coming off a Stanley Cup championship with the New York Rangers. Look, not to take anything away from Keenan, but New York won that Cup thanks to Mark Messier's leadership. Everyone knows that.

The Blues signed him to a contract that included an unbelievable clause that guaranteed he would be paid out to the end of the term if he was fired. Now, who offers something like that? They made him GM too, which gave him absolute power. Which you don't ever do. You can't give the keys to the car, the palace and the bank account to one person and then give them permission to spend at will with no repercussions. I don't care how good that person is. Ego takes over. But the Blues gave Mike all of that. They built the dragon.

Hully was friends with Chris Chelios and Jeremy Roenick, so he knew all about the crap Mike pulled when he was the coach in Chicago. We'd heard about how mean-spirited he was. How he belittled players. How he went after Dave Manson and made Dave mad. How Dave chased him down the tunnel in Chicago, sparks flying off his skate blades. Roenick gives a pretty funny account of the whole thing in his book *J.R.: My Life as the Most Outspoken, Fearless and Hard-Hitting Man in Hockey.*

Mike tried it with Tony Twist too. Like I told you, nobody wanted to fight Twister because of his fierce reputation. After a dry spell of four or five games, Mike lit into Twister on the bench. Tony didn't respond right away, but after the game, he walked into Mike's office and said, "Mike, I know what you did tonight. I'm not hurt about it. You went on me to have everybody rally around me. But make it a one-time move. Nobody's buying it and you look ridiculous."

Hully was the same. He'd stand up to Mike and it would drive Mike absolutely bananas. Hully came off the ice near the end of a game that we were losing 4–3 and Mike said, "We're never going to win unless you start playing." Hully's response was something like "Are you some sort of moron? I've got two goals and an assist. We only have three goals! I think you're talking to the wrong guy, dumbass."

Still, Mike had the ultimate say on all of us players, the same way Barry MacKenzie had with Notre Dame. But believe me, Mike Keenan was no Barry MacKenzie. The power Mike had was reflected in the way he spoke to us. He was incredibly arrogant. He talked down to us and to everyone else. On one of our first road trips, we made it to our hotel and he walked into the lobby and said, "Guys, get back on the bus. This isn't good enough." He was in control and everybody had to know it. His whole shtick was all about psychology.

Most of us had dust-ups with Mike throughout the season. I rarely talked to a coach my whole career. I remember Brian Sutter yelling at somebody about something, and then turning to me and going, "Stop the puck. I don't know anything about goaltending."

Goalies aren't ever on the bench. We spend the whole sixty minutes in the net. For me, what was important was communication with the defence and not who plays on your line or how many points you get.

I could see how hard Mike was on Brendan Shanahan, Steve Duchesne, Mike Grier. All the guys who weren't his guys. I knew he was going to dismantle the team. Even so, I was surprised when Mike called me into his office.

The way he was treating us wasn't sitting well with me. I knew my play reflected that. When I sat down, he started in. "You're not who I thought you were. You're playing like shit. You're nothing but an embarrassment to your team and your family, but what's worse is you don't give a shit about either of them, you selfish prick!"

I sat back and crossed my arms and said, "Mike, come on. I know who I am. I'm a team guy."

He sneered and said, "Bullshit, you're a team guy." And then he got really personal. "It's obvious you aren't part of this team, you don't go out with the guys, you hang around home with your fucking wife and kids . . ."

That was it. I stood up. He must have known he'd crossed the line because he jumped back against the wall. I leaned over and cleared everything off his desk, and then threw my chair across the room and walked out.

I called Donnie Meehan after that and said, "Tough day today." Donnie asked why, and I told him. Donnie was reassuring. He said, "Listen, Curtis, Mike has had a lot of things thrown at him throughout his career. He'll get over it."

At first, Keenan treated Brett like gold and everybody else like shit, but it was only a matter of time. You could see the writing on the wall. Hully wasn't going to take any of that crap. In fact, a while later, Mike called Hully into his office and blamed a loss on him. Hully started kicking Mike's desk over and over. In fact, I think Hully broke his toe. Hully told me it was sore all season. The next year, when Craig MacTavish joined the team, Mike told him, "You know, I may be nuts, but Brett Hull's crazy."

Mike wasn't afraid to embarrass people in front of other guys either. In hockey, there's a time and place to talk to a player, but he ignored all that. Our '94–95 season was shortened due to the lockout. I played a good regular season, I went 20–10–1. Donnie Meehan had started negotiating my new contract with the Blues for the next season.

After a short forty-eight-game season, we'd finished second in the Central Division. We met the Vancouver Canucks, who'd finished thirteen points behind us, in the Western Conference quarter-final. The series went back and forth, but we won Game Six 8–2, setting up a seventh game on May 19 in Vancouver. We were in the visitors' dressing room, and Mike had finished his pre-game speech. I was sitting near the door, so I stood up to lead the team out. Then Mike stopped me.

In front of the whole team, he said, "Curtis, you want a new contract?" And he started listing off the salary I was looking for and Donnie's negotiating points. "You want this, you want that. Well, then, you gotta step up like Mike Richter." Richter was the goalie for the Stanley Cup–winning Rangers the year before. "You're a long way from fucking doing what Mike Richter did in New York." And in front of the team he went on to tell me how I was failing and would never get my money, or a contract, and I had better pull up my socks or I was outta there.

Here's what Twister had to say about that performance: "You don't take your goaltender and tear him apart before a playoff game. Screw him over mentally and send him to war with a spoon! He was an asshole. A complete asshole."

I didn't cave. I did go to war, but it was a hard thing to get my arms around, mostly because it planted the seed in my mind that I was letting the team down. His words were extremely jagged. He kicked the wind out of every single one of us that night. We were very tight-knit, and when one of us was torn down, we all got torn down.

We lost the game that night, 5–3, and lost the series. I only stopped seventeen of twenty-one shots that night, and that's where I learned I couldn't be angry and play. I had to be confident. I know Mike wanted to get the most out of me by pissing me off. Maybe it worked for Eddie Belfour, his goalie in Chicago, but it didn't work for me. I wanted to be confident and on a roll, you know? I wanted to be aggressive in the net, but not angry. Focused. His bullshit distracted me from my focus.

I didn't know what to make of this guy. I was pissed at him, but more than that, I was disappointed in myself—in the way I played. I was better than that. I didn't go to his year-end meeting, and that was the end of me. I became a restricted free agent, and Keenan traded me that summer. I was on a golf course at a charity event somewhere in Ontario, and somebody came up to me and said, "Hey, you've just been traded to Edmonton."

I was devastated. The rejection. It's a knife in the heart. Truly. For me and Mike Grier, he got a couple of first-round draft picks—the same picks he'd had to give up when he signed Shayne Corson as a restricted free agent, so basically, he traded us for Corson. Wherever he went, and he coached or managed a lot of teams, Keenan brought in guys he'd had before. Corson was one of them—he'd played for Keenan in the 1991 Canada Cup. Mike liked Shayne and Shayne loved playing for Mike.

Keenan unloaded a bunch of key players that year, all to weaker teams. Craig Janney was traded to San Jose. Shanny went to Hartford. Steve Duchesne to Ottawa. Basically, he sent us to places where we couldn't hurt him and where we wouldn't be a threat to win a Cup.

He didn't trade Brett Hull, but he was shitty to him all the same. He tried to embarrass Hully into leaving. First, he pulled the *C* off his jersey. What happened was that Dale Hawerchuk's grandmother, Georgina Mitchell, was coming in to watch him play in Buffalo because she lived in Fort Erie. She was ninety-some years old and not in the best of health. They brought her in in a wheelchair. Hawerchuk was such a great player—he was inducted into the Hockey Hall of Fame in 2001. Amazing talent. And it was going to be the last time she would see her grandson play.

There was an article about it in the papers. That's how Keenan knew about it. And what did he do? He sat Dale out. He didn't play him. He sat out three or four guys that night, actually. As a result, the Blues were defeated 5–2 by Buffalo. Keenan told the papers that the players hadn't stepped up, blah, blah, blah.

That made Hully furious. He stormed into Mike's office and said, "What kind of a moron coach sits out four of his best players and then expects his team to win?" And then Hully gave him what-for about what he did to Dale Hawerchuk. "It's the worst thing I've ever seen anybody do to somebody in my life!" The next morning, Mike took Brett's *C* away, and Brett's response was, "That's it? Good. Now I don't have to talk to you anymore."

After Mike took away Brett's captaincy, he tried to trade Brett. You know, you heard the rumours. But Brett was Brett. He was the face of the franchise. He was the MVP of the league. Mike got fired before that happened.

CHAPTER 37

Chris McSorley and the Illegal Stick

I WAS PLEASANTLY surprised once I finally got to Edmonton, but I didn't get there right away. The Oilers' GM, Glen Sather, already had Billy Ranford in net and didn't want to trade him. Billy had led the Oilers to a Stanley Cup championship in 1989–90, winning the Conn Smythe Trophy as MVP of that year's playoffs. Glen liked Billy. But Edmonton had missed the playoffs for the last three seasons (1992–93 to '94–95), and the outlook wasn't good for 1995–96.

Meanwhile, I didn't have a contract for the upcoming season, and Sather was trying hard to sign me at a deep discount.

Against that backdrop, the big rumour was that one of us would be working for Harry Sinden, the GM of the Bruins and Glen's fishing buddy.

I was asking for pay that was appropriate for where I stood—the thirteenth-best goalie in the league. I think it was $2.2 million. It was fair. It wasn't off the charts. But Glen was only offering about a million. On Donnie's recommendation, I went to training camp without a contract as a show of good faith, to let the Oilers see I was healthy. It was a good camp and I was ready to go. But when it was over, Glen still hadn't changed his offer. So I packed up my stuff and left.

Two months into Glen Sather's one-man lockout, I knew I needed to stay in shape, otherwise I'd be a write-off for the entire season. I went to the Las Vegas Thunder of the International Hockey League to play for coach Chris McSorley—for free.

Chris McSorley. I love the guy. He's Marty's younger brother. Chris was known for his toughness and some pretty outrageous antics when he played. He was a lot smaller than Marty, but he still fought more than once every game. He once told me that the effect of fighting in hockey is equivalent to taking your hands and slamming them in a car door. That's the pain factor. And to have to do it twice a game? Well, it's not a lot of fun.

Chris did it because he loved to play. He said that during his first year of pro hockey in Kalamazoo, he was called into the general manager's office and was told, "Chris, your first contract is $9,286. The reason it's this amount is because we legally cannot pay you any less." And he said, "Great. Where do I sign?"

A couple of seasons before I met him, he'd been coaching in the East Coast Hockey League. The Toledo Storm—the toughest, most physical team in the league. He won two Riley Cups—the ECHL championship—with the Storm in 1993 and '94, and he was the league's all-time leader in coaching wins (193) when he left in 1994.

He'd been suspended a few times there. His favourite suspension happened during the playoffs. The Erie Panthers had a tough guy named Greg Spenrath who tried to get at Storm players by charging into the boards in front of them and launching himself into their bench area. Chris had been there, done that, a few times in his own playing career. When Spenrath started a Superman dive onto the Storm bench, Chris hopped up and kicked him right square in the face. Spenrath crumpled into a heap of flesh on the ice. It was the only time in history a coach was suspended for kicking an opposing player back onto the ice. I love that story.

The Thunder was a great team. We never lost, and Chris made me feel welcome. He always wore a big smile. Just a happy guy who treated me like an old friend. And he was a great coach. He called for a stick-curve measurement in the last minute of every game where we were tied or trailing. Under the rules, if the stick you challenge turns out to have a legal curve, your team gets a minor penalty. If the stick is illegal, the opposition serves a penalty and you get a power play. He had nothing to lose and everything to win.

Keep in mind that this was three years after the infamous incident in the playoffs in Montreal. On June 3, 1993, Marty McSorley was found to be playing with an illegal stick in Game Two of the Stanley Cup final between the Canadiens and Marty's L.A. Kings. There was a penalty and so L.A. was one man short when Montreal scored a last-minute goal to send the game into overtime. The Canadiens went on to win the Cup.

Some L.A. fans were of the opinion that, if not for that penalty, the Kings would have gone back to L.A. leading two games to none, with all the momentum on their side, and it would have taken them all the way.

I don't know whether Chris was inspired by what happened to Marty, but he won the ruling every single time. And it always led to us scoring the winning goal. I remember thinking, "This guy's the greatest. He finds a way to give us a chance to win every night!"

I enjoyed playing in Vegas. It was like ball hockey back on the playground at Whitchurch Highlands. No pressure, just fun. The total opposite of what I had just been through with Mike Keenan.

I was happy, as you'll see if you look at the results. Granted, it was the IHL, not the NHL, but I had twelve wins against just two losses. Not to mention a 1.99 goals-against average, which would've been even lower except I let in five goals in my first game, when I was still rusty.

Halfway through the season, the Oilers seemed doomed to miss the playoffs for the fourth straight year. So Glen and Donnie came to terms, and then Glen traded Billy Ranford to Boston. I became Edmonton's new number one goalie.

When I got to Edmonton, it was about minus 36 for an entire month, and all the locals would tell me, "It's normally not this cold!"

As I shivered while trying to pound the feeling back into my arms through my parka, I'd say, "Um, it's pretty cold."

But they were adamant. "No, not usually. Really!"

The fans there were nice. I remember being in Blockbuster Video one time, looking to rent a movie, and out of the corner of my eye I caught heads turning in my direction. But when I looked up, they were all examining the videos on the wall. I thought, "Did I imagine that?" And then, on my way out, everyone I passed made a little comment like "Good luck tonight" or "Great game last week" or "I'm a big fan, Cujo."

They were not invasive. They were very respectful. Sure, I'd catch people following my every move, but they didn't make it obvious. What great fans. Boy, they were hard-core. Edmonton fans live and breathe hockey. Everybody in the city, from the video clerk to the dry cleaner.

I was always tired from flying. We never chartered planes, and Edmonton wasn't an airline hub, so we had to take two flights to get to any city in the league except Calgary. That meant we'd stay on the road instead of going home for three days. Exhausting. In fact, I never even drank coffee until I got to Edmonton. Once I got there, I would stop at a nearby gas station on my way to practice and grab a cup. I hated the taste, but I needed the caffeine boost.

We rented a house in an area southwest of the city called Riverbend. Really nice place. Gorgeous hardwood. The neighbours were wonderful. I love people from the West. I'd drop my suits at the dry cleaner, and I can't tell you how many times I forgot to empty the pockets. Virtually every time. I am totally absent-minded. I'd go to pick them up and the guy at the counter would hand me a baggie of cash and say, "Mr. Joseph, you had $400 (or whatever) in the pocket."

I'd be like, "Oh man, thank you!"

CHAPTER 38

The Classy Guys

AFTER I TOOK over in the Edmonton net, we started winning at a 500 clip, which was more than the team had done in a few years. We'd gone 15–14–2 when we hosted Toronto on a *Hockey Night in Canada* game on Saturday, March 30, 1996. We were just three points short of a playoff spot. Then a player, I can't remember who, fell on my ankle. I missed the next four games and came back for the last two in the middle of April. Unfortunately, my ankle wasn't diagnosed as broken. In fact, the papers reported it as a sprained knee. That injury wound up causing me some major problems in the future. I was back for a couple of games, but I wasn't healthy and we didn't make the playoffs.

I had always made the playoffs and not being in them I figured it was just a one-off. I told myself, "I'm never going to miss the playoffs again."

If you get bounced from the playoffs early or you miss them altogether, you don't feel like you're finished playing hockey. It's early April and you want to play more. So I decided to go to the World Championship—it's a great opportunity to kind of bond with guys you wouldn't normally play with on other teams and to try to win a championship that was meaningful to people. So I joined Team Canada in Vienna, Austria. So did Paul Kariya, a super-talented forward with Anaheim. He was on our team along with Kelly Buchberger of the Oilers, Steve Thomas from New Jersey and Brad May of the Buffalo Sabres.

Marty Brodeur and I were the two goaltenders. We each played a couple of games, and then I was given the opportunity to run with the ball.

There was a lot of team-building prior to the tournament. By that, I mean the guys would go out and have some beers and have some fun together. I bonded quite closely with future Leafs teammate Steve Thomas. We enjoyed our time together. I remember one night he told me that he appreciated when I was in net because if the team made a mistake up front I was there for them.

We were a big-time run-and-gun type of team, so it was important that I never gave up on the puck. My philosophy was to get as much of myself as possible between the puck and the net. I didn't make a lot of clean catches, like, clean glove saves. I used my glove hand as a blocker almost as much as I did for catching.

In order to set up and make yourself a big target, you've gotta be smart. You've got to be able to read a play. You've got to be able to pretty much know what is coming next in order to set yourself up a certain way, position yourself a certain way.

Today on the morning highlights, you see lots of impossible saves. You'll see the goalie down and out, and suddenly he throws his arm up and stops the puck. Every so often, it might even go into his glove. I mean, he doesn't necessarily even see the puck. He just knows that it's better for his arm to be up.

I think I was one of the earlier goalies who did that. To me, the puck wasn't in until it was in. Even if the net is wide open and there seems to be nothing in the way of the puck going in, you don't give up on a shot because a save is always possible. The shooter has to beat whatever is in front of him, so you have to put something, anything, in the way.

As ridiculous as it may seem to sort of throw up an arm into this huge, open space, well, why not do it? You still have a chance because every so often, that arm is gonna get hit.

Dominik Hasek played a different way, but I think he had the same understanding. Put as much of your body as you can in front of the net. And when you do that, suddenly reducing the open space for the shooter, he kind of panics a bit. It becomes too hard to make the shot. He freezes, and a feeling of being defeated creeps into his consciousness.

I do remember that Kelly Buchberger broke his ankle at that tournament early and Team Canada was going to fly him back in economy class, so a few of us got together and went in to see the coaches. We managed to persuade them to fly him back first class so he would be a little bit more comfortable.

We got to the finals, so obviously we played pretty well. In the last nineteen seconds of the gold-medal game, Martin Prochazka scored the winning goal for the Czech Republic and we ended up with the silver. But that was a tournament where I enjoyed every second.

My next year was my first full season with the Oilers. I had a great training camp in the fall of 1996. My ankle was healed, my shoulder was great after being surgically repaired in St. Louis, and I was making what I asked for.

Ronny Low was our coach. A players' coach. One of Ronny's strengths was his insight into who was going good on a given night and who wasn't. If a player was playing lights-out, he'd leave him on the ice. He'd had a long NHL career as a goalie. Naturally, there was an instant connection there. He was an emotional guy who leaned towards nurturing his players. It's been well documented that, back in 1981–82, when he was a veteran player for Edmonton, he'd been a good mentor for Grant Fuhr. The classy guys, the good pros like Ronny, never pointed fingers, and that's one of the things he taught Fuhrsy.

The other thing about Ronny Low is that he'd be on the bike every morning, working out hard, the same as we were. There'd be a puddle of sweat around him. True, he was probably out the night before, having a couple of bottles of wine. So we might look down at the sweat and say, "Is that a puddle of red or white there, Ronny?" But Ronny was all-in, all the time.

We had a lot of young guys who were starting to hit their stride. Doug (Weighter) Weight, Ryan (Smitty) Smyth, Jason Arnott, Todd Marchant, Boris Mironov, Dean McAmmond and Dan McGillis. That added up to a ton of testosterone on the ice and in the dressing room as every guy worked to make a name for himself in the NHL. I felt it was important to try to be a stabilizing factor. You have to allow young teams to make mistakes and learn from them. Not many of them had much, if any, playoff success.

Kelly Buchberger was our captain, and I think all those guys learned a lot from him. Kelly was twenty-nine at the time and he was definitely the emotional leader of the team. In the dressing room, if Kelly spoke about the team needing to play tougher because we were playing like a bunch of ladies, I can guarantee that he'd follow that up by leading the charge—either by dropping the gloves or running over somebody on his first shift. He was a true leader.

We also got toughness from Bryan Marchment. Bryan was known for hitting low and blowing guys' knees out. I saw him come close to doing that to a lot of players, and then, at the last minute, he'd pull up. It scared guys to death. And as Bryan skated away, they'd be cursing him out like crazy. A knee injury could end a career. Bryan was suspended thirteen times in his first twelve seasons. He was tough. Or at least I thought he was tough until I met his dad. His dad was Clint Eastwood on steroids. When he shook your hand, his hand kind of swallowed up yours and his voice had the raspy resonance of a Harley Shovelhead engine. I was like, "Holy crap, look at this guy."

Bryan was not afraid of his dad, but it was obvious he respected him. His dad was a man's man. There were certain dads I'd meet and think, "I wish I'd been raised by you." And Bryan's dad was one of them.

Doug Weight was an emerging star. He was twenty-five years old and the Oilers' top scorer. A dynamic player, really flashy. A real fan favourite because he was fun to watch. Weighter was a great passer. A fantastic passer. Gutsy too. In 1996–97, he had 104 points and 95 penalty minutes. He wasn't one of those fancy guys who refused to grind. What a great power-play guy. He'd work the half wall over by the boards and set up guys from there. Boris Mironov was this big Russian defenceman with a wicked slapshot, but he had the damnedest time hitting the net. If Boris had been a little more accurate, Weighter would've had an extra ten or fifteen assists a year.

Weighter was a funny human being. He used to tell this story about being traded to Edmonton, and it's a great story. He was the Rangers' property, and in March 1993 he got traded to the Oilers for Esa Tikkanen. Neil Smith probably traded for Esa because he liked trading for veteran guys who'd won Cups. Anyway, Weighter got the news in New York on the morning of a game against Edmonton. He was told to pack up his things and head down the hallway to the visitors' dressing room.

He was devastated. Here he was, an American kid living in the Big Apple, playing for the Rangers, America's team. He knew his wife was gonna be in the stands, his family lived there and his friends were going to be at the game. What were they going to think when he skated out in an Oilers jersey? He was going through all these emotions. I mean, your first trade is such a kick in the scallops. You know, "The Rangers don't want me anymore. They think I suck. And now, I gotta tell my wife we're moving to Edmonton."

So, he's taking these zombie-like steps down the hallway and he runs into Esa, who's on his way to the Rangers dressing room with his stuff. There's a big smile on Esa's face and when he sees Weighter, he starts laughing. "Hey, Dougie!" He's jabbing the air with playful punches. "We got traded for each other! Ahahahaha! Can you believe it? We're playing each other tonight in the other jerseys! Isn't it funny?" Making light of it as only Esa can do. Meanwhile, Dougie's standing there destroyed, and basically in shock.

The first time Weighter and I met, I came into the Oilers dressing room to play Ping-Pong. The table was in the middle of the room. I missed a volley and turned to grab the ball off the floor. At the same

Playing in the 1996 World Cup of Hockey. Making the most out of an opportunity and having the time of my life! Courtesy Sun Media

Joining the Oilers in 1995. Edmonton turned out to be one of my favourite places to play. The fans there are incredibly nice. Courtesy Sun Media

Game Seven of our series against Dallas in 1997 and the desperation dive that stopped Joe Nieuwendyk's shot. We ended up taking the series. Courtesy Sun Media

Stretching evolved over the course of my nineteen-year career. Today's dynamic stretching, over static stretching, is the way to go! COURTESY SUN MEDIA

I had some really great masks. After my nickname, Cujo, caught on in 1995, we'd use the ferocious mad dog theme. It personified who I was on the ice, and I knew it'd be a hit. COURTESY SUN MEDIA

Any chance I got, I'd bring my kids out on the ice to play with me. Taylor is just three years old here. CourtESY SUN MEDIA

A desperation save in the 1998 playoffs against the Avs' René Corbet. Glen Sather made good on his promise to buy us all a set of Ping golf clubs when we came back from a 3–1 deficit to win the series against Colorado. CourtESY SUN MEDIA

With Ken Dryden as he hands me my Leafs jersey. It was a great fit in more ways than one. RON BULL/TORONTO STAR/GETTY IMAGES

Shaking hands at the end of a series with Ed Belfour, one of the toughest competitors I ever faced. COURTESY SUN MEDIA

A publicity shot from my early days with the Leafs. PAUL HUNTER/TORONTO STAR/GETTY IMAGES

Channelling my inner goal scorer while shooting on Steve Sullivan in practice circa 1999. PHOTO BY KEN FAUGHT/TORONTO STAR VIA GETTY IMAGES

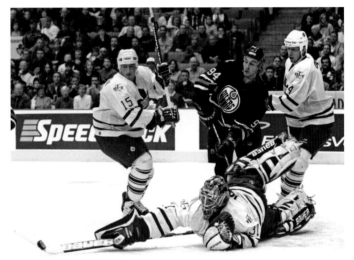

In 2005 I went back to goalie school, which cut down on the number of sprawling saves I made—like this one. COURTESY SUN MEDIA

I guess you could say playing brought out my competitive spirit. COURTESY SUN MEDIA

Announcing my retirement in 2009. Giving up something you love is tough. COURTESY SUN MEDIA

Mats Sundin and I started the 2000 NHL All-Star Game in Toronto on opposing teams (North America against the World). I knew how short I was going to feel in this photo, so I think I'm on my tiptoes here. COURTESY SUN MEDIA

Donnie Meehan is one of the smartest people I know. And he always had my best interests at heart. What else could you ask for? COURTESY DON MEEHAN

Tom O'Rourke, Barry MacKenzie, me and Rod Brind'Amour at Predator Ridge, celebrating the twenty-fifth anniversary of our Centennial Cup win.

Circa 2004, I spent many days with our trainer, Sue Leslie, and jockey Robbie Landry, dreaming of the "big horse" that would win us the Queen's Plate. Our silks were decorated with five hockey pucks.

With my good buddy from Newmarket, Mike Ham.
COURTESY MIKE HAM

Left to right: Terry Yake, Jeff Brown, Garth Butcher, Brett Hull, me and Kelly Chase. We'd gathered for Adam Oates's Hockey Hall of Fame induction ceremony.

time, Doug bent over to grab some socks from the drawers beside the Ping-Pong table, and so his bare ass was right in my face. I grunted in disgust, like, "ugh," and he looked over his shoulder and growled, "Oh, I'm Doug Weight, by the way." I enjoyed his sense of humour.

Mike Grier came over from the Blues with me. He was the nephew of the L.A. Rams' famous star defensive tackle Rosey Grier. Mike looked like a football player too. He was at least 225 pounds and he could run opposing players over like a semi. At the same time, he was the nicest, gentlest guy you could ever meet. Doug Weight used to give it to him. We all had big butts from skating, but Mike's was bigger than most, and Weighter would tease him—"Hey, Griersy, you wanna grab your wallet and pay for that?" And then he'd pretend to be Mike, reaching over his shoulder as if he was pulling a wallet out from behind his ear.

Ryan Smyth was only twenty, a young guy. He played on a line with Weighter that season. It was a breakout year for him because he'd just come up from the minors the previous season. He would go nineteen years in the NHL, and in his first full season he had his third-highest point total. Smitty didn't score a lot of goals away from the net, but in close, he was one of the best I ever saw.

Craig Simpson was like Smitty. Both had a great ability to screen the goalie, deflect shots from the point and jump on rebounds. But they paid a price. When you play like that, defencemen will cross-check you, butt-end you in the ribs, whack you in the head and find the tender part at the back of your knees.

Smitty was always picking himself up after the whistle. You get knocked on your ass all the time in that spot. That's why a lot of guys wouldn't go to the front of the net. But Smitty, it never fazed him. It was a testament to his courage, because as bad as you get beat up in that spot during the regular season, it's twice as bad in playoffs.

He'd screen, tip and then turn around and poke at the puck, jamming it under the goalie's pads. I'll bet you that on a third of the goals he scored, he was lying on his face, ramming the puck in. Having a guy like Smitty in our lineup was great for me, because he practised like that.

Smitty loved being an NHL player, and he loved being an Oiler even more. He grew up idolizing the Oilers. I remember how much confidence he had for a young guy. Not cocky confidence, but a quiet, you-can-count-on-me sort of confidence. He looked up to Kelly Buchberger.

Jason Arnott was an emerging player too. He also played on a line with Doug Weight from time to time. His plus/minus wasn't great at the start, but it improved each year. A lot of young guys come out of junior and they're focused on scoring. It takes them a while to realize they have to learn the defensive side of things. A "two-hundred-foot game," they call it. That means you're a good defensive player, working both ends of the rink. If you're labelled an "offensive player," it means you are there in body, but not in spirit.

One of the best things about the Oilers being a low-budget team was that, because they were paying me such a big salary, I played seventy-two of the eighty-two games. They wanted to get their money's worth. I loved that. When I played in St. Louis, I faced the most shots in the league. I faced a ton of shots in Edmonton, and again when I got to Toronto. What does that mean? It means you can make a difference.

Some nights, we were lucky to get out of a building allowing fewer than thirty-five shots, but the good news was that we were getting chances at the other end. I tried to fight every fight and be that difference maker. My first thirteen years in the NHL was run-and-gun hockey—exciting to play and entertaining for the fans.

And in Edmonton we had a grinding schedule. Nobody wanted to fly commercial, rack up the air miles and stay on the road as long as we did, but once we got to the rink, it was great. I had to adopt an attitude that worked, and I did. I discovered that run-and-gun was the kind of hockey I was made for. That's what I tell goalies today. "Your mindset every game should be 'I'm going to surprise them and make a difference tonight. I'm going to be a factor. *The* factor.'" Those are powerful words you can tell yourself. I always felt I could talk myself into playing well.

We made the playoffs that year for the first time in five years. The fans loved it. When you go into the post-season, you need guys in the dressing room who have experienced winning. Glen brought back Kevin Lowe because he was, well, Kevin Lowe. He had six Stanley Cups under his belt. If anyone knew about winning, it was him. He was part of the glue in the great Oilers teams of the '80s and early '90s. He's not in the Hockey Hall of Fame but probably should be if you judge guys by winning and being character players. He's a legend in the NHL. He was one of those guys who would get up and talk it and then walk it. A real steadying influence in the room, and that's what you look for in playoff hockey. Somebody who can settle people down when things get crazy. It can't always be the coach's job. More often than not, it's got to be a player.

CHAPTER 39

David and Goliath

THE DALLAS STARS were a powerhouse in the days before the salary cap. I'm not exactly sure what their payroll was, but it's safe to say it was triple what the Oilers were spending. In 1997, Dallas was the number two seed in the Western Conference, with 104 points, and we were the seventh, with 81. The Stars would bring home a Stanley Cup just two years later. It was like a David-and-Goliath matchup, no question.

They had great talents like Mike Modano, Jere Lehtinen and Joe Nieuwendyk. On the toughness side, there were Derian Hatcher and Richard Matvichuk on defence and Todd Harvey on the wing. Pat Verbeek was a really hard-nosed player with a scoring touch. He'd do anything to win. When it came to garbage goals, he was a master. And Guy Carbonneau, who captained the Canadiens to their last Stanley Cup, in 1993, was one of the grittiest and craftiest men in the game. They were just stacked with quality veterans.

Most people would've seen this as a bag-'em-up series for Dallas, but instead it went back and forth and lasted the full seven games, which was big for us. It was the beginning of a huge rivalry between Edmonton and Dallas, who would meet in the first or second round for six out of seven years. It rivalled the famous Battle of Alberta between the Calgary Flames and the Oilers.

There was a lot of emotion at the Reunion Arena in Dallas for that first game. An incredible atmosphere. You would lose ten pounds every game there because the arena had no air conditioning and it was eighty-five degrees Fahrenheit outside. I remember sweating during the warm-up—popcorn kernel–sized drops just pouring under my jersey.

Reunion was an awful rink to skate on too. Terrible ice. We weren't used to it. Edmonton had the best ice in the league every year. Period. Really fast. Dallas was like skating on slush, and the puck bounced all over the place. They had a great-skating hockey club too, but it was hard to skate on that rink. So they played a game that was physical as hell with a bigger, slower D, except for Sergei Zubov. Zubov was just a great player, a smooth-skating Russian who could handle the puck.

Zubov ran their power play. He got the puck a lot of the time, and every time, he'd either make a great pass or take a dangerous shot. Very cool, very confident, very patient. His head was always up. Never looked at the puck. He was a right-handed shot, and he used to walk the line. As soon as there was an eclipse, he'd shoot. I had to know that, because that way I could calculate when he was going to release. I could time it, and then dart out and look.

I was pretty good at dealing with being screened. It may look as though a goalie can see through a screen with X-ray eyes, but in reality, it's an educated guess. You see, the shooter has to miss bodies. And in order to miss bodies, the shot has to be on the side with the most room. If the puck carrier is a right-handed shot, he'll drag it to the left. Now, those guys in front are going to move to the right by the time he lets it go. That means I'll move over to *my* right (his left) and stop it. Basically, you play the odds, and it works pretty well. Unless the puck hits somebody's stick or shin pads or butt, in which case it can end up just about anywhere.

Dallas liked to do a lot of stuff around the crease. They crowded the crease and used the same old trick you always see—get in front, bump me, run me and then, if one of my defencemen gave a little shove, the opponent would fall on me "accidentally." Patty Verbeek must have skated through the crease fifteen times. Same with Carbonneau. They had their methods. They did stuff you can't even think about today. Nowadays, you can't touch a goalie.

It was important for me not to make it a problem. Not to retaliate with anything extreme. Sure, when I was pushed enough times, I'd give a shot back. But what our team needed was confidence. And the only way I could help them with that was by letting them know I was strong back there. Letting them know they could trust me.

We lost the first game in Dallas 5–3. We were down a goal with a minute and a bit left and Brent Gilchrist scored on the empty net. Dallas didn't play a smothering defence and neither did we. As a result, the game was end to end. It was entertaining, firewagon-style Oilers hockey.

I remember the change in the atmosphere in the dressing room. The players agreed. "We can play with these guys." When a game stays close, you believe in yourselves more, and this young, talented bunch of guys was starting to do that.

Fast-forward to two nights later, again in Dallas. Bryan Marchment was carrying the puck down the ice on a routine shoot-in, leaning towards the boards as he let the puck go, and it looked like his skate got caught in a rut because he fell over and crashed headfirst into the penalty box at the exact moment that Guy Carbonneau opened the door to leave. Bryan's head must have hit the jamb. His helmet popped off when his head hit the ice and he began convulsing. You see a lot of injuries, but there are some you have to turn away from.

I remember saying a prayer. "Please don't let him die on the ice, God. Give him a chance. Let him be safe." The only other time I prayed that hard for a teammate happened much later in my career, when Bryan Berard's eyeball was sliced in half by Marian Hossa's stick right in front of me.

We all skated over to the bench with our heads down. As worried as we were for him, in a situation like that, you can't help but think of yourself too. It brought the risks of the game to the forefront.

Bryan was taken away on a stretcher. We knew he was hurt bad. Ronny Low knew they weren't going to stop the game, so he called everybody around and said, "Hey! Snap out of it here! The one thing Mush wouldn't want you to be doin' right now is quitting 'cause he just went down! Get your asses in gear and go out and win the game for him."

We played hard that night. It was a rallying point around a tough guy who took a bad hit.

We scored on a power play in the first period and then an early goal in the second, followed by a power-play goal by Mironov from Weight and Smyth, and finally Smitty scored and we beat them 4–0. They say if you can win on the road, it's going to be a long series.

Game Three is always the big game. The swing game. If you're up 2–0, then winning Game Three solidifies the series. If you're down 2–0 and you win Game Three, it gets you back in it. If the series is tied 1–1, like ours was, Game Three starts tilting the balance of the series towards the ultimate winner. Game Three is critical. We won it in overtime in Edmonton, 4–3. Dallas took Game Four by the same score.

The morning of Game Five, Ronny told me in practice that I would have to steal the game. We were all on the ice when he said it. I was standing in the corner, and suddenly Ronny turned to me in front of all the guys and said, "Hey, Cujo. You need to start stealing games." In other words, "You're not playing the way you can."

We won that night 1–0 in double overtime. Ronny knew he could get more out of me, and telling me that in front of the team was his way of doing it, and it worked. It was the game that turned the tide.

We came home and lost Game Six in Edmonton. It was pretty close, 3–2, and it was still tied with a little over five minutes left. They were a much more experienced team. Mike Modano put in the game-winner—a deflection off Weighter's stick. I'd played against Mike in the World Cup of Hockey in 1996. Originally, it wasn't all that obvious that I was going to be part of the World Cup. Glen Sather was the head coach of Team Canada and I think he did me a favour. He's a loyal guy.

It was really good for my career to play on the world stage, and I thank Glen for that.

Mike told the papers, "We've had so much trouble beating Curtis. We've had to scratch and claw." It was a real pat on the back, and I appreciated his comment.

We went down to Dallas for Game Seven. The Stars took a charter flight. As usual, we flew commercial. We were big guys, covered in bumps and bruises and aching muscles, crammed into those uncomfortable seats.

After our morning skate, Ronny Low came to me privately and told me he was going to play my goalie partner, Bob Essensa. Now, Bobby was a good goalie. Look at his record. He had a good goals-against average. I didn't say anything for a few minutes, and then I strode into Low's office. I said, "You are not playing Bob."

Ronny looked at me and said, "I've made my decis—"

I cut him off. "You. Are. Not. Fucking. Playing. Bob." And I walked out and started preparing for the game that night.

April 29, 1997. A play that remains clear as day in my mind. Dallas defenceman Darryl Sydor found the puck in the corner and managed to get away from Boris Mironov, who tried chopping at him, but Sydor kept coming. I moved to the side and stopped the wraparound. I tried to deflect the rebound into the corner, but it skipped and came to rest on Joe Nieuwendyk's stick, right in front. Joe was one of the NHL's best scorers at the time, the last guy in the world you'd want to have that kind of chance. Luke Richardson was blocking him, but Joe fell sideways and managed to get off a shot along the ice towards the empty net. I dove across in desperation, reaching with everything I had. The puck hit my hand and died under my glove, just in front of the goal line. I had to adjust a little to see where it was, and when I saw it wasn't in the net, I couldn't believe it.

After the faceoff that followed, we went down ice and Toddy Marchant scored on a breakaway against Andy Moog. With that save, and Todd's goal, we won the series. David had taken down the giant.

CHAPTER 40

Over and Out

IN THE CONFERENCE semifinal we met the Colorado Avalanche, the number one seed in the West. This was another team whose player budget dwarfed ours. Joe Sakic, Peter Forsberg, Valeri Kamensky, Claude Lemieux, Jari Kurri, Adam Deadmarsh and Patrick Roy. It was practically an NHL all-star team in one city. We dropped the first two games, 5–1 and 4–1, and then beat the Avs 4–3 on home ice in Game Three. We dropped Game Four in overtime, and then were eliminated in another one-goal decision in Game Five.

The next year, 1997–98, was strikingly similar to the '96–97 season. We finished just a hair under .500, grabbed seventh place in the Western Conference, and again met the number two seed in the first round of the playoffs. This year, that team was Colorado.

Halfway into the season, we were out of the running with a record of 11–22–9, and then we traded Jason Arnott to New Jersey for Billy Guerin, a big, strong power forward. Billy was a great skater, big body, and had a nice scoring touch. He and Doug Weight were our two offensive stars. The acquisition paid off. We went 24–15–1 the rest of the way.

Here's an example of what Billy meant to us. One night in Colorado, late in the season, we had three D-men go down within the first ten minutes. Ronny Low looked around the bench and said, "Okay, which one of you forwards can play defence?"

Show me offensive players who want to play defensively. There's no glory in backchecking unless you're winning championships. In St. Louis, Shanny and Brett Hull were the stars. Goals equalled big contracts and fame.

But Billy Guerin was a funny guy. He had these Marty Feldman eyes, kind of big and bulging, and when he rolled them around and got his eyebrows going, it'd make you laugh. He turned around, gave Ronny a look and said, "I've been playing for Jacques Lemaire for four years. Trust me, I know how to back up in the neutral zone." Ronny put him on and he played the rest of the game as a defenceman. Scored a goal too.

In the Colorado series, Billy played a man's game. He was very, very gritty. I think both he and Dougie Weight rank among the top ten American-developed players of all time.

I remember Kelly Buchberger in that series too. What a great leader. He blocked shots, put his body in front of the hardest shooter. Whatever it took to win, Kelly did it. Bucky was tough, but I saw him fight way too many times when he was in over his head. He would fight guys he had no business fighting, just to change the outcome of the game. I'd be standing in the net, with a front-row seat, thinking, "Bucky, don't do it. I'll make an extra save, man. Don't go there." He was a heart and soul guy, and I loved him for it.

We were down 3–1 in the Colorado series, and then Glen Sather pulled an old chestnut out of his bag of tricks. It was something Oilers owner Peter Pocklington started back in the 1987 conference finals against Detroit. He took our whole team out for dinner at the Chophouse in downtown Edmonton and said, "I'll tell ya what. You guys come back and win this thing, and I'm going to buy you all Ping clubs." Ping golf clubs—complete set, with a bag and everything. We went to Denver for Game Five and won 3–1.

Then it was back home for Game Six. This was a bitter game. Our fans were going absolutely out of their minds. I remember them chanting, "Roy sucks!" every time the Avs goalie touched the puck. I am going to let you in on a little secret. Most goalies love that. If you're on the road and the fans hate you, it means they respect you. It tells you they fear what you might do. Fans taunt you to get you off your game, but I know it made me stronger when I heard my name chanted by the other team's fans.

You could feel it. The electricity in the air carried over to the benches, and at the very end of the game, Ronny Low, who never had much use for Colorado coach Marc Crawford, just lost it on him.

We were leading 2–0 in the last minute of the third period. Ronny threw Kelly Buchberger out. Crawford responded by throwing out two tough guys, Warren Rychel and their other big tough guy, Jeff Odgers. Odgers wouldn't sucker anybody. He told Bucky, "I don't wanna do this, but I've just been told to drop the gloves." A brawl started and Warren went after Mats Lindgren, who wasn't a tough kid, but he played hard. Warren beat up Mats pretty bad, and Ronny called it the biggest chickenshit move ever. First of all, what was Rychel doing out there that late in the game with no match? In Ronny's mind, if you are going to change the momentum with a fight, do it about halfway through the second period, not in the last few seconds of the game after it's too late.

When Ronny saw Mats getting beat on, he tried to get down the bench to go after Crawford, but our guys restrained him. It was chaos. Ronny was giving Crawford the finger on national television while Claude Lemieux jumped off the bench and onto the ice, screaming at Ronny, "It's on right now, you bastards! You gotta come to our building tomorrow!"

In truth, we couldn't wait to get there. Two nights later, in Denver, we took the series with a 4–0 win in Game Seven, and a lot of it had to do with that fricking one-second incident at the end of Game Six. Players don't forget that stuff. Crawford inspired us to win that final game. In terms of motivation, it works just as well as somebody mouthing off in the paper and then the coaches sticking it on the blackboard.

I mean, dropping Mats Lindgren. *Seriously?*

CHAPTER 41

He Looked Like Bobby Clarke

I LOVED EDMONTON—both the team and the fans. I didn't want to leave. We'd pulled off another big upset in the first round, beating Patrick Roy. You aren't really playing the other goalie, but when the other guy is a Hall of Famer and you win the series, it feels pretty special. With what we were building, I was confident we could make it past the second round in 1998–99. But my contract was up, so Donnie Meehan and Glen Sather were back at the bargaining table.

Remember, I sat out more than half of my first year with the Oilers. So in the end, I had played two and a half years instead of three. I'd earned $2.3 million a year, minus the money I lost missing that first half-season. Now Glen was offering four years at $3 million a year. Listen, I'm not trying to be arrogant and say it's not a lot of money. It is, and I was grateful. But there was a clause in our collective bargaining agreement that came into effect that year, 1998. It was the only clause in the CBA that I knew about, and it applied to me. Previously, you had to wait till you were thirty-two to become an unrestricted free agent. But in 1998, halfway through the six-year collective bargaining agreement, the age changed to thirty-one. That was me. I had turned thirty-one in April.

If my contract had expired a year earlier, Edmonton would have had me under their thumb. They could easily have signed me for

$3 million a year because I would have been a restricted free agent—an RFA. Outside of a few notable cases (like Scott Stevens in St. Louis), nobody makes an offer to an RFA because they have to give back too much in terms of draft picks, players, money, or a combination of all three. But if you're unrestricted, any team can make you an offer without losing anything. It's a huge bargaining advantage if you're still a good player. You're a bargain, even with a few more zeros on the cheques. It was kind of like when I left Wisconsin as an undrafted player, and any team in the league that was interested had a shot at signing me.

And I had had some great runs in the playoffs. I was thirty-one, but I think I was playing a little younger. The Oilers had been the last Canadian team standing both years and had knocked off two giants, Dallas and Colorado.

Donnie Meehan and I had many conversations about what to do next. He was like, "The free-agency market is crazy good for a guy like you right now. You can make double what Edmonton's offering, I guarantee it."

On the ice, I played the percentages. You know, "This guy likes to shoot, so I'm going to come out. This guy likes to pass, I can play deep and make all the saves that I want." I was the same way with contracts. My internal dialogue was "Wow, I think I should roll the dice. I still feel young and healthy. I love playing and I'm not going to make less than $3 million anywhere else."

Look, kudos to Glen. He always spent the Oilers' money as if it was his own. I really don't think he could've gone beyond $3 million. Remember, we were still travelling on commercial flights, and by that time we were the last team in the league still doing it.

The market was strong, because aside from me, there was only one other top goaltender on the market—Mike Richter. Lots of teams dipped their toes in the water, and four came to the table with offers of $6 million a year—the New York Rangers, Toronto Maple Leafs, Tampa Bay Lightning and Philadelphia Flyers.

Who wouldn't jump at $6 million a year rather than $3 million? I'm sorry, Edmonton. But what if I blew a knee out? I had to plan for life after I was done hockey. I thought, "I'm going to live until I'm ninety. I have to make this money work for me a long time."

From my talks with Donnie, I was under the impression I was going to Philly. The Flyers had gone to the Stanley Cup final in 1997, and they had the Legion of Doom line. Eric Lindros at centre, John LeClair at left wing and Mikael Renberg on the right side. Those boys each weighed over 225 pounds, and all three were tall. I think LeClair was the short one at six foot two. The Flyers looked like they were poised to win a Cup. They had all the pieces on offence and defence. All they needed was a goalie. But then I picked up the morning paper and read that the Flyers had signed John Vanbiesbrouck to a two-year contract worth a total of $11 million. Flyers coach Roger Neilson had been John's coach in New York, and again in Florida in 1993–94 and '94–95, and the next year with John in goal, when the Panthers made it to the Stanley Cup final before being swept by the Avalanche.

His signing seemed to come out of the blue because I thought the Flyers and I were very close to a deal, but I wasn't in the inner circle. It was the second time Bob Clarke had passed me over. Back in college, at the University of Wisconsin, I was getting ready for a home game when somebody said, "Bobby Clarke's here!" And I do remember seeing him on the catwalk behind me. I remember what he looked like— he looked like Bobby Clarke. I didn't play very well in that game, to be honest. Maybe that's why he signed Bruce Hoffort of Lake Superior State instead.

The Leafs were late in coming to the party. It was a case of Donnie Meehan being in the right place at the right time. Donnie ran into Leafs president Ken Dryden in Toronto one hot afternoon in late June. They met at a corner store at the bottom of Ken's street. Ken walked down there to pick up some Haagen-Dazs ice cream to make a milkshake. Donnie's office wasn't far. He had ice cream on his mind too, and decided to drop in to grab some. Ken was on his way out the door and Donnie was on his way in.

They didn't know each other well, but they knew *of* each other, and so they stopped to talk. It was a natural conversation. Initially, Ken didn't know that Donnie was my agent. So the conversation didn't start with my being a free agent, although it sure ended up going in that direction.

The Leafs were in a time of transition. They had had good teams in the early '90s, and some not-so-good teams in mid-decade. Ken joined the Leafs in June of 1997, and he was determined to make the team more competitive. A year earlier, assistant coach Mike Murphy had been promoted to head coach, and in each of his two seasons behind the bench, the team finished last in the Central Division, winning just thirty games and missing the playoffs both times.

So Ken went looking for a replacement. He talked with Terry Murray, Marc Crawford and Pat Quinn. Murray was hired by the Florida Panthers, while Crawford was under contract to the Avalanche, who wanted a first-rounder and cash to let him go. But Quinn, who had taken the Vancouver Canucks to the finals four years earlier, was available. He and Ken got together and decided there was a fit. Pat came in as coach for the 1998–99 season.

A team that is looking to become competitive overnight needs a goalie. What did legendary coach Pat Burns always say? Goaltending is 70 per cent of it, and if you don't have goaltending, it's 100 per cent. But the Leafs weren't actively pursuing a goalie. They had Félix Potvin. Félix was a very good goalie, but as Donnie pointed out, not every good goalie fits.

An award-winning goalie himself—he'd won the Vezina, the Conn Smythe, the Calder Trophy and several Stanley Cups—Ken knew that. He knew there was such a thing as goalies who were suited to play for good teams and goalies who were made for bad teams, and the first group doesn't necessarily succeed in the other scenario. And vice versa. He'd seen it a lot.

Ken and Donnie talked about how some goalies really have a hard time playing for poor teams or even mediocre teams. They can't deal with the prospect of not winning. When you play for certain teams, you have to face the fact that goals are going to go in. Ken also knew that on a team like that, a goalie had to be able to get past the goal he just let in and maybe make an emotion-changing save on the next shot. An inspiring save that could turn the game around when the team needed it.

A really good team doesn't need that so much. All teams need big saves, difficult saves, to win. But not all teams rely on their goalie to prime the pump with inspirational saves. That's a special component that can jump-start an average team and make it overachieve.

Donnie told Ken, "Curtis is able to do that. Look at what he did for St. Louis and the result in Edmonton."

Ken didn't know a lot about me, but he did know that both St. Louis and Edmonton were not that much different from the Leafs at that time. St. Louis was a bit better, maybe, but Edmonton was in the same category. Ken felt I had played well for those teams and taken them farther than expected in the playoffs. But he had a hesitation. He told Donnie I wasn't a textbook goalie. I had a style unlike anybody else's.

Donnie admitted that was true, but he called it a strength. He said I was capable of the spectacular save that could really get the crowd and the team going. He said, "Really good goalies can make remarkable saves. But due to Curtis's unique style, he can make *unusual* remarkable saves. Curtis can do better than textbook. He can do the unbelievable.

"Some are able to make only the routine outstanding saves as opposed to the truly one-of-a-kind outstanding save," he continued. "Curtis is the kind of goalie who can do that night after night in Maple Leaf Gardens."

Ken was quiet for a moment, and then he said, "From our perspective, that would be a good fit."

By the time Ken left the store, my playing for the Leafs was making a lot of sense to both men. In fact, the discussion went on so long that Ken's ice cream melted and he had to throw it away and go back into the store to pick up another container.

Ken went back to Pat Quinn and general manager Mike Smith the next day and said, "What about Curtis Joseph? Going after him as a free agent?"

Meanwhile, Donnie phoned me as soon as he got home. He was *really* excited. He told me all about the encounter. He said Ken was "captivated." "I convinced him that they needed you! It's a great fit for them and for you. But first, what do you think about the Leafs?"

I said, "Oh wow, that'd be cool."

But you know me. I always take a step back and process everything first. In this case, I had time. I didn't have to make a split-second decision.

I was extremely flattered. Anytime there's interest from a team, especially an Original Six team, it's a big deal. And the Leafs are Canada's version of the New York Yankees. Toronto hadn't been on my radar because they had Potvin. I started thinking about all the possibilities and the worries. One thing that niggled at me was that a couple of Toronto locals I knew about, Dave Gagner and Larry Murphy, hadn't been a great fit for the Leafs. Murphy had been traded from Pittsburgh to Toronto in the summer of 1995, and even though he scored 100 points in 151 games, they booed him.

I knew it was going to be a fishbowl, but nothing beat the Canadian experience I'd had in Edmonton. *Hockey Night in Canada.* Bob Cole, Ron MacLean, Don Cherry. I listened to Cherry—a lot of players did— and when Don said something, it was like the prime minister saying something. Actually, if Don went up against the prime minister on TV, he would win in the ratings.

Seemed like he was a fan of mine. He always had my back. When Don said something nice about me, all my friends would call and say, "Did you hear what Cherry said?"

I knew that if you played well in Canada, there was tremendous exposure. Especially in the playoffs. If you were the last Canadian team standing, as we'd been in Edmonton the last two years I was there, well, the whole country watched those games. I never thought about failure. Glass-half-full guy. I always believed in my ability, and that seemed to take the pressure off.

I signed for $24 million over four years. And you know who was more excited than I was? Tyler Stewart, my baseball buddy from Huron Heights. Like I told you before, he's the biggest Leafs fan ever.

CHAPTER 42

Gothic Meets Country

I'D BEEN RENTING a place in Edmonton, and when I moved back to Newmarket, I rented again while trying to find the right place to buy a house. It became common knowledge where I lived, and that was insanity. Another level beyond anywhere I'd ever played. People would just walk down the street and knock on the door to talk to me or to grab an autograph. Often, on Saturday and Sunday mornings, I'd go outside and sign for the kids lined up out there.

I bumped into a guy I'd never met before at the local gas station while filling up my truck. He told me he had a daughter the same age as Madi, who was about nine years old at the time. We had a casual conversation about kids, and that was that. A week later, this guy came walking up the driveway with his little girl. He said, "Hey, Curtis, remember meeting at the gas station?"

I had no idea who he was but didn't want to embarrass him in front of his daughter. I shook his hand and said, "Oh, yeah, yeah. How are you doing?"

He said, "Remember we were chatting and I suggested our kids should play together sometime?"

I smiled and nodded. "Yeah, yeah."

"Well, here she is." The little girl was staring up at me shyly.

I sighed. "Madi's in the backyard." We all walked around the house together and Madi welcomed the little girl right away. And then the guy turned to me and said, "Thanks, Curtis, I've got some errands to run." And he left her there for the rest of the afternoon.

Our neighbours two doors down were Mike and Julie Ham. Their boys, Taylor, Connor and Liam, played with my boys. We became good friends, although he, like everyone else, didn't know much about my background. I was embarrassed about how I grew up. I knew it wasn't normal, and so I hid it from almost everyone.

The Hams were good to us and kept an eye out for our family. One summer day, Mike was out on his front lawn, cutting the grass, when he spotted this beat-up green van rumbling down the cul-de-sac. It was the kind of street you'd only find yourself on if you were lost or looking for an autograph. This old beater was going really, really slow and coughing up black smoke. As it got closer, Mike saw from the licence plates it was from Nova Scotia.

It pulled up in front of his driveway and the driver, an older Black gentleman with a huge Afro, waved him over. He said, "I'm looking for Curtis Joseph's house. Do you know where that is?"

Mike said, "Yeah, he lives on this street, but I don't think he's home right now. Can I help?"

The guy nodded. "Yeah, I'm just here to visit."

"Oh, okay. Are you a friend?"

The old guy shook his head. "No, I'm his dad."

═══

I BOUGHT A farm in King City, where hockey had started for me. The first rink I'd played on was right down the street. It sat on fifty-three acres, and it was fifteen minutes from Newmarket. Sixty minutes to Maple Leaf Gardens. I'd make the commute to and from the arena. Traffic wasn't like it is today, bumper to bumper. The drive was my time to unwind. I learned about myself on those drives. They gave me a chance to sit back and evaluate. "How did I play tonight? Could I have been better? What could I have done to be better?" Sometimes the answer was as simple as getting a good night's sleep before games.

Why did I buy such a big place? My thinking was that a lot of the great Western Canadian guys I played with came from the farm. Kelly Chase was a typical example. A farm-tough guy with good values. Guys like Kelly talked about their dads and horses and playing games on the hay in the barn. The Western guys I knew were brought up to work hard and do the right thing.

Mine was more of a gentleman's farm. I mean, I never took the dog out behind the barn and shot him like in the stories the guys told me, but I had horses. Two, three, sometimes four at a time. The biggest factor was that it was a good place to raise my kids. Madison was seven, Taylor was four and Tristan was two. Taylor would watch hockey games on TV from start to finish, not just the highlights like most kids. Still does.

When I first drove through the gates of the farm, I saw rolling hills and black fences and a pond. I thought, "Wow, the kids will have a chance to run around and skate on the pond." There was a toboggan hill and a forest—a winter wonderland!

There was a guest house on the property, a beautiful cottage that overlooked two ponds. My in-laws could have their own place. Madison's middle name is Jacqueline, after my mother-in-law. Jacqueline was a wonderful human being. She's passed now, but I loved her. She always treated me like one of her own. She used to call me after every game. I'd be on the bus and she'd be tickled by the stories I'd tell her.

The main house looked like something you might find on the Hudson River in New York State. You might call it stately, with board and batten siding. It had high peaks and weather vanes. Gothic meets country.

I built an indoor rink on the property. I used Dave Gagner's company for the boards and glass. It was like a little NHL rink, three-quarters regulation size. Everybody in York Region skated there—

teams, schools, friends. My elementary-school friend Martin Harding ran the rink and the barn. We lived there for twelve years and saw a lot of kids come through.

Connor McDavid has a 1997 birthday, so he played hockey for a number of years with my son Tristan, who was born in '96. They played lacrosse together too. Connor's mom, Kelly, tells a funny story about Connor. He was always super-excited to play any sport, so when he was seven and they signed him up for lacrosse, he jumped out of bed and basically dragged her out the door so that they'd be early for the first practice. He placed his bag on the bench in the dressing room and then ran outside to kick the ball around. Tristan and I arrived, and Tristan took a seat across the room. Connor ran back into the dressing room, saw us there and whispered to Kelly to move his bag over beside Tristan's.

Ice wasn't always available, and so Tristan's team would sometimes come over to the barn and practise. Hockey's about having fun, and I remember the kids practising with all that energy and excitement. It was contagious. A lot of the dads were good players too. Connor's dad, Brian, played junior hockey at St. Mike's in Toronto and he coached Connor's older brother Cameron, so he knew a fair bit about hockey too. In 2004–05, the year of the NHL lockout, Brian and I got to know each other as we stood together at the glass, watching our kids play.

Connor was always quick and a great skater, with good hands and the ability to handle the puck in tight spaces and tight areas. Brian told me he would always try to lengthen Connor's stick, trying to find the right balance between reach and control over the puck. We talked about the length of sticks. I'd give him my theory about reach. If you want to get to a loose puck and you've got a short stick, you've got to move your body. A longer stick makes it more difficult to handle the puck, but when you're in front of the net and you're battling for pucks and positioning, if you can reach for it and gain control, you've got an advantage.

When kids are seven years old, you're not thinking they are going to make it to the NHL. You're just trying to figure out how your kids fit on the team. But Connor was exceptional. The boys were nine when Brian and I were at the Richmond Green arena in Richmond Hill, standing behind our goalie. Connor picked up the puck, like he usually did, and raced up the ice, zigzagging between a couple of players. Then he passed over, got it back in front of the net and took a shot. I leaned over to Brian and said, "Brian, it's unbelievable. Every time he touches the puck, he makes something happen that puts us on the edge of our seats." I shook my head. "He's always just a breath away from putting the puck in the net."

My sister-in-law Teresa ran the horse part of the farm along with her best friend, Laurie Marriot. They'd groom the horses and feed them in the morning, and then let them out at night.

Leeane was another sister-in-law. Her husband was a handyman, Danny "Bernie" Brinovick. I had a tractor, and he used it to mow the grass. He painted the fences and did general upkeep and maintenance work on the place. The lawns looked like a golf course. It was gorgeous. We had the ponds and big pine trees. Country living, fifteen minutes from where I grew up. It was a piece of heaven. It really was.

CHAPTER 43

"Never Mind Him!"

GOALIES HAVE DIFFERENT personalities. Fundamentally, there is not a huge difference in the way each of us approaches the game, but there can be quite a difference in the way every goalie relates to the rest of the team.

The position can create a kind of fear amongst your teammates. "Don't do the wrong thing, because this goalie will let you know about it." On the other hand, there are goalies who inspire players to want to play for them. I am not even sure it's a conscious decision. Some goalies are one way, some are the other.

I think when you look back at goalies throughout history, most of the award-winning goalies and the ones who made the First All-Star Team belong to the first group. Terry Sawchuk and Jacques Plante were vocal. I think Ken Dryden might have been a little bit more like that as well. He may not have expressed himself outwardly as much as Plante or Sawchuk, but I suspect there was an unspoken message that the rest of the players got. In my generation, Eddie Belfour, Patrick Roy and Dominik Hasek were like that. Steely-eyed, deadly serious goalies. When they were interviewed after a game, you'd hear answers like, "Yeah, we were lousy tonight and I wasn't very good, but we have no right to play that way. We have only a right to play a lot better, because we've got a lot better in us."

There's another kind of goalie. A glass-half-full type. A little more positive. Like Glenn Hall with the Chicago Blackhawks. Kelly Hrudey with the L.A. Kings. Marty Brodeur with the New Jersey Devils. They tell the reporters, "Well, the guys were really working hard and the puck just didn't go in for us, but they were really trying." I would say I'm probably in this group.

Glenn Healy, one of the funniest guys on the face of the planet and another of my goalie partners, is definitely in the second group. As I said, when the Leafs signed me, Félix Potvin was still there. It was a little bit awkward. Okay, a *lot* awkward. Félix had been the number one goalie and I respected him. I'd had a playoff series against him when I was with St. Louis in '93, when the Leafs were very strong, and they beat us.

I felt real compassion for Félix because the Leafs had had a run of mediocre and poor seasons, and now I had just signed a huge contract and seemed poised to take his place. Healy always says, "Never mind him! When you came in, *I* got sent to the minors!"

Félix was traded to the Islanders a few months into the season for a solid defenceman named Bryan Berard.

I adjusted quickly and played well right off the hop. The playoff experience behind me gave me lots of confidence. This was a team that hadn't made the playoffs in two years and we started winning. Winning with no expectations. The media in Toronto were very cynical. I wasn't used to it. The journalists in Edmonton were optimistic and generous. Jim Matheson and Cam Cole were just so nice. But when I first got to Toronto, there was a lot of negativity. After a few wins, that negativity began to dissipate and then it was like "Hey, wait a minute!"

I had great teammates, which made it a lot of fun. Derek King, Mats Sundin, Steve Thomas. We called Steve "Stumpy."

Heals would always entertain us with the story about how one of Stumpy's shots severed his finger when they played together for the

Islanders in the early '90s. They were on Long Island after a morning skate. Stumpy stayed on the ice to shoot some pucks. He took a shot—not a hard one—and the puck spun in the air like a circular saw. When Heals lifted up his blocker to stop it, it hit his index finger in a weird way and sheared off the tip.

Now, Heals is a fun-loving guy, a character guy. Stumpy and the boys had no idea Heals was injured because he didn't take off his glove. So when Heals left the crease, skated off the ice and then ran down the tunnel, the guys were chirping him. "Come on, Glenn, you big baby! Get back in net. What's wrong? You tired? Were we shootin' it too hard?"

After a while, when Heals didn't come back out, they looked at each other. "Oh. Maybe he really *was* hurt." The boys headed to the dressing room to check on Heals and found the trainer using a long pair of tweezers to fish the end of Heals's finger out of his blocker. The trainer dropped it into a bag full of ice and took off with Heals to the hospital. A hand surgeon named Charles Malone sewed the tip back on. His finger looked a little banged-up, but it worked. Could've been a career-ender there.

Another one of the funniest guys I ever played with was Derek King. He was a character without a doubt. "Character" is a really good word. Our team was successful because we had a number of characters. You have to have talented guys who go out there and just play, but you also have to have guys who bring something else, that fun personality that's infectious. That was Derek King. When you have a number of people like that, that's when you really come together as a team.

Kinger could score. When he played for the Islanders, he was on a production line with Pierre Turgeon as his centre. But that first season with Toronto, for some reason, Pat Quinn wasn't giving him a lot of minutes. So every morning, Kinger would come in early and head into the bathroom in Pat Quinn's office and leave him an unflushed present. Kinger would bounce into our room, grinning like the Cheshire

Cat, tucking in his shirt and clapping his hands together. "Hey, guys! Time to stretch?"

Pat would go into his office and then come out searching for the culprit. "What the hell? Tell the arena workers to use the GD crapper out in the GD hallway. Every GD morning!?" We just stared at the floor and worked hard not to laugh.

One time near the end of the regular season, Kinger got hit in the finger. It might've been broken, but he played through it. His fingernail was the colour of a plum and just as round. Really swollen. It was super-painful. He couldn't touch anything. We were in the dressing room and Kinger was standing there, holding it up to show it to the doctor, who gave it a little squeeze. "Does this hurt?" The next thing you know, Kinger passed out on the floor from the pain. When he opened his eyes, Stumpy, who was standing over him, said, "Hey, Princess, did you have a nice trip?"

Kinger's dad was from Scotland. Kinger was pretty skilled at ripping guys in the room when he imitated his dad's accent. That way, it didn't really offend anyone, and everyone got a good laugh.

We had a great dressing room. In his book *Cornered*, Ron MacLean calls a hockey dressing room the happiest place in the world next to Disneyland. That's a good analogy. Sometimes I wonder if the new arenas are a good thing. Some of the best times I ever had in the sport of hockey were in those old locker rooms. I loved the spirit of the dressing room and I loved being around the team. I even loved being on the planes and on road trips.

You prepare with each other. You go through the battles, the wars, the ups and downs. You enjoy the times after the games together. In the dressing room, you can be yourself. Players are remarkably respectful of each other. Yeah, you make fun of the other guys' quirks, but you allow them to be themselves. The guy who is loud and front and centre is allowed. The guy who's really funny is allowed. The guy who's really off the wall is allowed. And so is the guy who's quieter. There's a place and a space for everybody. And everything that happens in the room really just stays in the room. That's trust.

I talked about this with Tony Twist one time, and I agree with his take. In the locker room after the game, you literally have to sit and look across at your teammate. Look him in the eye after your performance. That accountability to your teammates makes the locker room the best place in the world. To me, it's like church. A place you want to be. I had the thrill of sitting in the same room with some of the greatest Leafs ever. That, to me, is what makes the sport of hockey different from any other. Soccer? Baseball? Everyone spreads out and then they're gone. But in hockey, you sit there with coolers in the middle of the room, having a beer. Having a laugh. Or sometimes helping a buddy who's going through a tough time. It can be a confessional too.

There's no better feeling than knowing your teammates have your back in all the situations, whether it's on the ice or off the ice. They have your back in a heartbeat.

CHAPTER 44

"I'll Kill Alfredsson Next Shift"

TIE DOMI AND Glenn Healy were the two guys who specialized in keeping the dressing room loose. They would go at it because, unlike most guys, Heals was never afraid to talk back to Tie. Their lockers were side by side, and it was entertaining to watch.

Tie was a little sensitive when it came to getting jazzed in the room. He didn't like people talking about him. Of course, that's what made it so much more fun. Tie would say something, and then Heals would say something about Tie's head, and then Tie would get personal with him and it would go back and forth. Everyone got the same treatment. You have to have a thick skin to be on a hockey team.

Tie had 333 fights in his career and never fought once for himself. Every time he fought, it was on behalf of somebody else. It was funny. At training camp, he'd get the puck and would score something like fifty goals. You didn't dare hit him, and if you did, look out! On the other hand, you didn't dare say anything to our bench, not even hello. He would defend any teammate, any time, any place. He was very loyal. If you took a run at me or Mats Sundin, good luck.

I always knew he was there for me. I remember a playoff series with Ottawa, which I will get to in a minute. He'd skate back to the net and say, "Cujo, tell me if somebody's bothering you. Tell me if somebody touches you. I'll kill him. In fact, I'll kill [Senators star Daniel] Alfredsson next shift." His threats were not idle.

I never had to hand him a name, because nobody dared run over me. That was the good thing about the game back then. The tough guys policed the game. Nobody took liberties. It was a safer environment for the talent.

Here's an example of how intense and loyal to the team Tie was. During one TV timeout, there was a player standing at the faceoff circle, talking to Heals, who was on the bench. They were talking about Christmas. You know, "Merry Christmas" and "Good luck to the family"—all that kind of stuff. Tie thought the player was chirping Heals, so he came over and proceeded to knock him out.

Heals said, "Tie, I just wished him Merry Christmas."

Tie looked at him and said, "You shouldn't be wishing anybody Merry Christmas."

Heals nodded. "Okay, fair enough."

What made Tie so strong? His head, for one thing. You couldn't hurt him. You could punch him in the head and it was like hitting an impenetrable concrete dome. And he was strong. Compact. Guys would tell me that with a quick punch less than six inches below your chin, he could knock you out. Bulldog strength. Like Bob Probert said in his book, *Tough Guy*, "Domi was just a hard guy to fight. The shorter guys often are. He was a lefty too. And to his credit, he was a tough little bastard. He could really take a punch."

Shorter guys like Wendel Clark or Tie Domi were going to hurt you because they punched up. They hit your jaw, not the top of your head.

Tie was a great skater too. Good balance, low centre of gravity. When he got into a fight with a guy who was really good, like Bob Probert or Sandy McCarthy, Tie would start skating them, turning them with him. He'd position his legs at ten and two and skate his opponent in what I called the death circle, all the while pushing and pulling with one arm to get them off balance. If his opponent started to go down, Tie would punch him in the face. Fight over.

Listen, you won't get me to say anything bad about Tie. I don't want him mad at me. Nobody does. We're still scared of him twenty years later.

CHAPTER 45

"No Stopping Behind the Net"

IN TORONTO AS well as in Edmonton, I had young defencemen playing in front of me. I enjoyed that because I found that I could be the voice of reason with them. My guys had to learn to trust my air traffic control. They couldn't see what was behind them, but I could see it all. I'd tell them, "I'll keep you safe. You won't get hit. If somebody's lining you up, I'll yell, 'Heads up!' You'll know a few seconds before."

I'd warn them when their heads were down. If a guy was coming at one of my defencemen, I could feel his speed and know his intention by the way he was carrying himself. I'd yell, "Heads up! Heads up!" and immediately my defenceman would protect himself and make a play.

When any of my guys were coming back, I would give them options. "Forward checkers coming on you." If the second forward checker was taking the wall away, I'd say, "Keep coming! Hurry! Go, go, go, go." Or if the path was clear behind them, I'd yell, "Reverse!" which meant they should bank a pass off the boards backward to their defence partner.

If a guy didn't listen to me and instead stopped and rimmed it around, which meant the opposition could pick it off, I'd discuss it with him at the whistle. "I told you to keep coming because the other side was closed off. If you keep coming, at least you've got time. In fact, you've got a lot of time, and you're going to make a play, and it's not going to go in our net."

I was selling something out there.

Cory Cross came to us in a trade a year after I got there. Cory was a big guy with a gentle soul. He was put in an aggressive role because of his size. I noticed he had acquired a habit of going behind the net, picking up the puck and heading into the corner. Meanwhile, an opponent would come across, line him up and come barrelling in. Cory would get hammered and turn the puck over. While this was all shaping up, I was yelling, "Heads up! Stop, stop, stop!" But he wasn't listening. When I got the chance, I called him over and said, "Cory, why don't you stop behind the net? You're getting lined up and hit."

He said, "Pat doesn't want us to stop. No stopping behind the net."

I looked at him and said, "Tell Pat I said it's okay to stop behind the net!"

The next morning, we were in the dressing room, watching highlights from a Boston Bruins game. I called to him. "Hey, Cory, come here for a second." He came over and I said, "Look at Ray Bourque. He's stopped behind the net. There he goes, he stopped again and made a play on the other side."

I said, "Stop behind the net, because I can see what's coming. I'm the traffic cop. You have to trust me." Again, how do you gain trust? By being a good goalie. And it's more than stopping pucks.

In Toronto, thanks to Pat's leadership, I was able to run the penalty kill. Normally, an assistant coach works out the penalty kill. But Pat let me put in my two cents' worth. And we were successful—by the end of the 2000–01 season, we were killing off just under 85 per cent of our shorthanded situations, good for tenth in the league. My first year there, we were ranked twenty-fourth.

We'd huddle or plan it out in the dressing room ahead of time.

"How do you want me to play this two-on-one?"

"When guys are coming down, I'll identify the shooter. Listen, be aggressive on him, and he'll pass it over and I'll have the other guy, no problem. If you make an early decision, I'll make an early decision, and we will never get scored on. Because when you take him, the shooter has got to make that pass over your stick, or he's got to catch it and corral it and get by. It's not going to happen."

We spent hours and hours discussing defensive scenarios. "This is the dangerous guy. I want you to crowd him. Always. Don't let him shoot, because if he gets a step, he's got a 50 per cent chance of scoring. This guy over here, if he gets a step, he only has a 5 per cent chance of scoring. So this is how we're going to play it." And when the play was on, if the dangerous guy was coming down, I'd be yelling, "Crowd him, crowd him, crowd him. Crowd, crowd, crowd!"

I always tried to get the guys to do two things—close their legs and be there early. That way, I told them, "The shot will miss you and I will have only 50 per cent of the net to cover. Percentages. And when you are there early and set up, don't move! If you set up and then you move, the shooter has the whole net, but I'm playing only half the net." Bobby Orr had a rule—"Early easy." Get to the puck early. Make the move early. Make the pass early. Make the block early. Get your stick in the way early. Bobby Orr won the Norris Trophy as best defenceman eight years in a row, along with three Hart Trophies as MVP. "Early easy" works.

I think the reason I was good with the penalty kill and power play was because I was observant. A goalie sees the game maybe better than any other player. Look at the colour commentators on hockey broadcasts—a lot of them are goalies. If somebody had a different tape job on their stick, I would know. That's where I had to look to see the puck. You learn the stick, you read the stick, because you don't have time to look at the face. More often than not, the stick will tell you where the shot is going. You know what? If scorers were smart, they'd change their tape jobs.

I remember getting beat one time by Bob Corkum in Anaheim. Bob had a bullet shot. Initially, that surprised me. I looked at the game notes and passed him over, thinking, "This is not one of the guys who can hurt me. Doesn't have a lot of goals." Turned out he had an amazing shot. I learned his stick immediately.

If it was the Bob Corkum blade, I came out, making him miss the net or forcing him into an uncomfortable position. That's what I did to guys who could beat me with a shot. If it was a guy with a not-so-good shot, like Adam Oates or Doug Gilmour, I stayed deep and played the other guy. Oates in particular was one of the great passers. More than a thousand assists in his career. Just ask Brett Hull. I'd watch for a pass from Oates or Gilmour until they got really close, and then watch out. Because Adam and Doug were smart. Abnormally smart players.

CHAPTER 46

"That Kah-vellov"

WE HAD A lot of Russians come through Toronto while I was there. Sergei Berezin was already on the team before I signed. Dmitri Khristich played a year with us in 2000–01. Igor Korolev, a former St. Louis teammate, was there when I came in. What a sweetheart of a guy Igor was. Family guy, really down to earth. A solid individual— never partied. He became a Canadian citizen in 2000. He was great on the penalty kill. He and Alexander Karpovtsev, who played two years with us in 1998–99 and 1999–2000, both died in that terrible plane crash in Russia in 2011, the one that killed the entire Lokomotiv Yaroslavl team from the Kontinental Hockey League. Korolev and Brad McCrimmon were the two Canadians killed on that flight.

Alexander Karpovtsev—we called him Potsy. One of the first Russian players to have his name engraved on the Stanley Cup when he was a rookie with the New York Rangers in 1994. Potsy was a different bird. Hard to get to know. Very quiet. The blade of his stick was only about an inch and a half high. When the puck came back to him, it would bounce over his stick and he'd have to corral it. I'd be thinking, "Oh no, Potsy, please just get a wider blade on your stick." He was always fumbling the puck. Why he played with a blade like that, I will never know. It was less than half the size of an average blade. I have one of his sticks at home because it's so unusual. The shaft of his stick was weird too. Rounded like a broomstick, with the knob filed down almost to a point. The weirdest thing. But he blocked shots like nobody's business.

Potsy, Dmitry Yushkevich and Danny Markov were all shot-blocking phenoms. The pain tolerance those three guys had was crazy. I'll never forget Potsy's face when he would go down in front of me after getting hit in the ass or the leg. He'd be on one knee and his head would swivel towards the net. He'd squeeze his eyes so tight that his eyebrows were resting on his cheekbones, and his mouth would be open wide with his teeth bared. Like a big dog in the middle of a yawn. A lot of pain.

I remember saying to someone, "Wow, Karpovtsev is a shot-blocking machine. I've never seen anybody block shots like that." And I can't remember who I was talking to, but he said, "Yeah, because he's never in position."

We had two of the most atypical Russians you could ever meet in Yushkevich and Markov. They were tough as nails. Some people stereotype the Russians. Supposedly, they're cute, they like to play with the puck, they're skilled, but they're mercenaries. That's not what I saw.

During one playoff round, I remember Yushkevich having a broken finger, a broken rib and a broken foot all at the same time. And he played. Dmitry Yushkevich was a friend to all. Another great guy. And then, of course, in 2001, we got Alexander Mogilny. Alex should be a Hall of Famer. An incredible talent. Inscrutable. Quiet and serious. But at the same time, a little nonchalant. Nothing you could say would throw him.

What a talent. When he got the puck, I'd think, "Wow, this guy is out of this world." You know when you are watching a player who's got the puck for an awfully long time and you're like, "Wow, how does he keep it so long? How does everything open up for him?" It's because guys won't go near him. Very few challenged Alex because they didn't want to get beaten and look like a goat. That gave him a little more room. When you play a guy like Alex, who is such a great skater and has such great hands, all you can do is try to contain him. There aren't very many of that kind of player, but they make it look like the game's a little easier than it is.

If I had to compare Alex to any other player at the time, I guess it would be Alex Kovalev from Pittsburgh. Pat Quinn always mispronounced his name. He'd say, "That Kah-vellov . . . " I'd look at Heals and go, "Kah-vellov? Did they get a new player?" There were a few names Pat mispronounced. Any Russian name gave him trouble, that's for sure.

I never played with anyone tougher than Danny Markov. He was a rebel. He used to come up to my farm and saddle up one of the horses and ride at a hundred miles an hour through the fields full of potholes. Same with my Harley. I had a Harley-Davidson and he'd jump on that thing and take off. I'd be like, "Oh my God, he's gonna kill himself."

I was up at the barn one time and watched him make his way back to the house, walking my bike with one hand and holding a broken rear-view mirror in the other.

I will always remember a one-timer in Ottawa that Danny blocked with his face. The whole rink went silent and our trainer ran out to help him. Luckily, the puck hit him dead flat on his cheekbone, so it didn't break anything. Danny got up, not a cut on him, no injury, nothing. The Ottawa guys were slapping their sticks on the ice and everybody was cheering because he was okay. And Danny looked at the Sens and sneered, "Fuck you, you motherfuckers! Fuck you!"

CHAPTER 47

"I'm Gonna Punch Ya in the Tomato"

PAT QUINN PLAYED me a ton, so we had a good working relationship. He was a player's coach. Not an Xs and Os guy at all. His game was all about heart. It was about the will to win. "There's the puck. Who wants it more? You show me."

I liked that, and I liked that Pat stayed away from Glenn Healy and me. We had no goalie coach. Instead, we worked together ourselves. Glenn knew the players in the Eastern Conference, which was really helpful because I had played most of my career in the West. Now that I was playing in the East, I'd ask him, "Okay, who are these shooters and what are their tendencies?" He'd take me through them. "This guy's a backhand deke on a breakaway. That guy's top shelf. This is what this team's power play does." We worked together as a team, in tandem. And then, of course, there's always the psychological support. Only another goalie can fully understand some of the things you feel in the game.

Pat had respect for his players. Not just the goalies, but the veteran guys too. He left them alone. Mind you, if he walked into a room and was unhappy about what he'd seen that night on the ice, there was no filter, no speed bump between the brain, the mouth and the tongue. He'd tell you what he thought, which I loved. Don't baby your way around it. Tell us the way it is.

He had a confidence that inspired confidence. His famous line was "Have pride in your craft, son!" There was no question that he knew where he was going and how to get there. No denying the respect he had earned around the league. Pat's name would be in the same conversation as Al Arbour's.

Pat was a big, burly Irishman with a presence. Before a game, he'd come into the room, dressed to the nines. Three-piece suit, usually. Shirt with French cuffs and cuff links. Dressed for battle. He had a big, booming voice, and he'd use it on the refs and linesmen.

Pat had to weigh close to 260 or 270 pounds, maybe even north of that. In practice, he wore these old, beat-up Lange skates. They had rivets on the side that looked like they were gonna pop. Whenever he moved, his skates creaked—*eeek, erk, erk, eek*. I'd think, "Oh my gosh, those old Langes, they're gonna explode!" He had terrible bunions or corns, so he would cut pieces out of the sides of his skates to stop the corns from pressing against the boot and hurting his feet. He wasn't a good skater to begin with. He kind of shuffled around out there.

When Pat wasn't looking, Tie used to pass pucks into Pat's feet. The puck would sting, so he'd yelp and then look around to see who was doing it. Tie would continue skating around, looking innocent, as if he didn't know anything about it. Stumpy would often watch Tie do this and start chuckling.

One time, Pat had just had it. He was mad. He called Steve over and said, "Stumpy, if you shoot another puck at my fuckin' feet, I am going to punch ya right in the tomato!"

Every practice, Pat would go to the dry-erase board that was set up by the glass. He'd blow the whistle and call everybody. "Okay, over here. I wanna talk about the neutral zone." He had these big hands and big sausage fingers. The dexterity wasn't there. With one glove under his arm and his stick in his other hand, he'd try to pull the cap off the blue marker with one hand. He'd yank at it, and every single time, he'd drop the cap on the ice. His hips were bad, so he'd teapot over with one leg in the air, grabbing for the cap with his bottom arm while it rolled around, until somebody—usually assistant coach Rick Ley—would pick it up and hand it to him before he fell over.

Pat would then straighten himself up and turn to the board, where he'd start to draw out a play or a drill. He'd rub it out with the palm of his hand, and then he'd scratch his face and write something else on the board, and then rub *that* out with his hand and put his hand on his face again. By this time, everybody had stopped listening, instead we were waiting for him to turn around and face us. And then he'd turn around, and his whole face would be covered in blue marker ink. He'd turn back to the board, and we'd nudge each other and do the silent laugh.

Sometimes when he was drawing on the board, he would go off topic and talk about how we'd messed up the night before, and he'd continue down that road. Outlining all the mistakes we made in the game. He'd draw lines representing our two guys coming down and the other team going the other way, and he'd yell, "Shit through a goose!" That meant "They skated right through you guys."

Another one of his favourites was "It's a goddamn double-cross." He'd pull that one out when talking about anyone who turned over the puck by trying to go one on one instead of making the simple play and getting it deep. "A goddamn double-cross!" he'd yell. And he'd smash the whiteboard marker into the board to emphasize his point.

If he got too worked up, he'd dismiss us and order us to go and do the drill. We'd skate away, thinking, "What's the drill? He never got to the drill."

Three-quarters of the expressions Pat used couldn't be used today. He was very passionate, no question. Pat never really got angry with us between periods, but about once a year, Rick Ley would say, "You might want to shut the door for this one, because the paint's gonna peel off the walls." When Pat wanted to let it out, he could really let it rip. I remember one time in Florida, when we were scheduled to have a day off, but we hadn't played well against the Panthers the night before. We were called in for practice, and some of the guys were upset. Pat let them know in no uncertain terms why we were there, and it was actually one of our better practices.

Like I told you, Pat cut a pretty wide swath, because he knew that at the pro level, we didn't need a pump-up speech. But he was a great orator, and once in a while, he would launch into a long, powerful speech. Often in the playoffs. One time, he set a chair in the middle of the room and talked about a war defence strategy called "box plus one." According to him, it was the foundation for defensive play that he wanted our guys to use. He went through this detailed story about how Britain won the war against Germany with this "box plus one" system. He got really passionate about it, slamming his fist into his open hand. And he ended with "This is how we're gonna win, and this is how we're gonna defend!" It was a powerful speech, and it really got us going. We got up ready to go through a wall for him.

On our way out to the ice, our three big Russian defencemen, Yushkevich, Karpovtsev and Markov, rushed over to Heals and said, "Glenny, what the fuck is a British box plus one?"

CHAPTER 48

Moment of Majesty

GLENN HEALY, CORY Cross, Alyn McCauley and I would all sit together on the plane. You know the row just behind first class, after the divider? That is where we'd sit. Four across.

Heals was big into playing the bagpipes, so he carried his electronic chanter (a practice tool) with him. Cory would sit across from us with this gigantic seven-hundred-page history book about World War II that would put him to sleep fifteen seconds into every flight. In a full season, I think he read about seven pages. I don't know if he's finished it yet.

As for me, I had an absolute passion for horse racing, and breeding too. The owner of the Leafs, Steve Stavro, was a breeder. He owned the Knob Hill Stable in Newmarket. Mr. Stavro bought me a yearly subscription to *BloodHorse* magazine. I was fascinated by the Kentucky Thoroughbred Sales and would follow the champion bloodlines very closely, so on team flights, I'd be reading my breeder magazine and talking about horse semen.

Horse breeding relies heavily on genetics. So, considering my family background, you don't have to be a psychologist to figure out why this kind of stuff would interest me. You look at traits kids have and you wonder where they come from. Do you smile like your mom? Are you good in school like your dad? Horses are no different.

I was always looking at how a horse's bloodlines nick. You know, what kind of a horse will you get if Northern Dancer's line nicks with Secretariat's? Generally, you can't get a great horse from ancestors that were crappy horses.

I was with St. Louis when Donnie Meehan and a few of his clients, including me, first threw in about $5,000 towards a horse we called Ice Agent. That horse ran until he was ten years old. Normally they run three, four, maybe five years, if you're lucky.

Back then, it cost $25,000 a year to keep a horse. We divided the cost between five guys. And if you win a race, obviously, it offsets the costs. Ice Agent paid for himself every year.

Ice Agent was entered in the Queen's Plate, a race that features the best three-year-olds in Canada. Over time, we were lucky enough to have two other horses enter the Queen's Plate, Millennium Allstar in 2001 and Moment of Majesty in 2010.

One horse led to another, and so on. Donnie and I had pieces of twenty horses over the years. Initially, we were all minor partners, and we were warned, "You know, you're probably not going to make money, but you never know." True enough, but it was fun. We'd go to the races and bet on our horses. You can't bet on your team in hockey, but you can bet on your own horse. For the first four or five years, we broke even, which is an achievement in horse racing.

I loved it. We'd go to the barns at the back of the track and see all the jockeys. We always used the same jockey, Rob Landry. Wonderful person. He'd train the horses in the morning and we'd be looking for immediate feedback—"What's he like? Can he run? Is he smart?"

Millennium Allstar was the best horse we had. Donnie said I was an NHL All-Star in 2000, so I guess he named the horse after me. What an amazing horse. Fearless. Best body ever. He was the Rod Brind'Amour of horse racing. His half-brother won the Belmont Stakes, the last leg of America's Triple Crown.

I started to breed horses at our farm. For me, it wasn't about the competition as much as the breeding and the challenge of making something out of nothing. The last one was the daughter of a filly I had, the granddaughter of A.P. Indy, the winner of the Belmont in 1992. We called her Moment of Majesty. She won $627,000 in purses over five years. We ended up going to the Queen's Plate with her in 2010, and when I met Queen Elizabeth after the race, she said Moment of Majesty was her favourite horse.

CHAPTER 49

Conveying a Message

ON FEBRUARY 13, 1999, the Toronto Maple Leafs played their last game at Maple Leaf Gardens. I grew up watching games on that rink on TV. Such a unique building. The seats at the Gardens were on a steep incline. People sat right above your head. And there were seats along the rail, right next to the backup goalie. The golds, closest to the ice, were always known as the best seats in the house. They certainly weren't the most comfortable. But they were basically right on top of the action—and each other. Steep and hard.

The key thing about the old barns is the nostalgia factor. Fans will never feel that same emotion, or closeness to the action, or sense that they were part of the game in any of the new arenas. Not like they did at the Gardens or the Forum in Montreal.

Some of my own history was there, in fact. I never really had a temper off the ice. But on the ice, you're a competitor. Winning and losing are all-encompassing. And as a goalie, you don't have the kinds of outlets you do as a skater. You hate getting scored on, but you can't skate harder. You can't go and lay a hit on somebody. You can't take your frustration out in any of those ways. You're standing there and you get scored on. The foghorn sounds—*Hhhooooooommm! Hhooooooommm! Hhhooooooommmmmm!* Instant feedback that you're not doing your job. Of course you take it personally. So, occasionally, I'd come off the ice and leave a few scars and dents in the dressing room walls and doors.

I don't see myself as a perfectionist. Nobody in my personal life would say that I am, but I once asked the trainers, "Do you think I'm a perfectionist?" and they were like, "Oh yeah. Are you kidding?" I know I had preferences about the condition I wanted my equipment to be in, so that I could play the best I could play. When you love something or do something for a living, you make sure everything is in your favour, that it's set up to give you the best possible chance of success.

And when you're not successful, you look for a way to let the frustration out. My first six or seven years, I used to break sticks over crossbars. It calmed me down, especially when the wood shattered into a thousand pieces. I don't know what the science behind that is, but it felt good. I didn't want to yell at teammates or single them out. I wasn't that kind of guy. Also, I was always aware that I played poorly sometimes too. I knew how badly I could play.

Every once in a while, after a bad game, I'd come into the room, lift up the Gatorade tub and toss it. Just grab the Gatorade and dump it, and then sit and stew by my locker while it flooded the carpet. I didn't even think twice about it. I was making a point. I was in a leadership position and I was conveying a message. The way we played was unacceptable. We had to be better the next time. It seemed to work. I didn't have to say anything else. We always played better the next game. We never lost more than two in a row.

When I first got to Toronto, we played a game at the Gardens and we lost. And I was pissed off about it. When the players left the ice, we had to pass the boxes as we turned the corner to go up a set of stairs leading back to our dressing room.

I was so mad that I shoved my stick into the drywall of one of the boxes as I came off the ice. I did it with such force that the blade stuck in the wall while the shaft quivered violently—*dwing-dwing-dwing!* I left it and stomped up the stairs. Next time I came out, I noticed that they had covered the bottoms of the boxes with metal sheeting.

CUJO: THE UNTOLD STORY OF MY LIFE ON AND OFF THE ICE

Blowing up wasn't calculated, but it was sometimes part of the game. I remember going to Washington one time and there was a huge dent in the door to the visitors' room. One of my teammates pointed it out and told me, "That's a Cujo dent. It's known throughout the league." And I was like, "What? *I* did that?"

———

THERE WAS A big buildup around that last night at the Gardens, so the atmosphere was intense. But that meant our focus wasn't on winning, which was not great for me.

The arena that night was foggy. It was hot. There was no air conditioning in the building and it was packed. It was electrifying, to say the least. The Leafs were doing well, which meant our popularity was off the charts. Part of it was also thanks to all the alumni—those guys who won in the '60s, created the Leafs culture and strengthened the fan base by winning Cups. All that history was on the ice with us. You could feel their eyes, the energy of those who were alive and of those who'd passed on, there with us as we carried on the tradition. We got to walk the roads they had. And to have legends like Johnny Bower, Bobby Baun, Frank Mahovlich, Davey Keon all back in that building, as a fan who loves the history of the game, it was absolute gold. Pure gold.

But as a player, it was distracting. We were signing memorabilia out the ying-yang every day, starting weeks ahead of the final game. Everybody and their brother was taking a dressing-room tour. People were phoning night and day for tickets. I felt bad having to make excuses to close friends because I couldn't get tickets for them.

They were auctioning off everything, from the seats to the Zambonis, the Cup banners and the signs over the men's room doors. Now, all NHLers are collectors. For example, I have a few sticks from opponents—I'd ask the other team's trainer for them. Pavel Bure, Wayne Gretzky, Brett Hull, Mario Lemieux, Ray Bourque, Mats Sundin, Alex Ovechkin, Bobby Hull, Tony Esposito, Jeff Batters,

Félix Potvin. Not all are Hockey Hall of Famers, but like I said earlier, I focused on the sticks during games. Hundreds and hundreds of hours. It was my job to know an enemy's weapon and how he was going to use it.

Heals thought it would be great to buy the big copper bar in the Gardens lounge, the Hot Stove. He walked in there for our last pre-game meal and saw that every living Leaf alumni had autographed it. He said that's when he knew it was out of his tax bracket. The stools from the Hot Stove were going for two grand each!

That day was so crazy that some of the players had trouble parking. At that time, we could park across the street from the Gardens for $11. On the day of our last morning skate, it was $70.

All told, it was an ideal scenario for a visiting team to come in and steal the game.

Bah. I hate letting in goals. Final score was Chicago 6, Toronto 2. Bob Probert scored the last goal ever in Maple Leaf Gardens. Good player, Bob Probert. He was underrated. He got a lot of room, thanks to his toughness. But you had to respect him as a player. You had to respect that he had a good shot and he was good around the net.

I didn't play well to close out the Gardens. I wish I'd done better. For me, the game was almost anticlimactic, and you never want that.

CHAPTER 50

Powerful Stuff

SOMETIMES WHEN YOU have so much, you want to share your good luck. I'm not special as far as that's concerned. Most, if not all, NHLers give to charity or sponsor people in need. We are blessed with some skill, but the fans are the reason we make the money in the first place.

I called Donnie up in 1999 and told him I wanted to help out somehow. He asked me, "What's the most important thing in your life?"

"My kids," I said.

"That's a great start," he said.

After warm-ups every game at the Gardens, I would look up at the seats behind the net and see the kids from Toronto's Hospital for Sick Children. So when the Air Canada Centre (now called the Scotiabank Arena) was being built, we picked out a sixteen-seat private box near the home net, the east end, and we had it tricked out for kids in wheelchairs and their families.

Then the Powerade people came to me and asked if I would endorse their product. They were competing with Gatorade. I sat down with the president of Coca-Cola Bottling, who just happened to be a neighbour of mine. In a weird coincidence, he lived up on the hill behind me. I had a mile-long driveway that wound through the woods, and he was the only neighbour who could see my farm. His name was Jarratt Jones and he was from Texas.

He asked me, "Okay, what's the charity component?" And I said, "Well, 100 per cent." We set up Cujo's Kids Foundation for the Hospital for Sick Children. It's a special hospital—one of the top three children's hospitals in the world. They do so much good there and the doctors and nurses are wonderful.

Powerade set up a Come Shoot on Me contest where you peeled off the label of your Powerade and a hundred winners across the country could try their luck on a breakaway on me at the Air Canada Centre. All expenses paid. There were in-store likenesses of me, drinking Powerade. You know, those big cardboard cut-outs.

I sat down with the doctors at SickKids and said, "You are here every day. What do you guys need?" And they said, "We need a room for pain management. And there's this machine that puts the kids out for about fifteen minutes." They compared it to a bubble-gum machine for anaesthetic. When the staff had to do things like bone marrow taps or changing bandages on kids who are burned, the little guys would cry because it hurts. But this $280,000 machine administered a light anaesthetic so the procedures could be performed safely and pain-free. It would make everybody happier. Staff, kids, doctors.

We created a room called Cujo's Crease Satellite Anaesthesia Room. It's dedicated to pain management. Sterile rooms with lots of metal can be really scary for kids, so we had this room painted like the Leafs locker room, complete with my teammates' names on the lockers. And then, when the kids were lying down, they'd look up and see Don Cherry and Ron MacLean on the ceiling. Which was really cool. There was also a treasure chest full of prizes. About 150 kids use the room each month.

Over the four-year association with Coca-Cola, we raised more than a million dollars. I got a lot of credit but really didn't do anything for the room except raise the bursary, so when a philanthropist named Harold Groves asked to match it and have his name attached to the room, my response was, "Yeah, sure. Of course." His generosity doubled the amount and helped it continue to spin out every year.

People come up to me all the time about it. "You're Curtis Joseph? I don't know anything about hockey, but my son spent a year going to your room. And we are so thankful." Hearing things like that? Wow. Powerful stuff.

To this day, I think about one little guy in particular. The staff had arranged a little thank-you party for me. I went, and this one little guy—five years old, maybe six—had cancer. He stood up and gave a short speech about how these procedures he was having didn't hurt anymore. It was so touching and brave. He was such a lovable kid. Kept pushing his glasses up on his nose because he didn't have any hair to hold them up, you know? I dropped in a week later just to say hi, but he had passed. That memory still chokes me up.

CHAPTER 51

Guns a-Blazing

AFTER CLOSING OUT one of the most historic buildings in the National Hockey League, we moved into the Air Canada Centre. The move came with a parade from the Gardens down to the ACC.

Parades . . . hmmm. Parades are for the Stanley Cup. A few of us were a little concerned about what the hockey gods might think about it.

The organization paired older players with current players. I was in a car with Mike Palmateer. Mike was a Leafs goalie between 1976–77 and 1979–80, and again from 1982–83 to 1983–84. A phenomenal, athletic goalie who was sidelined by knee problems. He's had something like twenty-one operations on his knee. But in 1977–78, when I was ten years old, I couldn't get enough of watching him play. It was his second year with the team and he went 34–19–9. He took the Leafs all the way to the semifinals—the first time they'd been there in eleven years. During all four years in his first stint as a Leaf, they made the playoffs. Punch Imlach got rid of him because of his knees, but he came back and ended his career as a Leaf.

Turns out the hockey gods weren't mad at us about the parade. We made the playoffs in 1998–99. In fact, we went deep into the playoffs. Past the Flyers, past Pittsburgh, and then we faced the Buffalo Sabres in the Eastern Conference final. The final four! For the first time in five years. The city was just upside down. We were crushing it. It felt great.

But we lost to the Sabres in five. I believe it was a combination of playing so much hockey, being a little tired and banged-up, and a false sense of security when we learned we weren't going to have to face Dominik Hasek, who was injured for the first two games.

I remember Steve Thomas saying that when they heard that, everyone in the room breathed a sigh of relief. "Okay, good. We don't have to play Dominik Hasek." Hasek was literally the most dominant player in the league for five years. He won Hart Trophies and Vezinas. The guys thought, "It's gonna be a little bit easier." That kind of thinking can creep into your game.

It's a fine line between winning and losing, and when you know that Hasek's backup, Dwayne Roloson, is going to be in net instead, you have to come out with your guns a-blazing. We didn't take advantage of Hasek's absence, and then, when he came back, he was good. Very good.

We should have beaten Buffalo. Unfortunately, we didn't. It was a huge disappointment.

Because he had been a player, Ken Dryden knew that, except for ceremonial moments during the season and playoffs, players were meant to interact with coaches, not executives. If he had an observation or something to say about a player or the team, he'd speak to Pat. "I was noticing this or wondering about that."

Ken might've been the team president, but deep down, he was still an NHLer. It's the same with all of us. No matter what exalted position you might get to in business or the league, at heart, you are a hockey player.

One thing Ken really seemed to enjoy was conducting exit interviews at the end of each season. He'd invite each and every player into his office for a one-on-one chat. It's customary for players to sit down with the head coach for this kind of season-ending conversation, but the way we did it in Toronto was to meet with Pat and then head up to Ken's office.

Ken was open and friendly. He'd start with "How did you feel about the year?" and follow up with "Now that it's over, what are you taking into the summer?" That's what he always asked us, because he believed that the groundwork for a lot of what happened the next season could be laid during the summer—if only by training, making yourself stronger and working on a few improvements.

Ken would tell us that each new season is its own story. "During the summer, you start writing next season's story." For example, every fifteen-goal scorer can write a story that has him scoring thirty. He can tell himself, "Geez, I got my fifteen. I missed so many chances, this way and that way. I can work on this move to help me score, and that'll get me a little bit more ice time, or get me on the power play."

He also liked to talk to us about how we saw ourselves—who we imagined we wanted to be like. He'd ask each of us, "Are there any players in the league that you'd like to emulate?" And the answers he got were revealing.

Years later, Ken said there were times when he'd get an answer and think, "Oh man, there's no way this guy can be like that player. He's got the wrong image in his mind. He's going to try to write the wrong story, and that's going to send him down the wrong road."

But most players are pretty self-aware. They would have in mind somebody who was better than they were but played a similar game and was enough like themselves that, with a bit of work, yeah, it could happen. Ken would tell us, "That's a good person to keep in mind over the summer as you're beginning to write next year's story."

Ken didn't usually ask me that question, because I was far enough into my career and playing at a high level. I know the answer he was looking for, but no way would I mention an adversary. Honestly, I wasn't a goalie nerd growing up. I was a forward.

I felt I was at the top of the heap, so I'd say, "Yeah, Mike Palmateer." Ken and Mike played each other a lot. Ken was a veteran goalie for the Montreal Canadiens when Mike Palmateer was playing for Toronto.

Ken nodded. "Mike Palmateer is a little bit like you in the way that he could make the amazing save. But you are more disciplined." He smiled. "Mike would fairly often put himself into impossible positions and have to make the impossible save. Thankfully, he was better than most at doing that. He might have let in fewer if he'd put himself in situations where he needed only to make a *possible* save."

"But you are right in that I can see you are similar in the pleasure and joy you both get out of it."

We went on to talk about things I might work on or think about. "What are those things that are keeping you from having an even better season next year?"

Finally, he threw out some food for thought. "Curtis, you're not a good puckhandler. I think the biggest reason for that is that you catch left and shoot right. So in order to handle the puck, you have to flip your stick around in your hands, and that takes time, which means you've got maybe a second less against the forecheck. It's just a fact. I am not saying it's a problem."

It's true. In an ideal world, I would shoot left, but I did not. And as a kid, I'd never had any instruction, and playing goal as I moved up, I never played the puck. Can you imagine an NHL goalie today who never learned to play the puck?

Once I became a pro, I was like, "Okay, I need to do something." I was constantly trying to solve the puzzle.

Goalie gloves—the catcher and blocker—are like lobster claws. They really limit your dexterity. I used a glove with no padding— barely any plastic—because I needed to feel the top of the stick. A leather glove without cushioning is more supple. It was hard on the hand, but you get used to it. I'd tape up each finger like a boxer to cushion it a little. That way, I wouldn't break my hand.

For a few years there, I was voted the goalie with the best glove hand in different magazines and other surveys.

I often thought about designing a glove where I could pop my hand out the top so I could hold the stick. I considered a one-piece stick that looked like a hockey stick and acted like a hockey stick, maybe curved right. In practice, I'd shoot with a normal stick and then I'd flip it over and take shots. I thought of all kinds of things, but nothing really worked.

I learned to flip my stick over to the left side. It was like swinging a golf club left-handed. How hard is that, right? It didn't look pretty, and I was a good skater, so I was able to get to a lot of pucks. It was something I continually worked on until it wasn't a weakness, just different.

CHAPTER 52

"His Eyeball Is Split in Half"

WE HAD A young guy, Bryan Berard, who had been a number one draft pick for the Ottawa Senators in 1995. While still playing junior, in 1995–96, he was traded to the New York Islanders, where he became the rookie of the year in 1996–97. When he was traded to us in January 1999, he was in his third season. Bryan was on track to become the best two-way defenceman in the league. With his size, strength and skill, he made a difference in the 1999 playoffs. He played all seventeen games. Mats Sundin really liked him, which is why he played so much. And then, something awful happened.

On March 12, 2000, we were playing the Senators. Our biggest rivals. We were doing well, leading 3–1 in the second period. We were on a four-on-four—both teams had a skater in the penalty box. I went down and blocked a shot. The rebound came out and Bryan came in to clear it. Marian Hossa, who was following and saw an opportunity to intercept the puck, got there first and angled himself back because he wanted to escape being hit. It looked like he lost his balance a little as he followed through, and at the same time, Bryan reached for the puck. The blade of Hossa's stick got him right in the eye.

It was really unfortunate. You see similar plays often. A puck will come up and cut a guy along the eyebrow, forehead or upper cheek. There will be stitches, but no serious harm.

Bryan went down fast. I was within ten feet of him and had been tracking the shot. I could tell he was seriously hurt right away, not from the way he fell, but by the tone of his screams. It was a primal wail, so full of despair that my chest tightened.

That was a big red flag because it never happened. Bryan was one of those players who would try to hide his injuries and never show he was hurting. Skate back to the bench and maybe have it looked at after the game. So when he started yelling, "I can't see! I can't see!" I started praying, "Please, God, take care of Bryan. Stay with him. Don't let his career be over."

I skated out with my arms and stick in the air, waving the trainers over. Our trainer, Chris Broadhurst, jumped out and just rocketed across the ice. He reached down to press a bench towel against Bryan's injury. When Bryan lifted his head a little, you could see how much blood had pooled under his head. Chris was trying to assess whether Bryan had cut an artery, which happened in 1989 to Clint Malarchuk, the Buffalo Sabres goalie, when a skate sliced open his jugular vein and he was actually bleeding out.

Chris was trying to gauge the danger. Was it a cut? Or was it a facial fracture? If it was a cut above the eyebrow, it would be gaping. But all the skin was intact, so Chris knew immediately that the brunt of the force had been absorbed by the eye, which is a very sensitive structure with a lot of nerve endings. That's why Bryan was screaming in so much pain. Once Chris applied pressure with the towel, he wanted to get Bryan off the ice as quickly as possible. With the amount of pain Bryan was in, he could go into shock at any moment.

Chris and one of our left wingers, Jonas Hoglund, grabbed his arms and skated him over to the bench. They got him back to the dressing room as the game continued. Once he was laid out on the treatment table, the doctors irrigated the eye to see what damage had been done.

It was bad. The blade had slit his eyeball, clean across the iris. It had opened up and lost its shape. Vitreous body, a clear gel, was oozing out, bubbling up out of the eyeball. There was a real threat that he could lose his eye. Think of a water balloon full of water. You slit it with a sharp knife and . . .

In the playoffs, you carry your whole medical team, including your doctors and orthopaedic surgeons, because you don't want the other team's doctors treating your players. That way, the other team doesn't find out anything about your players' injuries. But this was the regular season and we didn't have the full medical team available. We were extremely fortunate that Ottawa's doctors were fantastic and that the city has an incredible eye institute connected to the Ottawa Hospital. The paramedics had come so quickly that Bryan was still in full hockey equipment when he left the building. They rushed him to the eye institute, where a surgical team was waiting.

Mats Sundin and Tie Domi went to see him after the game and find out how he was doing. When they came back into the room, they were both white as ghosts. Cory Cross, who was Bryan's defence partner, got up to go see for himself, but Mats put his hand on Cory's shoulder. "Don't go in there." Cory froze for a second, then sat back down. The bench went dead quiet. Tie said, "His eyeball is split in half."

It was one of those injuries everybody dreads. We were a close team, and Bryan Berard was a big part of our success. It was a really tough night for everybody in the building.

CHAPTER 53

Goalie Gone Wild

LOSING BRYAN WAS tough. We weren't the best team in the league. We were the kind of playoff team that other teams described as "hard to play against." But it took a lot out of us to play the way we did— that tough, physically risky game. We were always going to have injuries. When you're playing every second night in a series that way, and when most of them are going to six or seven games, you're going to wear down. By the time we got to the end of the second round, we had less left in the tank than the team we were facing.

Now, if you make it to the final, you find an extra level of energy. At that point, you are so close to the Cup, you don't think about aches and pains, you don't think about how tired you are. There is only one gear. But on our way up, we were ground down.

The four years I played for the Leafs, the team to beat, year in and year out, was New Jersey. They were a pain in the ass for everybody because they were so well coached and so well managed by Lou Lamoriello. They were a real thorn in our sides, and they won Cups—three while I was in the NHL. In the West, it was Detroit, Colorado and then, sort of laterally, Dallas. After those four teams, I think we were maybe fifth best. That didn't mean that we couldn't win. Every one of those years, we won the first round. Twice we lost in the second round and twice we won it and went to the Eastern Conference final.

The team that everybody else seemed to think was better than us in the East was Ottawa. Often, our regular-season games were close—one-, maybe two-goal games, or they'd beat us in overtime. But then we'd play them in the playoffs, and we beat them every single time. We always found a way, but it took a toll. And that's how I ended up on TSN's show *Top 10 Goalies Gone Wild.*

We were facing Ottawa in the first round in 2000, the first time the teams had met in the playoffs. Right away, the press started calling it the Battle of Ontario, like the great Battle of Alberta matchups between the Calgary Flames and Edmonton Oilers. I was confident. They outshot us 30–21, but we won the first game 2–0. In Game Two, the shots were a bit closer, and we came away on top again, 5–1. Then came Game Three. We were not ourselves. It was really frustrating.

The visitors' dressing room at the Corel Centre (later called Scotiabank Place and now Canadian Tire Centre) in Ottawa was right underneath the stands. You could hear the fans, almost as if they were right on top of you. There's not another rink like that, where you can hear them chant and shout, and the Gatorade is actually rattling on the tables in the dressing room when they stomp their feet. You don't really get a break. And that damn horn in Ottawa—*argh!* If I ever hear a horn like that again . . . When Ottawa scores, it's the loudest, most annoying horn ever, and it lasts for what seems like thirty seconds. It's like a train horn. You know what they say about goaltenders—"When you go to work and you make a mistake, does a big horn go off while twenty thousand people call you a sieve?" I'd let in a goal and that horn was like *buh-waaaaahhh.* Brutal.

In the third period of Game Three, we were trailing 3–2. Ottawa's Rob Zamuner fired a slapshot from the point, and it looked like an easy stop. I moved to the post, but Daniel Alfredsson was driving the net and Cory Cross wanted to send him a message, so Cory gave him an extra shot and drove him into the crease. Alfredsson was crafty, and he stuck his leg out and ended up right on top of me. The puck went in. When you play against a guy like Alfredsson, you realize how good he was. He'll be in the Hall of Fame.

I was so frustrated with the game and how we were playing, and especially my own performance, that I went after ref Mick McGeough to dispute the goal. It was obviously interference, as far as I was concerned. The situation escalated.

Okay, you may read this next part and think, "Wow, that Cujo's a maniac!" Trust me, I'm not. At home, with my kids, with my teammates, friends and family, I never lose it. Never. Maybe it was all bottled up, I don't know, but I saved my anger—or rage or whatever you want to call it—for war. I'm not saying I was a saint. Of course not. Could I get grumpy? Sure. But lose my temper and yell and scream and throw things? I'm just not that guy. I like to get along.

Two things. I'd had a problem with Mick McGeough long before this game because he never, ever talked to me. I'd ask him questions and he'd always hold his hand up in my face like a stop sign. That would piss me off to no end. In the heat of a game, if you get riled, most refs will try to defuse the situation—"Curtis, Curtis, calm down. Did I miss something?" But not McGeough.

Getting hit by Alfredsson and then seeing the red light come on and hearing a big blast from that damn horn, combined with the fact that, as a goalie, I couldn't go out and whack somebody . . . that triggered a little road rage. I decided I needed to change Mick's mind before he got to the penalty box to call it a goal. I would give him my perspective, and maybe after that, he'd confer with the other officials and give us a chance.

As I said, I got up in a hurry, threw off my catcher and blocker, threw down my stick, skated out to him at full speed, slipped and knocked into him. This is technical, but goalies are constantly hitting the posts with their skates, and when that happens, they lose their outside edges. You play on your inside edges, and so you don't know you've lost an edge until the next day in practice, when you start skating and doing crossovers, and then it's like, "Oh, I lost an edge last night."

When I chased down Mick and followed him towards the corner, I shifted my weight to the outside edge of my right skate to turn, and down I went. My legs took out his legs, and he fell on me.

What's funny is that I didn't even acknowledge that we collided. I continued to yell and argue even as we struggled to get up. McGeough, he was just trying to get away from me.

Colin Campbell, who was one of the league disciplinarians, called me the next day, and the first words out of his mouth were "You know, I should suspend you."

I said, "C'mon, Colin. Do you actually think I wanted him to fall on me? Intentionally made him fall on me?" He knew it was an accident, and so he let it go.

Anyway, I always say it worked because, while we also lost Game Four, we won Games Five and Six and took the series.

We came up against New Jersey next. We made it to Game Six, losing 3–0, but in that game the shots were 27–6 for the Devils. We'd run out of gas.

You know how Gordie Howe always used to say, "Get a number and get him next time"? Cory Cross wound up playing for Edmonton a couple of years later, and as he went in to check a guy, McGeough stepped in the way. Instead of stopping and trying to go around him, Cory went right through him. And then he got off the ice as quickly as he could, sat on the bench and grabbed his water bottle. McGeough got up and skated down the ice. As he passed the bench, he gave Cory the side eye. But Cory focused on the play and looked so innocent that he didn't get a penalty.

I loved the referees that you could talk to. Andy Van Hellemond was one. And Kerry Fraser. Oh yeah, you could talk to Kerry.

We were playing in L.A. once—it was a game I was sitting out. If I had been playing that night, I'd have been focused and serious. I got my hands on a rule book and thumbed through it. I had a question about a rule I found, so I headed down the hall to the referees' room just ahead of the game. The door was open, so I walked in. That's when I caught Kerry Fraser in the act. He had the hairspray out and he was lacquering up the do. The room was foggy with it. He didn't see me come in, and so he was still going at it. Hard. I pointed at him and I yelled, "Aha!"

He jumped a little and then turned and looked at me. "You caught me," he said. No wonder Kerry had the best hair. It never moved. It was a perfect pompadour. Maybe that's why Pat Quinn yelled at him all the time.

Paul Stewart was just the best. Before he became a ref, Paul used to be a tough guy. His only season in the NHL was 1979–80, with the Quebec Nordiques. Paul had a little bit of an ego, which was normal. I always used to get to him by pointing out a guy I thought deserved a penalty and saying, "Paul! That guy's diving all over the place. He's making a mockery of you!" And every once in a while, he'd call it.

You always tried to plant that seed in a ref's mind. They're human, and if you can, you want to influence them to your team's advantage. They're smart guys, so you're not going to fool them, but you can call attention to things and complain. Squeaky wheel gets the grease, right?

You have to walk the line. Go too far and you can end up embarrassed or with a penalty yourself. But I'd try everything. Steve Yzerman, Wayne Gretzky, Sidney Crosby—just look at those guys. They all went to the ref to get a point across. Trevor Linden was the king of making sure he was heard. If you have Crosby or Gretzky in your grill, yelling at you, it's going to have an effect, don't you think?

CHAPTER 54

Reach

ON DECEMBER 27, 2000, Mario Lemieux made his comeback in Pittsburgh. Mario had retired in 1997 at age thirty-one, having averaged 2.01 points a game, just under Gretzky's 2.03. Mario packed it in fairly early in his career due to back pain and Hodgkin's disease. He didn't want to end up in a wheelchair. But three years later, with rest and rehabilitation, Mario decided to return.

We went to Pittsburgh for that game, and every media outlet in the world was there, even those that didn't cover hockey. We pulled up to the rink and it was wall-to-wall semis and vans and cords snaking along the ground like a root forest. I had never seen anything like it. Man, did we feel the anticipation.

Coming out on the ice for the warm-up, I thought we were late for the game. The rink was already packed. Everyone had taken their seat. And there was Mario, all six feet, four inches of him, with Jaromir Jagr beside him on the power play. Like two Bobcat loaders coming down on you.

Thirty-three seconds in, Mario got an assist. And in the second period, Jagr went behind the net, spotted Mario, passed it out and Mario one-timed it for his first goal. The place went crazy. You couldn't have written a better script. I should have been on my knees right away to make the save. I would have covered the whole bottom of the net and had a better chance. I was probably the only person in that whole arena who wasn't clapping.

There are no bigger fans in hockey than the players. When one of us has the opportunity to see a guy like Mario play, up close like that, it's hard to take your eyes off him. We caught ourselves watching a lot. At the end of the second period, after that goal, we filed into the dressing room and someone said, "Hey, guys, wake up! We're standing around, watching *The Mario Show*."

I watched that goal on YouTube with a buddy recently and joked, "Geez, I didn't see the puck go in back then, and watching the replay today, I missed it again."

Mario had such great hands. He was so quick and so gifted. He was big, with tremendous reach. When he came in on you, if you challenged too much, he'd simply go around you. Guys with huge reach and soft hands are so tough to stop.

Let me give you an example. Joe Thornton, whom the Bruins selected first overall in 1997, is still playing at age thirty-eight. He signed a one-year deal with the Sharks for $5 million in 2018–19. He has great hands and he's tall—six foot four—with a long reach. I always had to respect his shot. He came in on me during one game, and I came out. He faked the shot. I moved back. He went around me and put it in.

In the same game, Joe's teammate Sergei Samsonov, who had great hands too but stood just five foot eight, tried the same thing. I came out, cutting down the angle. He came in. I backed up. He went around me. I stopped it. He couldn't get it by my pad. The difference? Reach.

Mario's reach went from the front door to the dining room. His wingspan was incredible. He was like a pterodactyl. Remember, goalies guard on angles. Lemieux was so quick, he could change the angle in the blink of an eye, with just a slight stick movement. So smooth. As a goalie, you end up flipping back and forth across the net like a maniac, trying to stop him.

I mentioned this earlier when I was talking about Alex Mogilny, but the D did not want to challenge Mario or guys like him. They would just try to contain him. If defencemen went at Mario, he could so easily make them look like fools. Mario could dangle it through a defenceman, put it between his legs or between his stick and his skates, move around him, and make it look ridiculously easy. Nobody wants that on the highlight reel.

Mario was an incredible athlete with an incredible story. I was not happy to be part of the 5–0 loss that night (he added an assist, giving him three points on the night), but I was privileged to be part of that game and to watch his comeback. A valiant, courageous comeback.

CHAPTER 55

"Oh My God, My Career Is Over"

LIKE MARIO, GARY Roberts made an incredible comeback too. In 2000, the Maple Leafs brought in Roberts and Shayne Corson at forward, along with Dave Manson for help on the blue line. That brought us real toughness at three positions, and scoring punch too.

As I mentioned, when I left St. Louis, I got traded for Shayne, kind of. Blues GM Mike Keenan signed him out of Edmonton. He was a restricted free agent, so the Oilers were in line for compensation and the league valued him at two first-round picks. Nowadays, they would never award a team two first-round picks. That's a heck of a lot. But Edmonton said, "Okay, you can have your two first-round picks back for Curtis Joseph and Mike Grier." So in the end, the Blues got Corson, and the Oilers got Mike Grier and me.

Shayne and Gary became significant parts of our team in Toronto, that's for sure. Gary (we called him Robs) was a machine, an absolute powerhouse. We also called him Robocop because he was very stiff, muscular, a physical specimen. He'd make protein shakes for everybody. Whenever we went on the road, he made sure we had a supplement trunk with us. Nobody turned those shakes down.

Robs was a real leader, on and off the ice. He was one of the best teammates I ever played with. He had a tremendous impact on our team. His intensity was off the charts when it came to pretty much everything, whether it was on the ice or in his off-ice workouts, the way he treated his body.

When he first started out with Calgary in 1986–87, he lived an unhealthy lifestyle. And then he hurt his neck in the early '90s. He would be the first guy to tell you how that injury changed his life. He did a 180. He started working out and training and dove into that whole lifestyle.

You'd see the scar on the back of his neck, and he'd tell you the inspirational story of his comeback. Even though we were all professionals and kind of jaded, when Gary started talking, we'd all shut up and listen.

At his first Flames training camp back in 1984, Gary was just a skinny kid. Over six foot one, but only 170 pounds. He was so weak, he couldn't do a single pull-up. Not one. Badger Bob Johnson, the coach, was furious and let him have it in front of the whole team. Gary didn't understand. Yeah, he smoked, drank, ate fast food and never worked out, but he scored goals.

And then, in November 1991, Bob Rouse hit him from behind in Toronto on a line change. He was badly hurt and had to leave the arena on a stretcher. His body was paying a price for the years of taking a beating in front of the net when he was only 185 pounds yet played a physical game and didn't live the healthiest of lifestyles.

Even so, he barely missed any action and set career highs in 1991–92 with fifty-three goals, ninety points and 207 penalty minutes. He continued to absorb a lot of punishment, in games and in practice. Then, during the 1994 playoffs, Gary couldn't raise his arms. He played in a neck brace, which only made him more of a target. By February 1995, his neck was injured so badly, he couldn't feel his arms. Scary.

Gary had what they call cervical spinal stenosis, a narrowing of the spinal column. There were also bone spurs that were pinching off the nerves leading to his arms. He was told he needed a three-level fusion to his spine and that his career was over. He went for a second opinion and a different surgeon agreed to operate. He drilled though the discs on the right side of Gary's neck to relieve the pressure and allow the nerves in his neck to regenerate and heal. Next, the surgeon went back and opened up the same scar and operated on the left side. Gary went through a lengthy rehab to try to strengthen his arms and neck enough that he could play hockey again. If his neck had been fused, as the first doctor had advised, he would have been so incapacitated, he wouldn't even be able to drive a car today.

He came back and played the second half of the 1995–96 season for the Flames, winning the Bill Masterton Trophy for perseverance and dedication to hockey. He'd played thirty-five consecutive games, putting up twenty-two goals and forty-two points, when, on April 3, Dana Murzyn of the Canucks cross-checked him. Doctors said he tweaked his neck and would have to sit out two games. In June, he announced his retirement. He spent the summer hanging out with his hockey buddies, drinking and partying at the Calgary Stampede. That September, the phone stopped ringing because everybody was back at training camp. Meanwhile, he was retired with nothing to do. He woke up one morning and said to himself, "Oh my God, my career is over." He was only thirty years old.

At first, he thought about becoming a golf pro, but his neck was too messed up to play eighteen holes. He was losing the strength in his upper body because he was living an unhealthy lifestyle again. Early in November 1996, a strength and conditioning coach named Lorne Goldenberg called him and suggested he go to Colorado Springs to see a progressive chiropractor named Mike Leahy who was using a new method called "active release techniques," or ART.

Gary hung up the phone. He wasn't happy. He knew that if he didn't do something pretty soon, it would be too late. He decided to take a leap of faith. He flew to Colorado Springs, spent five days with Dr. Leahy, and it changed his life.

Gary flew from Colorado Springs to attend the funeral of Joe Nieuwendyk's mother. Joanne Nieuwendyk had died of stomach cancer. Joe was one of Gary's best friends since childhood. They'd played hockey and lacrosse together—the latter game gave them both remarkable hand-eye coordination. Saddened by Joanne's passing, Gary and some of his friends spent the night of the funeral toasting her. The next day, Gary embarked on his comeback bid, beginning with a decision to stop drinking.

From November 1996 to August 1997, Gary reinvented himself. He announced he was going to make a comeback in Calgary. But the doctor in Calgary said, "Gary, you look amazing, you pass all the tests. But when I look at your MRI, I just don't think you have a chance at any longevity." The Flames felt the insurance risk was too high. They traded him to the Carolina Hurricanes that summer.

Gary played three years in Carolina and then became a free agent. That's when he signed with the Leafs for the 2000–01 season.

I remember Gary's first exhibition game with us on the road. He was just hammering guys. He scored a few goals too. When you are in net, you have time alone in your own end to think about things. I remember saying to myself, "Wow, wait till the Leafs fans see this guy at home. They're going to love him." Leafs fans love guys who give that kind of effort, and sure enough, they did.

Chapter 56

Hellbound Train

BRYAN MCCABE CAME to us just prior to the 2000–01 season in a trade with Chicago for Alexander Karpovtsev and a draft pick. Gary Roberts saw Caber as a wonderful human being. He was a younger player—not the fittest, but he had a really good frame. Bryan was never in the best shape, and then Gary got a hold of him and there was a new sheriff in town. Gary was the elder statesman.

Caber was this solid, skilled, athletic defenceman who hadn't quite put it all together. I think he was looking for a mentor, and Robs was ready to mentor everybody and anybody who would listen. He had discovered a fitness regimen that had given him a new career and he was eager to share the secret. That summer, Bryan started training with Gary and Lorne Goldenberg, Gary's strength-training coach. Bryan became a disciple of Gary's healthy lifestyle.

Caber went from being a good defenceman to a great one. He was very popular in the room, partly due to his self-deprecating sense of humour. His teeth weren't straight, so he'd say, "I hope I get all these Chiclets knocked out this season. Then I'll get the team to buy me a new set."

Bryan McCabe's signature move was the can opener. That's when a forward skates in on you and slips his stick between your legs. It takes virtually no force, just leverage, and there's no escape. When his opponent tried to escape the stick with a crossover, Caber would punch him in the shoulder and the guy would be so far off balance that, with Caber's stick there, he'd go down. Bryan made an art out of it. Lots of guys did it, but nobody could do it at high speed like he could. His timing was perfect. He had the best can opener I've ever seen. The league had to make the play illegal because of him.

Caber would step up for guys when needed. Unless you sat along the glass, I'm not sure it was possible to grasp how impressive some of the fights could be, especially when the opponents were so huge. I remember a game in Ottawa one night when Caber mixed it up with Zdeno Chara. Caber is six foot two, 230 pounds. Chara is what? Six foot nine, 260? Just watching them jostle made me cringe. A normal human being might end up in a body cast. A couple years later, after I was gone, in another Leafs–Ottawa contest, Chara picked up Caber and helicoptered him. Honest to goodness, Caber's feet were off the ground and Chara was spinning him in a circle. That's like a refrigerator picking up a washing machine and throwing it around.

Caber was our guy when it came to the music in the room too. The game creates enough pressure, so an important dressing-room tradition is to have one person in charge of the music. Bryan had everything going. A lot of rap and songs to get you pumped up. We all loved it. It was great. I noticed Glenn Healy wasn't into Caber's playlist, so I asked him what he thought of it. He said, "Terrible." Heals was a musician himself. He played the bagpipes. He was only allowed to play one song, one time, on the bagpipes in the room, so he picked a song from the Victoria Police Pipe Band called "Hellbound Train."

He talked about how everyone was going to love it and how it was the best song ever. "Really edgy," he said.

It was the third game of the season. We were all getting ready, and Heals pulled out the pipes and started playing. His eyes were closed and he was really giving 'er. He finished playing and opened his eyes and looked around. He was the only one left in the locker room. He told us later that he said to himself, "Wow, the guys really love this song. I open my eyes and it's just me. Nobody else left. Not even Aki Berg, one of the nicest guys on the team. I guess I have to consider the possibility some people don't like bagpipes."

CHAPTER 57

Under His Shirt

WE WERE DEFINITELY the underdogs in our conference quarter-final series against Ottawa in 2001. They finished the season second in the East (and fourth overall) with 109 points, nineteen points ahead of us. We clinched the seventh seed in our next-to-last regular-season game with a 1–0 win over Chicago. Had we not won, Boston and Carolina could've overtaken us and our season would've ended early.

The first two games were in Ottawa, and we shut them out both times, 1–0 and 3–0. After Game Two, we got on the bus and Heals was showing me the zone times—how much time the puck was in each team's end of the rink. We were in our zone something like forty-four minutes—nearly three-quarters of the game. "That's a long time to spend in your own end," he said.

And then we heard some of the guys saying, "Wow, what a great job we did checking Yashin tonight."

Heals, being Heals, turned to me and said, "Really?"

But truth be told, Shayne Corson did a great job shadowing Alexei Yashin, the Sens' leading scorer. Pat Quinn had asked Corson if he was willing to stay on Yashin and frustrate him. Shayne was more than happy to take on that role. He really took on that responsibility.

Shayne prepared by watching a lot of tape to scout Yashin's tendencies, strengths, weaknesses, what he liked to do and what he didn't like to do. Shayne worked on a plan to shut him down. Yashin was one of the league's true skill players at the time. He could be dangerous, but not if he was running in neutral. Shayne relished that challenge. He really got under Yashin's shirt. Like we said in the dressing room at the time, "If Yashin went to take a piss, so did Shayne."

We didn't have a clue about this at the time, but Shayne was struggling. He roomed with Darcy Tucker on the road. They were like brothers. In fact, Tucks married Corser's sister. But even Darcy didn't know how bad Shayne's anxiety was. Nobody did. He hid it from everybody.

Shayne wanted to keep playing hockey. He didn't want to lose his job. He knew a player could be moved, or sent down or bought out, pretty quickly. And he wasn't sure how the team would react, or if we'd even understand. He couldn't tell anybody that he needed help. Meanwhile, it was taking over his life.

I found this out much later, and Corse is cool with me writing about it now because he wants to bring these kinds of issues out of the shadows.

Back then, unbeknownst to anyone, the only way Corse got through the day was by self-medicating. At first, he tried drinking, but the relief he got was short-lived. When he got up the next day, the anxiety would be ten times worse because alcohol's a depressant.

He started having full-blown panic attacks. Then shame and depression followed. He hid all this really well. To us, he seemed to be in a good mood all the time. Maybe that's because, when he got to Toronto, he stopped drinking and started taking Ativan like it was candy. From six to ten pills a day.

He says there were some really tough days. At times, it was tough in practice, or sitting on the bench. He'd start having an attack and feel like he couldn't breathe. He felt like he was swallowing his tongue.

Everybody saw him as a tough, macho hockey player. He felt he couldn't afford to show weakness, so he tried to power through it on his own. Now he says he should have dealt with it early on and gotten proper help, because it just got worse and worse as time went on.

He lost weight. He dropped down from 207 to 180. He was having acid reflux, which caused painful spasms in his throat when he lay down, so he didn't want to eat. Steve Thomas would talk to him about the weight loss and encourage him to eat more.

Corse would get exhausted from fighting his thoughts, and sometimes he felt like giving up. Thankfully, he would hear a voice in his head that would tell him, "No, I can't do that." For some people, the voice says the opposite. He never thought about shooting himself or hanging himself, but he'd be at a buddy's condo and look over the railing and think, "I should just jump off here. I've had enough of this shit." Then, right away, he'd say to himself, "But that'd be stupid."

The only place he felt totally free was on the ice. He hated getting introduced by the announcers. Just hated it. But once he stepped onto the ice and looked out at the ocean of light and colour and heard his blades ripping over the surface, felt the sensation of surfing along the boards, he would relax. His brain stopped obsessing and stressing and he focused on the job he had to do.

Corse finally found the right doctor. And he went out and started to talk about it to help other people. It was therapy for him too.

Shayne says it broke his heart when he heard about our teammate Wade Belak's death. Wade was another guy who hid it really well. You'd never know. He was always smiling, always in a good mood. He was just an awesome guy.

We claimed Wade off waivers in February 2001. He was a great person—funny, wonderful sense of humour. He was that ironic paradox you often meet in hockey, a sweetheart off the ice and a seriously tough guy on the ice. Big and strong, really built, he looked a little like Dolph Lundgren in *Rocky IV*. Wade was a protector on the team. He knew the game well and could play defence or wing. Wade played really well for us in the 2002 playoffs.

I remember watching a game much later in his career—March 20,

2007, in New Jersey, the season before Wade was traded to the Florida Panthers. The Devils' Cam Janssen hit Wade's teammate Tomas Kaberle late in the game. Wade was patient, but the next time he and Cam stepped on the ice on a line change, Wade dropped the gloves at centre ice. They had one of the longest, hardest fights I've ever seen in my life. That epitomized everything. Wade waited for the chance to defend his guy.

Wade and Tie Domi were pretty tight. Tie taught Wade the ropes on how to become a better fighter. But when I think of Wade, it's his sense of humour that stands out for me. He was incredibly funny. Tie used to get ingrown hairs on his shoulders sometimes, and Wade would put on a hockey helmet, pull down the visor and pop them for him. So funny.

Everything that came out of his mouth was accompanied by a little smile at the corner of his bottom lip. It would curl up and say, "Got you with this one."

Wade had a ten-year career, which is long in the NHL—even longer for a tough guy. The first season after he retired, he was practising for Ron MacLean's reality figure-skating show, *Battle of the Blades*, and he died alone in a hotel room in Toronto, apparently a suicide by hanging. I remember reading that his parents said it was an accident. Who knows? Maybe so. When I heard about it, it was shocking because he seemed like such a happy guy when we played with him. Three enforcers died in that summer of 2011—Wade, Derek Boogaard and Rick Rypien.

All I know for sure is that they are missed.

CHAPTER 58

"Fill Me Up"

IN GAME THREE against the Senators, things were going our way. We led 2–0 with about three and a half minutes left, and then Marian Hossa scored at 16:51. They pulled goalie Patrick Lalime late in the third, and Daniel Alfredsson tied it up with thirty-six seconds left on the clock. At the intermission before we went into overtime, we were saying to each other, "Hey, we just woke these guys up. We had them on the ropes." When the other team gains momentum like that and ties it up late, it's a mental hurdle you have to get over.

Every player has a spot they really like to shoot from. For Cory Cross, it was just outside the slot, at the edge of the right circle. He would practise shooting from there all the time. As a defenceman, he never scored more than seven goals in his career, but Cory actually had a good shot.

Just over two minutes into overtime, Nik Antropov let a shot go at Lalime's blocker side. The rebound bounced past Ottawa's Mike Fisher, right up to Cory in the high slot. He stepped into it and nailed it, off the post and in. Rob Zamuner was on the ice and didn't pick up Cory on the backcheck, so he just stepped into it. The roof blew off the Air Canada Centre.

That goal triggered one of the most memorable dogpiles of my career.

In Game Four, we took it to them pretty good again, winning 3–1, and that was it. A sweep. Four in a row against the hands-down favourite.

Our building would get oven-hot in the playoffs. I'd face more than thirty-five shots a game and I'd be completely dehydrated coming off the ice. You cannot drink enough water as a goalie to replenish, so I was put on IVs after every game—two bags of saline. It made me feel so much better the next day. I would peel off my upper-body gear and head to the training room, throw myself down on a table with my arm out and say, "Fill me up." The St. John Ambulance guys were always happy to help out in whatever way they could. They would rub their hands together and say, "All right, what d'ya need?"

Dehydration is dangerous. Like I mentioned earlier, in the 1993 playoffs when I was with St. Louis against the Leafs, I was so dehydrated, my groin muscles felt like they were off the bone. When you get like that, it's only a matter of time before your muscles pull. In fact, two ways you can pull a muscle is if you are dehydrated or you're not properly warmed up. It's automatic.

In the Toronto playoff runs, I was hydrating like crazy. After those two bags of saline, I'd come home and go to bed and get up in the morning and not even have to pee.

On the flip side, that last game against Ottawa, I only faced twenty-two shots, not a lot of action, so I didn't have to work as hard. I got the saline pumped in, jumped in the truck and headed home. I was on the highway when I had to pee so bad, it felt like I had electric Vise-Grips biting into my bladder. I got to our gate, threw the truck in park, jumped out and peed on the gatepost. I couldn't even make it up the drive.

CHAPTER 59

And Then It All Went Sideways

NEXT UP, THE dreaded New Jersey Devils. Pat Quinn was a really straight-ahead coach. "Drop the puck and let's go" was his philosophy. With Pat, we didn't really have a system or a plan, but we kept winning. I think he didn't want to burden us, especially our high-end guys, with systems, so he just let guys go. It definitely was good for Mats Sundin and Gary Roberts and guys like Sergei Berezin, who had scored thirty-seven goals just a couple of years earlier. We had a run-and-gun offence and it seemed to fit our style until we matched up against New Jersey, a very system-oriented team. New Jersey had an answer for us. Not because we lacked anything, but because sometimes your opponent has something that one-ups you.

In this case, it was called the trap. They'd used it for years, since the early '90s. They'd won two Cups using it. Instead of an aggressive forecheck, New Jersey would hang back and wait in the neutral zone. One winger was always bringing up the rear, so he could angle the puck carrier into the boards. It was patient, defensive hockey. Maybe it was boring to watch, but it won Cups, and pretty soon other teams copied it.

The Devils' goalie was my old nemesis Marty Brodeur. Despite Marty and the trap, we came away from Game One with a 2–0 win. In

Game Two, the play opened up and they won in overtime, 6–5. Game Three was another squeaker—3–2 for the Devils. And then it all went sideways.

We went into Game Four with a lot of confidence. You never say this stuff out loud during the series, but I think we were all thinking the same thing. "We're going to do it. We're going to win this."

I watched Tie play the entire time I'd been with the Leafs, and that night in Toronto was probably one of the best games I'd ever seen him play. He was incredible. Leading the charge, blocking shots, making a huge difference. In the first three games, they outshot us by 32–17, 33–21 and 45–28. In Game Four, the shots were almost even.

Tie wasn't just playing his usual tough game. He was scoring too. He assisted Shayne Corson on the first goal in that game. The fans were ecstatic. He had them on their feet. I'd never heard the building so loud. We were winning 3–1 with eight seconds to go when Tie elbowed an unsuspecting Scott Niedermayer in the head as he was coming up ice along the boards. Niedermayer had already passed the puck, so he wasn't expecting it. Scott was one of the league's most talented defencemen, a great, effortless skater. The elbow caught him and knocked him out. Everyone went quiet. The hit sucked the energy right out of the building. The mood went from jubilation to concern over the severity of Scott's injury and hope that he was going to be okay.

Scott regained consciousness on the ice, but he was groggy. I remember Chris Broadhurst saying that you could tell he had definitely received a head shot and was concussed. Scott was taken off the ice to the dressing room on a stretcher.

It was unfortunate, because up until that point, the game had been such a high point for us. We had played a really great game as a team.

The entire incident started with something that happened in Game Two. Scott hit Tie along the boards with his stick up and didn't get a penalty. That really got Tie's goat. In Tie's book, *Shift Work*, he calls the elbow "the dumbest thing I did in my career."

Colin Campbell, the league disciplinarian at the time, banned Tie for the rest of the playoffs and the first eight games of the following season. It may not sound like a lot to some, but for a competitor like Tie to sit through the playoffs, that was like denying him food or water. It was one of the toughest suspensions in league history to that point.

Look, Tie was a big part of our team. He was like the cop out there. No one messed around when Tie was on the ice because they knew better. He knocked everyone so far off their game and intimidated everyone so much. He added value to our team, big value. Our team was an inch taller when he was out there. He did his job exceptionally well and he knew when it was time to get into a fight and when it was time to rattle the cage.

Tie was one of the big reasons we'd made it past Philly two years earlier in the playoffs. Philly had two heavyweights, Craig Berube and Sandy McCarthy. During one game in that series, both Berube and McCarthy were skating after Tie, and he just kept backing off.

Tie could be controversial. Just before the 2001 playoffs, in late March, we were playing in Philadelphia. Tie got a penalty, a minor infraction. Remember, nobody in Philly liked Tie, especially since that series two years earlier, when we beat them.

There were maybe five or six fans behind the penalty box that were just giving it to Tie, calling him a plumber and a plugger—all kinds of crap. Tie grabbed a water bottle and gave them a squirt. This really bothered one of the fans in particular, a bigger fellow. He came over to the glass, leaned on it as if he was reaching for Tie—and the glass broke.

As a result, the fan fell into the lion's den. Tie grabbed him and then realized at the very last second that it wasn't a good idea to go off on a fan. They're paying customers. They contribute to the success of the NHL.

Kevin Collins, a veteran linesman, got in there quick, thank goodness. Cooler heads prevailed, but it could've been a tough situation if Tie had been in the wrong mood. Tie could've killed the fan.

I remember talking about it with Cory Cross after that game. He said, "You know what? I think you're fair game if you fall in. If you're leaning on the glass, reaching over, chirping and pulling all that crap, you're fair game. And to his credit, Tie was able to maintain his composure when it happened."

In an interview the next day, the fan was a puppy dog. Not so tough. There's a big difference when there's a piece of glass between you and the guy you're harassing. It's like being at the zoo.

In any case, the Niedermayer elbow was a bit of a turning point in the series. After pulling ahead three games to two, we ended up relinquishing that playoff series to New Jersey. We were beaten by the reigning Stanley Cup winners. I guess you could say we had that going for us.

CHAPTER 60

Salt Lake City

I THINK IT was Pat Quinn who convinced Wayne Gretzky and the rest of the Team Canada brass to give me a shot at the Winter Olympic Games in Salt Lake City, Utah, in 2002. Pat was the head coach, and he was really pulling for me. I got to play the first game, against Sweden, and I wasn't very good. I'd had too much time off and I was rusty. We lost 5–2. Sweden, led by Mats Sundin, was firing on all cylinders.

The game was on February 15, a Friday. Some of the guys had come in just the day before, on Thursday, after playing NHL games on Tuesday and Wednesday. I hadn't played in nearly a week—against the Montreal Canadiens on Saturday the 9th. I sat out our next game, against Atlanta, on Monday the 11th. In retrospect, I would have been better off playing the Atlanta game, and then flying out to Utah the day before the Sweden game. That suits my style way more. I can't have too much time off.

Pat played our other goalie, Marty Brodeur, in the next game, which made sense, and he beat Germany 3–2. After that, Pat ran with Marty. But that's what happens. I get it. You gotta play the hot hand.

That's the threat for every goalie. You never want to get out of the crease. I'd been on the other side of it with Marty Brodeur. At the 1996

World Cup of Hockey, we split the first two games, and then I got to play the rest of the way. Same thing with the World Championship in 1996—Marty and I split and then I got to play. On international teams, everybody is an all-star, and some of the best players in the world end up playing minimal minutes on the fourth line.

You know what, though? It was a big deal for me just to be named to Team Canada. I remember my first Olympic experience, in Nagano, Japan, in 1998. One of my greatest memories was getting on the bullet train from Tokyo to Nagano. It was a two-hour trip, and they pack you in like sardines. I am not exaggerating. They push people through the door with what looks like a plunger. These huge hockey players were taking up all the room.

Wayne Gretzky was on that team, and when we got off the train, the cameras were waiting. A group that could fill a small auditorium, all taking pictures with flashes, surrounded him everywhere he went. He had to take baby steps because he was constantly surrounded by this pack. When it came to the rest of us, it was just, "*Pfft*, who are you?" I have to say, it was interesting—and quite funny—to watch it all unfold.

Wayne gave me one of his sticks. He sat beside me at the last game, the Finland game. We lost, and so we were out of the medals. We were all so disappointed. As we sat there absorbing the loss, I looked at his stick, the last stick he would ever play with at the Olympics, and asked, "Do you mind?" He said, "Take it."

Another thrill was meeting up with my buddy Tyler Stewart again. Drummers and goalies are similar in that we both play at the back of the stage. We're a little weird. We see everything. My career and Tyler's were intersecting. Here we were at the Olympics. The Ladies performed a concert in the Olympic Medals Plaza in front of a crowd of about twenty thousand. Canadian pairs skaters Jamie Salé and Dave Pelletier were up on stage with them. This was right after the figure-skating judging scandal. Salé and Pelletier deserved to win gold after just a really beautiful, incredible performance. Days later, it came out that there had been a conspiracy to give the gold to a Russian pair. The International Olympic Committee ended up awarding gold medals to Salé and Pelletier as well.

But what really sticks with me is being on the ice when our team was introduced, and looking over at the Barenaked Ladies. They'd just finished a song. Tyler looked at me and I looked at him and I could see he was feeling the same thing I was. Here we were, in front of the world—two local kids from Newmarket who went to Huron Heights Secondary.

In my mind, we were the best team at the 1998 Olympics in Nagano too, no question. But we came home empty-handed. Our chance at a gold medal came down to a shootout. And unfortunately, Wayne Gretzky wasn't one of the five guys tapped to compete in it. I remember what Wayne said about it in 2016 in his book *99: Stories of the Game*. "We were crushed. Such an empty feeling. We hadn't even lost the game. We were knocked out of the tournament because of an event."

Marc Crawford was our coach in Nagano. He was also Patrick Roy's coach in Colorado. We flew over to Japan on a two-level plane, the kind you'd think the Rolling Stones might own. As soon as we took off, they started the individual meetings and called me up right away. I went upstairs and the coaches were sitting there. Crawford told me, "It's Patrick's time. He's going to play all the games." End of meeting.

I nodded and said to myself, "It's going to be a long flight."

Yeah, I was disappointed. Of course I was. But I tempered it with the excitement and knowledge that I was on the first Olympic hockey team where elite NHL hockey players could play. I went back to my seat and proceeded to have a drink and watch a movie.

Both Olympics were a lot of fun, just being there and working with the players every day. I wanted to play, but so did the other guys. And let's face it, in 1998 I was backing up a first-ballot Hall of Famer, Patrick Roy. Marty Brodeur was a first-ballot Hall of Famer too. So I really can't complain.

CHAPTER 61

Fist Bump

WHEN WE GOT back from Salt Lake, there were all kinds of media reports claiming that I had been promised another start at the Olympics—specifically, against the Czechs. Listen, I wasn't promised anything. I didn't even know I was going to start the game against the Swedes. Taking a week off, I wasn't sharp. Period. Of course I wanted another chance, but that's not how it works.

Have you ever heard Ken Dryden's Wally Pipp story? He's written about it a couple of times, but it is a great story with a lot of truth to it. Wally Pipp was the first baseman for the New York Yankees in the 1920s. As the story goes, one day, he wasn't feeling well, so he decided he couldn't play. He was benched for that game, and the next time there was a chance to start at first base for the New York Yankees was 2,130 games later, after Lou Gehrig's iron-man streak ended. Very few people know the name Wally Pipp these days, but everybody involved in sports knows the lesson. Once you're there, you find a way to stay there, because if you don't, you may never be there again.

My situation was similar. I had my chance to be there, play huge and make it impossible to pull me out. I didn't play well, and I missed my window. Pat Quinn probably didn't want to make a change. As a player, you've got to give the coach a reason to think about making a change. That's sports.

It was too bad it worked that way, but once the shift was made to Marty, and Marty got stronger and stronger as the tournament went on and started playing lights-out, it was done. I felt I would have been the same, but that's okay. I was genuinely happy we won the gold medal.

I liked Pat. He was a nice man. A great man. But my relationship with him wasn't a cozy one. It didn't need to be. I respected him. I thought he was a great coach and loved what he was doing with the team. Our relationship was a professional one. We didn't talk much. I wasn't a forward. He wasn't a goalie coach. I rarely, if ever, went into his office.

I do think a strain between us developed, but not because he didn't play me in the Olympics. After we got back, he called me into his office for the first time in a long time. I wondered what he was going to say. Maybe something positive about winning gold at the Olympics? Or focusing on something now that we were back? Maybe he wanted to share a penalty-kill strategy? Who knows? I went in with a smile on my face.

He was sitting at his desk with his arms crossed, frowning. I sat down across from him and he said, "It was my decision not to play you at the Olympics."

Not knowing what was coming next, I said, "Okaaay."

But that was it. I was dismissed.

At the time, I wasn't sure what to think. Take it at face value? "It was my decision not to play you at the Olympics." Why would he have to say that? Was he saying I let him down? It didn't shake my confidence. I knew what I was capable of, and we both knew how well I played for him.

Another thought occurred to me. Earlier in the season, the Leafs had opened discussions with my agent, Donnie Meehan, about a contract extension. Donnie was handling all that. That was his job.

My work was on the ice. But as I understood it, the organization had offered a shorter term than what we wanted and they hadn't come up with a dollar value. There was still no offer on the table after I got back from the Olympics. Crickets.

Maybe in that brief meeting, Pat was saying that the Leafs weren't interested in re-signing me anymore. I was worried that they might not come back with an offer. What if an offer didn't happen?

The gold medal had been won, and the Leafs, like every other team in the NHL, were going to acknowledge Team Canada in a pre-game ceremony. Of course, the two people on our team involved with Team Canada were Pat and me.

After warm-ups, prior to our February 26, 2002, home game against Carolina, Pat and I were on the ice—they rolled out a red carpet, the whole bit. I had all my equipment on—glove, blocker, stick, everything. The announcer was saying, "Yada yada yada, gold medal, yeah!" Cue the loud music. Pat put out his hand to shake mine and I gave him a fist bump. Big mistake.

Two things. One, I didn't know I was going to be shaking Pat's hand. After our meeting in the office, shaking his hand would seem pretty phony, but I would have set that aside and done it. Two, the fact that the ceremony was happening ahead of the game was not a great thing for me.

As a forward, it's hard to be embarrassed. You miss a shot, so what? A goalie? You can be pulled. And that's embarrassing. You have to be prepared to be out there for sixty minutes. You have to be focused. Before every game, I would get into a quiet zone. It wasn't like, "Hey, I need my quiet time, get away from me," or anything like that. I'd find my quiet place. It might be a physical place, or it might just be that I would turn inward mentally. As a game approaches or between periods, most goalies become quieter. There's a certain introspection that is part of being a goalie. Before a game, even if I was smiling and appearing friendly, I'd be thinking, "I have a job coming up for the next two hours, and if I mess it up, I let my team down and I embarrass myself." No way was I looking around thinking, "Oh my goodness, wow, look at this fanfare about the Olympics!" Maybe after a game—if we won, that is. But not before.

The media tried to play it up as this thing where Curtis snubbed Pat, Curtis was hurt because Pat broke his promise at the Olympics, and Pat and Curtis were at war. None of it was true. A big hullabaloo over nothing.

And you know what happened to make matters worse that night? I broke my hand. Six weeks before playoffs. We were ahead 4–1 with a little over eight minutes left in the game. I was right by the net, and like I'd done a thousand times before, I put my glove, knuckles down, on the ice to make a save and then give myself a little push back up. But my hand was caught in the netting on the side of the net, and the netting gave way. I rolled my wrist and snapped the bone—the fifth metacarpal, near the knuckle next to my ring finger. They call it a boxer's fracture.

There was a whistle, and I got up and skated right off the ice. Our backup goalie, Corey Schwab, finished up for me.

All heads on the bench were turned my way as I stepped into the tunnel. We had an X-ray machine in the dressing room. You could see the crack down the bone. Thankfully, our trainer, Chris Broadhurst, was pretty progressive. Twice a day, I wore a contraption called the Exogen that we Velcroed around my hand. It vibrated every few minutes to stimulate bone growth.

Chris employed a lot of sports science. He was a great resource on how to improve my performance. Until I joined the Leafs, it would be fair to say I just played on raw talent. The Leafs helped me develop as a player.

The Leafs were early to the table not just on fitness but on injury prevention, going back to the days of Grant Fuhr in 1991–92. I was told to take body maintenance days. Once in a while—say, every six to eight weeks—I might come in and my body was a little stiff and cranky. I'd try to loosen up a little bit, but I was either too fatigued or too sore, so I didn't practice. When you are beat like that, you can suddenly tweak a hip flexor or a groin in practice. Instead, we had the pools there, so I'd do contrast pools—hot, cold, hot, cold. We also had the steam room, and I'd go in there, and I'd ride the bike, stretch and get a massage.

When this happened, Scott McKay, who was our equipment manager, and Chris Broadhurst would go in net for practice because it was usually too late to call in a practice goalie. Those guys always said they liked body maintenance days because they got to pretend they were pros.

The biggest issue about my hand, aside from missing all those games ahead of the playoffs, was that we didn't want to tip off opposing teams at such a crucial time, so we concealed it from everybody. I still practised, though I was cutting down the size of my blade because, every time a player took a shot and I stopped it, the force of the puck hitting the blade would vibrate up the shaft of my stick. It was agony for my fractured hand.

The media were all wondering why I was doing this to my stick. I told them, "Oh, I'm just working on some balance stuff."

I used a regulation stick and tennis balls after practice. One day, I called my buddy Tyler, who was on a break from touring with the Ladies, and he came onto the ice with a hundred tennis balls and just fired them at me. That was a bright spot.

CHAPTER 62

Webb Was Dangerous

WE ENDED THE 2001–02 season in third place overall, and just one point behind the Boston Bruins for top seed in the East. In the first round, we met the New York Islanders in a kill-or-be-killed series. Guys were getting hurt left, right and centre. It was brutal. And we went into the series with a lot of injuries already.

My hand was healed, and I was ready, but I was worried about the long layoff. Coincidently, Tom Barrasso—the goalie they brought in at the trade deadline to fill in and who was now backing me up— broke his hand too.

Dmitry Yushkevich hadn't played since early February because of a blood clot in his right leg. Gary Roberts had a torn rib-cage muscle. Mikael Renberg had a pulled hamstring and Robert Reichel had sprained his left knee in practice. Garry Valk had a bad shoulder and Shayne Corson was playing with a hip flexor injury.

In the opening game, Mats Sundin and Claude Lapointe were standing in front of me, jockeying for space. Mats held up his left arm to block a shot, but the short cuff on his glove left his wrist exposed. When the puck hit, it fractured one of the two main bones in his forearm, the ulna, which, along with the radius, runs up to the elbow.

Mats was a right-handed shooter, which means he used his left hand as his control hand at the top of his stick. When you're shooting, you follow through with the bottom hand. Being the kind of player he was, a real gamer, Mats had his left hand frozen and played the next two periods. He came back for the next game wearing a playing cast made of fibreglass. The doctors cast his wrist in playing position so that he could hold a hockey stick. They made it thin enough that he could wear a stretched-out glove over top.

We won the first two, close-fought games. It was a hard-hitting series. By Game Three, the hostility between our two teams had built up. On every shift, someone was getting a slash on the laces or the back of the leg. On every line change, the benches were yelling at each other. It was an intense battle.

One of the Isles' fourth-liners, Steve Webb, was a one-man wrecking crew. He would hurt guys. One hit and he could take you out of the game, or the series. As he ran around our zone, it was like watching a driverless car with the gas pedal stuck down. He didn't slow up. Usually, when guys hit somebody, they brace themselves so they don't get hurt. Not him.

When Webb was on, I'd tell my D, "Guys, heads up! Webb's out there." And I'd yell at them if he was behind them.

He ran every D when he was out there. He hit Cory Cross and separated Cory's shoulder. For him, it was like there was no puck on the ice. He was effective and he was dangerous. He went after our skill guys. He checked Mats into the boards. Mats connected hard with his cast, and the pain was almost unbearable. It took him out of the series.

After the final buzzer, Gary Roberts, being the great teammate and team player that he is, decided to repay the debt. He went after Mariusz Czerkawski to send the message back to the Islanders that if they were going after our skill players, we'd return the fire. There was a big scrum and the gloves came off, which resulted in a pileup. When it was over, Robs found Czerkawski again, and Brad Isbister, one of Long Island's huge young power forwards, who played on Alexei

Yashin's left wing, grabbed Robs and they started to fight. Isbister was throwing down. He landed one on the top of Gary's head and broke his hand, taking him out of the series. Who knew Gary had a head as hard as Tie's?

Fans in the Nassau Coliseum were chanting Webb's name. He was named first star of the game, and as we were coming off the ice, someone saw their coach, Peter Laviolette, literally hugging him.

We lost that game 6–1, and the Islanders tied the series with a 4–3 win in Game Four. Webb kept going out there at the start of every game and, just to get the ball rolling, he'd run someone through the glass. Five seconds into the fifth game, the level of intensity was ratcheted to the max. And it stayed that way for the entire sixty minutes.

Webb didn't just hit. He antagonized by chirping. He went to work irritating some of our tougher guys, like Darcy Tucker and Shayne Corson. We knew what his job was. He was out there to take guys off their game. I'm sure if any of us met him off the ice, we'd think he was a great guy, but on the ice, none of us could stand him. Webb was in the Sean Avery or Matthew Barnaby mould. Shayne wanted to literally pop his head off every time he played him, but he knew he couldn't lose it because that would result in a penalty and maybe even cause us to lose the series.

We were no angels either. They played hard, but so did we. We crossed the line sometimes too. There was an incident in Game Five where Tucks hit their captain, Michael Peca, below the knees. Harry Neale on *Hockey Night in Canada* called it a low-bridge hit. It was a legal hit, but Peca was out for the rest of the series with a torn anterior cruciate ligament in his left knee. The NHL introduced a penalty for clipping soon afterward because of it, but I have never heard of it being called.

The same game, Robs skated into the offensive zone, just flying on the forecheck, and hit one of their defencemen, Kenny Jonsson, into the boards. Jonsson went down and was out with a concussion for the rest of the series.

What a thrill to spend time signing autographs with Johnny Bower. He told me that the money he made for one signing event was better than what he made playing hockey for a whole season back in the day. Wow!

At the Centennial Classic—Leafs versus the Detroit Red Wings—in Toronto in 2017 with some of my favourite people: Mayday (Brad May), Robs (Gary Roberts) and Joe Nieuwendyk.

With Tie Domi and Robs. Notice how I have my hand around Tie's arm? That's to stop him from putting me in a surprise chokehold. Could happen any time.

Bill Ranford and Dwayne Roloson both had great careers. This outdoor game in Winnipeg was a blast!

I'm honoured to be a part of this great group of Leafs goalies. I'm holding Mike Palmateer's legendary pads! I'm in the front row, next to Félix Potvin. Second row: Johnny Bower and Mike Palmateer. Third row: Freddie Andersen and Antoine Bibeau.

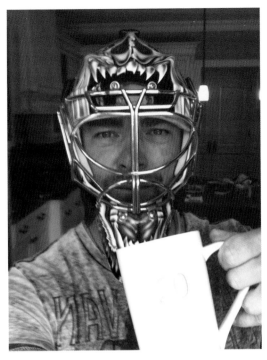

I loved my Toronto mask . . . but it made it tough to drink my morning coffee.

This guy told me he was my biggest fan. Then he showed me his tattoo. Uh . . . he wins!

The infamous photo of me pretending to check out Danny Ardellini's car when I'm actually trying to meet Stephanie. COURTESY DANNY ARDELLINI

With Kailey, Hef and Stephanie at the Playboy Mansion.

With Don Cherry and Steph in 2009. Don didn't know it at the time, but what he said on "Coach's Corner" back in 2003 inspired me during one of the toughest times of my career.

Steph and me with Nick Kypreos and his wife, Anne-Marie, at Tie and Heather Domi's wedding in New York in 2017.

At our wedding reception on the beach on June 4, 2012—one of the best days of my life. COURTESY THE SCOBEYS

With Kensie Shayne, Jason, Kailey, Rita Casio (Stephanie's mom, a five-star chef and the best mother-in-law a guy could ask for) and Steph.

Madi, me and Steph. Like Madi says, "He's lucky to have us!"

In Virginia Beach with four of our seven kids and my mother-in-law, Rita.

With Steph and all of our kids at the Leafs–Coyotes game, Christmas 2017.

My son Tristan cracks me up. Here he's using a vase we had in the house to make fun of me for not winning a Cup.

With Luke, Taylor and Tristan
on a road trip to Yankee
Stadium and Fenway Park.
Awesome time!

When you hear your kids
encourage each other
while climbing a tough
mountain . . . priceless.

We took the game 6–3, putting us ahead 3–2 in the series. Game Six at Nassau Coliseum wasn't just hockey. It was all-out war. Dirty and mean. If we'd had guns instead of sticks, I swear players would have killed each other.

The Coliseum was a big, no-frills barn. Built in the early '70s, it didn't have anything in the way of soundproofing. In the dressing room, you could hear the fans, and as you came down the tunnel to the ice surface, they were right there on top of you. It added to the anticipation. You could feel the building buzzing.

The Islanders had won all those Stanley Cups in the early 1980s, but after that they had some tough times for quite a while. This was their first post-season appearance since 1994. The pent-up demand for playoff hockey on the Island had exploded, feeding the intensity level of fans and players alike—our team included.

When the Canadian anthem started, Islanders fans booed. I looked up and saw why. Tucks and Robs were being shown on the Jumbotron and New Jersey fans hated them because of the toll they were taking on their players.

Steve Webb was back out there, hitting everything in sight, and every time he took it to one of our guys, the Isles fans would chant, "Peca! Jonsson! Peca! Jonsson! Peca!" It got the hairs standing up on the back of your neck.

With 1:50 to go in regulation, they were ahead 5–3. Shawn Bates hit Corson, sending him down flat on his back. As he was getting up, Corse grabbed Bates's jersey and Tucks jumped in on Bates. As Corse tells the story today, "And then I got stuck with six-foot, five-inch Eric Cairns." Cairns was one of the toughest guys in the league that year. During their matchup Corse lost his balance and they both fell down. Corse jumped up right away and the officials came in, but by that time, Corse says his wires were crossed and he was out of his mind with anger. He tried to knee Cairns in the head. He knew he shouldn't have done it, but he paid the price and got a one-game suspension. It was a hard thing for him to sit out and watch Game Seven, which we played at home.

After Mats was hurt in Game Three, Robs stepped up. So did Alyn McCauley, who played on Rob's line throughout the whole series. Alyn played unbelievable hockey for us in that series. Here he was, a fourth-line centre most of the time, and suddenly his contribution was off the charts. He was probably one of our best forwards. Robs, McCauley and Jonas Hoglund were attacking like army ants.

Yashin opened the scoring, but Robs put in the equalizer, and I remember watching their goalie, Chris Osgood, go down on his back with a charley horse. I felt his pain, and I remember thinking, "Ooooo, not good."

Tyler Stewart lived and died for hockey, especially the playoffs. He was such a big fan. I would get him tickets, but only when he needed them, and he always offered to pay. If I got an extra set, I'd call him. That night, a Gary Roberts chant filled the building and went on forever. Afterward, Tyler and I met up in the visitors' room. He said, "You heard the Gary Roberts chant in the crowd?"

"Yeah, Gary was on fire. He was running over people, scoring goals, he was a force to be reckoned with tonight."

Tyler said, "I started it."

He did too. He's so musical and he's got this great voice and perfect timing. *Ga-ree Rob-erts! Clap clap clap-clap-clap. Ga-ree Rob-erts! Clap clap clap-clap-clap.* His whole section started to do it, and then the whole building caught on, like the wave.

I played average throughout the series, maybe because of the layoff from my broken hand, but in Game Seven, it all came together for me. I played well and made thirty-one saves. Alex Mogilny scored our second goal, Travis Green put us ahead, and then Alex clinched it with an empty-netter that made it 4–2. We won the series.

I looked around the dressing room. There was more ice in there than in a Dairy Queen truck. We weren't quiet, but nobody was ready to celebrate yet either.

CHAPTER 63

"Bless You, Boys"

BELIEVE IT OR not, even with everybody injured, our next series, against Ottawa, was the most fun you could ever imagine. When you have really good chemistry on a team, it's like being in a family. A big, close Italian family. You don't always agree, but there's definitely support all around. We all had each other's backs, thanks in part to a great leadership group in that dressing room. Mats was our team captain, but now that he was out, we had Gary Roberts.

We'd call up five or six guys from the St. John's Maple Leafs, our minor-league affiliate, and four of them would be out for the warm-up. We had no idea whether all four would play, or just two or three of them. It depended on whether our regulars were healthy enough. Pat Quinn would come into the coach's room just before opening faceoff, and even he didn't know who was going to be playing that night. He'd go through the list. "Joe can't go and Tommy can't go, but so and so can, so we're gonna insert this guy and that guy."

We had a couple of those call-ups in the lineup for Game 1—Alexei Ponikarovsky and Paul Healey, but winning that rough seven-game series with the Islanders had taken everything we had. So the Senators won Game One, 5–0, at the Air Canada Centre. We didn't mean to take a step back, but we really weren't there for that game. We thought we were, but we weren't.

Remember my hesitation about using the last name Joseph instead of Munro just before college because I was worried about the fans calling me a sieve? Well, the headline in the *Toronto Sun* the next day read—you guessed it—JOE-SIEVE. Right there on the front page of the paper. I was like, "Okay, come on, we just won a Game Seven!"

We took a 2–0 lead into the first intermission in Game Two, and then Ottawa tied it early in the third. We went to overtime. Twenty extra minutes solved nothing. Neither did forty. Finally, at 4:30 of the third OT, Robert Reichel won a faceoff, the puck found its way to Robs, and he fired the winner. I was really blown away after the game when I looked at the stats and realized that Bryan McCabe had logged fifty-two minutes of ice time. Fifty-two minutes! Holy cow.

I remember thinking that, despite the injuries, despite the fact that we were exhausted and Ottawa had had some time off, we could grind them down. And we did. After four games, the series was tied 2–2. Late in Game 5, at the ACC, Tucks was checked from behind into the boards by Daniel Alfredsson. It was a controversial hit because, just seconds later, Alfredsson scored off the turnover he had created with the hit. Our fans went nuts. I was as pissed as any of them. I was sure the ref would call a penalty, but there was no whistle, and the next thing you knew, the puck was in the net.

Darcy was laid out on the ice in our end. The hit pushed him into the boards at speed and he went in at an awkward angle. He came out of it with a broken bone and a dislocated left shoulder. He was out for quite a few games. It was a shame to lose Tucks. He was such a fierce competitor and he hated to lose. I'd compare him to Brad Marchand of the Boston Bruins. Brad's a little bit better scorer than Darcy was, but they had the same ability to agitate, the same competitiveness, the same do-anything-to-win attitude.

Tucks was helped off the ice, and we could see there was no way that he was going to be playing in the next game. We lost that fifth game at home and now had to go back to Ottawa for Game Six.

The Sens got off to a quick start and went ahead 2–0. We were being outplayed and going nowhere. Later in the first period, we scored on two power plays. Caber put it in with assists from Robs and Alyn McCauley, and then Robs scored off Jonas Hoglund and McCauley, tying it up. In the second period, Robs got another on assists from Travis Green and Caber. But the Sens got that one back with twenty-five seconds left in the period and we were all tied up again.

Tyler Stewart and his brother-in-law Chris travelled to Ottawa for Game Six. It was a crazy game that went back and forth. And then, about four minutes into the third period, Alex Mogilny scored off Travis Green. It was a huge goal for us. Tyler got so excited that he jumped up and down and started screaming, "ALLLL-EXXX-AN-DER MO-GILLLLL-NYYYYYY!!!!" until he ran out of air and fainted. He dropped forward, falling on an extremely frightened woman who was seated in front of him. Chris grabbed him by the scruff of the neck, pulled him back up and lowered him into his seat. That poor Ottawa fan. This whole game, she had had this bald, sunglasses-wearing man screaming in her ear, and then he fell on top of her.

During the last minute of the game, Ottawa pulled their goalie, Patrick Lalime. With about twenty-eight seconds to go, there was a faceoff in our zone. The Ottawa net was empty and . . .

Okay, we are going to pause for a moment while I tell you about Joe Bowen, our radio announcer.

Bonesy has called over three thousand games for the Leafs. And when he calls a game, it's exciting. He really puts you there. When I was playing, I didn't hear any of the games. But today, I enjoy getting in the car and turning the game on whenever I'm driving somewhere. And when I listen to Joe Bowen and his partner, Jim Ralph, I think, "Wow—once upon a time, that was me he was talking about."

Anyway, my guess is that nobody was listening to the radio for Game Six of the Toronto–Ottawa series. Maybe if you had to go somewhere in an emergency—if your wife was having a baby or something—but otherwise fans had either travelled to Ottawa to see it in person or they were watching it on TV. Nowadays, you can listen to the broadcast again on your computer. Back then, it went out over the air, and then it was gone. So, while I'm pretty sure nobody heard it—certainly none of the players—Joe delivered this classic call:

> *Green wins the draw, but it comes back to the blue line. Alfredsson with a shot off a leg. Into the corner for Bonk, trying for the side of the goal. Here's Hossa, trying to come out in front, back to the point—and a shot! Corson blocks! Another shot! Wide of the goal! Far side, Mogilny trying to get it out and can't. Twenty seconds left, McEachern in the corner, back to the blue line. Over it comes to Alfredsson. Shot goes wide of the Leaf goal, back of the net, centred in front! Knocked away, still loose in front, back to the blue line—stopped! Bonk can't get a shot.*
>
> *Six seconds left. Mogilny, along the boards, doesn't get it out. Back to the point—a shot blocked! Another shot blocked! Redden blocked! Another chance, game over! Game over!*
>
> *Bless you boys, what a game! Unbelievable! In our very small way of being a part of this team, I don't think I've ever been as proud in my entire life. What a performance. What a gritty bit of work over the last twenty-eight seconds. Travis Green, Shayne Corson, Alex Mogilny. Unbelievable.*

Mike Ferriman, a guy who worked in the Leafs front office, running the game presentation department and suiting up as the team mascot, Carlton the Bear, came into Ken Dryden's office the next day and said, "A guy from the radio station just came in with a couple of CDs of Joe Bowen's call of the last twenty-eight seconds of the game. You should hear it."

Ken put it on and said, "It's unbelievable. My God, we've got to share this with the office staff." He did, and the response was so positive, he called Mike back and said, "Here's what we're going to do for the next game . . ."

Remember, the series was tied 3–3 and the seventh game was being played in Toronto. So right after the anthem, while the arena was darkened, the video board lit up with the words MAY 12—LEAFS 4 OTTAWA 3—JOE BOWEN'S CALL OF THE LAST 28 SECONDS. And they played that audio to the arena. Of course, none of us had heard it, and neither had the Ottawa players. It wasn't like we needed any help to get us going, but hearing Joe Bowen's passion gave us an extra shot in the arm. We opened the scoring at 11:49 of the second period, and by 14:04 of the third period it was 3–0.

Ken knew we were playing Carolina next if we won. He didn't want to jinx us, so he waited until there were four minutes left, and then he went to our video people and Leafs organist Jimmy Holmstrom. Ken said, "Okay, here's what we're going to do with about a minute to go in the game. Wait for a stoppage of play . . ."

With about a minute left, the whistle blew. Up on the board appeared the words NOTHING WOULD BE FINER THAN TO BE IN CAROLINA . . . ON THURSDAY, while Jimmy played the old song "Carolina in the Morning" on the organ. It zipped through the crowd like electricity, and the fans started singing that song right through the final buzzer.

CHAPTER 64

A Tough Call

THE STANLEY CUP is the hardest championship to win in all of pro sports because you've got to go four rounds, and each of those rounds is a battle. There are tremendous highs and lows along the way. You think you're crushing it, and all of a sudden an injury like Mats's comes up.

I've been retired for just under ten years now and people are always asking me what I miss most. That's easy. The playoffs. No question. That's when everything's on the line. That's when you really get to see what you and your team are made of.

I made it as far as the semifinals twice, both times with Toronto—in 1999, against Buffalo, and in 2002, against Carolina. There are a lot of reasons why we lost that series against Carolina. Mats had been out a couple weeks with the fracture, so his return was a big morale boost for our team. But it's tough to play when the chemistry changes in the middle of a series.

By Game Six of the Carolina series, Sundin, Darcy Tucker, Jyrki Lumme, Garry Valk and Wade Belak had all returned at some point to the lineup. Fantastic players, all of them. But it meant the guys who had been killing it, playing out of their minds for us to get there, guys like Travis Green and Alyn McCauley, were losing their ice time.

There is something to be said about a team when it's rolling. When a lineup is winning, most coaches will be leery about changing it up. It's a tough call. When you look back on it, you ask yourself, "Should we have maintained the status quo and not put all the injured guys back in all at once?" With Mats back in the lineup, the chemistry changes. His line works around him. But is a team going to tell a guy who has been a big part of getting them to the semis, "By the way, we're gonna work you in slowly?" Probably not. The coach is going to say, "God bless you, we have you back." Even at 75 per cent.

I believe with all my heart that it came down to the fact we got banged up yet again in the Carolina series. After the two very physical series we'd already played, the injuries caught up with us. We were gamers. We could play with whoever they put on the ice. Pat and the coaching staff made the call on who was in and who wasn't.

To make it more complicated, Pat was having health problems. Coaches are like players when it comes to job security. We're always on the verge of losing our jobs, though I never really felt that way—glass half full, remember? But a bad season, a bad run in the playoffs, even a few bad games in a row, and that can mean you have to pack up and move on. That sense creates a lot of stress.

In Pat's case, he ate like the hockey player he used to be, but he didn't work out like the hockey player he was back in the 1960s and '70s. An NHLer can burn five to seven thousand calories a day. Players lose weight as the season progresses.

Pat still loved his huge steak dinners and his cigars. He'd been having trouble breathing, and after another big meal in Raleigh, it got worse when he got back to his hotel room. Pat was a stubborn Irishman, so he was sort of denying there was a problem. He wanted to be able to stay behind the bench. But our team doctor convinced him to go to the hospital and get checked out. It turns out Pat was on the verge of having a heart attack.

Pat missed Game Three, and then he came back, but you could tell he wasn't feeling well. He wasn't the same. What we all noticed the most was that he wasn't yelling at the refs. That wasn't like him. Our assistant coaches, Ricky Ley and Keith Acton, stepped up.

The series was incredibly close—low-scoring games, and all but one were settled by just one goal. Game Six was a seesaw battle all the way. The shots were close, and there was no scoring till the third. Jeff O'Neill scored for the Hurricanes, and then Mats tied it in the last twenty seconds of the game, sending us into overtime. At 8:05 of overtime, Martin Gélinas scored for Carolina, ending our season.

We had been able to find the win we needed in the Ottawa series to get to the conference final, and then to have Mats come back in Game Six and score that late goal was a real high. It gave us hope. It made us think we had a shot to take the series to Game Seven.

And then, it was over.

Carolina went on to play Detroit and lost in five games in the Stanley Cup final. If we'd won that series against the Hurricanes, it would been a Toronto–Detroit final. Can you imagine how much fun that would have been?

CHAPTER 65

"Is This How It's Going to Be?"

WE'D MADE IT to Game Six of the semifinals, farther than the Leafs had gone since Doug Gilmour, Wendel Clark and Dave Andreychuk got them to Game Seven against L.A. in 1992–93. Yet Donnie and I didn't get an offer for a new deal from the Leafs. So Donnie started canvassing, and he came back to me predicting that the Detroit Red Wings and New York Rangers might be interested.

Detroit made an offer of $24 million for three years. Toronto did end up making a last-ditch offer, but by that time, I'd had a lot of time to think about it. And I was arrogant. I wanted to win a Stanley Cup more than anything. That's what all players want. That's what we all dream about doing. Most players don't play the game for the money. I mean, of course the money is great. We're lucky that we get to do what we love and get paid so well for it, but a lot of the guys would play the game for free.

Detroit had Brendan Shanahan, Chris Chelios, Luc Robitaille, Stevie Yzerman, Nick Lidstrom, Brett Hull, Pavel Datsyuk, Igor Larionov, Sergei Fedorov. All these Hall of Famers. But it was an older team with a lot of miles on it.

Sometimes, when you become a veteran player, you think too much. You start questioning things. I started second-guessing management decisions when really, I would have been better off focusing on playing. My heart was in Toronto, and that's where I should have stayed. I didn't want to leave. I had success there. But on the other hand, they weren't breaking my door down to keep me.

I'd changed teams before, and it had always worked out for me, so maybe I had a false sense of security. I was thinking, "Detroit is winning Stanley Cups." They'd just won it in 2002. In my mind, I could go to Detroit, play for Scotty Bowman, win a couple of Cups and then come back to Toronto.

Some would call that ambitious. A voice in my head was saying, "I need Cups." My heart was saying, "Stay—you are a Leaf," but my brain was saying, "Curtis, you can have it all." A pretty egotistical thing to think, honestly. But that's what it takes to be a number one goalie.

There was the lure of winning Stanley Cups in Detroit versus the months of uncertainty in Toronto, not knowing whether they were going to re-sign me. It came down to my decision, and looking back, it seemed like it was a spur-of-the-moment one. I went with Detroit.

I remember being in Toronto, just after my signing with the Red Wings was announced. I went into the bank and held the door open for an older woman, a grandmother, like I normally do. She walked through it and said, "Traitor."

I was like, "Wow. Is this how it's going to be?"

CHAPTER 66

High Risk, High Reward

THE HOCKEY GODS were mightily pissed at my decision to leave Toronto. The first thing I learned was that I wasn't irreplaceable after all. The same day I signed with Detroit, the Leafs signed Eddie Belfour. He was two years older than me but a fearless goalie who was also a good fit with the Leafs' run-and-gun style of hockey. Eddie would become a fan favourite very quickly.

Detroit's training camp was in Traverse City, Michigan, about a four-hour drive northwest of Detroit. As I was putting on my equipment, one of the young guys, a prospect looking to make the team, turned to me and said, "You look better in blue and white." Just another sign of things to come.

I'm not whining here, okay? This is all on me. I made the decision, and I'm living by it. I'm just letting you know what happened. A friend of mine from high school told me, "Wow, you're in a no-win situation. You're going to have to win the Cup, four straight series in a row, without Scotty." Scotty Bowman had retired as the Wings' coach after the 2002 season. He had just won his ninth Stanley Cup and left the game with 1,244 coaching wins and a .657 points percentage in the regular season—basically winning two games for every loss throughout his career. Wow. All of those stats are all-time bests.

One of Scotty's assistant coaches, Dave Lewis, replaced him, along with Scotty's former right-hand man, Barry Smith. I had a good relationship with Barry, but the GM, Ken Holland, and the owner, Mike Ilitch, were also very involved.

I struggled in my first year with the Wings. In St. Louis, Edmonton and Toronto, I had fed off facing lots of shots and being a big part of wins. In Detroit, if we lost, it was my fault. We would win as long as I stopped a few pucks. And there weren't many, because we had a really, really good team.

Ever since I left Notre Dame, I had been on teams that faced thirty-five to fifty shots a game. High-risk, high-reward teams. That's when I played my best. The more work I got, the better I was. Now, instead of getting pelted, I was facing maybe seventeen shots a game, with two or three breakaways, and I sure as hell had better stop those. It was the complete opposite of what I was used to, of the way I had developed as a goalie. It was foreign to me and I had to learn to deal with it. Fast.

Even the way Detroit played defence was completely different. I was used to telling the defence, "Be aggressive! Take that guy! Pass it back, I'll go over and make the save." Nick Lidstrom, one of the best players in the world, on a two-on-one? He would back off and I'd have to make a save. It took a while for me to understand, "You're supposed to face the shot, dummy."

My defence would always come back and play the other guy, not the puck carrier. They'd cover the pass. I was used to playing for the pass across, so that meant I was usually playing too deep in my net. If all I had to worry about was stopping the shot, I needed to be more aggressive, come out and cut off the angle. It was a real challenge to change what was basically a lifelong habit.

And I had some small, aggravating aches and pains. There was a plantar wart on the bottom of my foot. Right on the ball of my foot. I'd never had a wart in my life before. It kicked me in the ass every time I'd push off in the net.

There was something wrong with my knee. I first noticed it when I got on the floor to play with the kids at home. I couldn't kneel. I was on the carpet and I thought, "Oh man, I can't put any pressure on my right kneecap!" It was diagnosed as patellar tendinitis. Some people call it jumper's knee. It comes from the stress of overuse.

And then it turned out I had os trigonum syndrome. In the normal human foot, there are twenty-six bones, but I had an extra bone right behind my ankle—the os trigonum. It's congenital. I didn't notice it until the bone started peeling away from my ankle. The next time you get out of the driver's seat of your car, notice how your toe catches under the brake pedal or sweeps it. When I did that, it caused my foot to bend in such a way that it felt as if somebody was digging out my ankle with a screwdriver. Every time I made a kick save that first year in Detroit, it felt like Freddy Krueger from *A Nightmare on Elm Street* was using his knife-bladed glove to go after my foot.

Suffice it to say that in my first year in Detroit, I underachieved. Yeah, if you scan my stats quickly, you'll think, "C'mon, Cujo, you had two amazing years there." Sixty-one games in 2002–03, thirty-four wins against nineteen losses, a .912 save percentage. Uh-uh. I didn't play well enough. It was a disappointment for me. When you play on a team that good, it makes your stats look better.

We made it to the playoffs and lost four straight to the Mighty Ducks of Anaheim in the first round. For the team with the third-best record in the league, which happened to be the defending Stanley Cup champions, that's terrible. I didn't make the big saves, while Anaheim's goalie, Jean-Sébastien Giguère, was on fire. The Ducks went to the final, where they lost Game Seven to the Devils. Giguère was awarded the Conn Smythe Trophy as the MVP of the playoffs.

CHAPTER 67

Battle Mode

AFTER MY FIRST season in Detroit, Dominik Hasek, who had retired after the 2001–02 season, told the media his batteries were recharged and he was ready to play again in the NHL. He was still the property of the Wings, so they brought him back in July 2003. To say it came as a surprise to me would be an understatement. Ken Holland announced he was going to try to move one of us.

Hasek never really spoke to me, so I wouldn't say we had any sort of relationship, the way I did with every other goalie partner I'd ever had. But he was the greatest goalie I ever saw. He just knew how to stop the puck. He was big and incredibly agile, with a great butterfly. He had long limbs too, like a spider. He played the percentages like I did. Hasek perfected the art of goaltending.

I went to a clinic in Cleveland that August to have the extra bone near my right ankle removed, and they told me it would be a piece of cake because it was just dangling inside my foot like a loose tooth.

In late October, the Red Wings called me in. They told me they wanted me to test out my foot with their AHL affiliate, the Grand Rapids Griffins, in a game against the Utah Grizzlies. Even though I was medically cleared to play, I knew I shouldn't play on the ankle for a while yet. But I felt that they were paying me so much, so I rationalized it by telling myself it would be good for me, that it would help me get back into playing shape. It was only a two-and-a-half-hour drive, so I took my truck.

The Grizzlies scored on me early in the game, and I remember being down on the ice, pulling the puck out of the net, as the guys celebrated near me. I heard one of them say, "Suck on that, Cujo!" I have to admit, I did find it pretty funny. But I got the last laugh because we ended up winning the game.

I hopped into the truck to head home, and my foot was killing me. Pain was pounding on the bone. I had to elevate it to drain some of the blood out of it and relieve the pressure. So I stuck my right foot up on the dash and operated the gas and the brake with my left.

It was pretty clear to me that it had been too early for me to come back and play hockey. I couldn't even jump on the trampoline for the next two years. The kids were always on the trampoline and they'd say, "Dad, let's go!" I'd look at the surface of the trampoline and shake my head, knowing how much it would hurt. "There's no way, guys."

The club had basically stopped playing me, even though I was ready and willing. They put me on waivers, but there were no takers. Of course not. Everybody in the league hated the Wings because they'd won three Cups in the past seven years. My contract was expensive, at $8 million a year, and unless Detroit was going to eat half of my salary or more, nobody was going to do them a favour and take me. Every other team saw the situation the Wings had put themselves in, investing $16 million in goaltending (Hasek also made $8 million that year). Why would any other team help Detroit? So now I was stuck. I was the team's embarrassment, and I had no way of working my way out of it. It was tough.

On December 6, we were in Toronto and they played Manny Legace. Look, it was their dime. They could do what they wanted in that situation. But most organizations will play a player against his former team. It shows that they have his back. Not to do so sends a different message.

Maybe I'm disrespecting the team. They were the Detroit Red Wings. They were a year away from a Cup championship. But I was disappointed. I was used to being a big cog in the machine. Now they were sending me a message. It made sense to them, but it didn't make sense to me. It could have just been my arrogance, but that's how I felt.

A month and a half after the Utah game, Kenny Holland called me into his office. The team had played twenty-eight games, and I'd started four. They were playing Hasek and Legace instead. The coaches were in the meeting too, but they were looking at their coffee cups or the floor or the ceiling, anywhere but at me. I took that as a bad sign.

Holland told me he was sending me to the minors.

"Kenny, hold on a second. Are you *telling* me to go to the minors, or are you asking me?" I looked around at the coaches, but nobody would meet my gaze.

"I'm telling you."

"Okay. What's your reasoning?"

Holland looked at me. "Manny needs the net for practice."

I flew down to Grand Rapids, and when I got there, I remember sitting on the edge of my bed, waiting to catch the bus, watching "Coach's Corner" with Don Cherry and Ron MacLean. I love Don Cherry. He's a great Canadian. Sometimes he's controversial, and he wasn't always very nice to the European players, but he is more supportive of the military than anyone else in sports in Canada, for sure. And when it comes to hockey, he just gets it.

Ron said, "You know, Curtis Joseph got sent to the minors. Just a year ago, he was just one series away from the Stanley Cup finals with Toronto."

And Don answered back, "Let me tell ya something, kids, this is just nonsense. He's resilient. Don't you worry, he'll be back, you'll see. It's only temporary. He'll be back and he'll carry that team . . . "

I will never forget how good he made me feel. Believing in me like that and telling the whole world about it. He gave me inspiration. I immediately felt stronger and ready to prove he was right.

Remember Derek King? My buddy from Toronto? He'd been down in Grand Rapids for a while, since the 2000–01 season. I love Kinger. He's a funny, funny man. He and I were at the back of the bus, and I was telling him what happened. I mean, it was fine. It's business, right? And I said, "I get it. I'm not a spring chicken, I'm thirty-six." But he knew it was hard on my ego.

We were dealing out the cards. Kinger was there, cheering me up, making me laugh. And I got a phone call on my cell. It was Barry Smith, the assistant coach in Detroit.

I liked Barry Smith, you know? I liked all assistant coaches. They act as a go-between between you and the head coach. "You must have pulled the short straw," I joked, because he was the one calling me. Listen, I was older, more seasoned. Not easy to intimidate anymore, and I was in battle mode.

Barry said, "Curtis, you ready to play?"

"Barry, you know me. I'm always ready to play." I thought he meant in Grand Rapids.

He said, "No, no, no, you've got to come up here. Dom hurt his groin in practice, and Manny hurt his knee. We're in Buffalo. Can you catch a flight?"

Both goalies had gone down in my absence. I was thinking, "Wow. The irony." Here I was, having just left Detroit, and now on a bus headed to Cleveland, needing to find a way to get to Buffalo. I said, "How far is Cleveland, Barry?" I was having fun now.

He said, "Geez, I don't know, I . . . Jiri Hudler, he's getting called up too." There was a long pause.

I let him off the hook. "I'll just rent a car. I'll put it on my credit card, and yeah, I'll bring Jiri."

I hung up and I looked at Kinger. "You're never going to believe who that was."

We got to Cleveland, and this being the AHL, we pulled up to a Days Inn or some hotel like that, and I looked across the parking lot and there was a Budget Rent-a-Car agency.

I told Jiri to grab his things, thinking it was about a three-hour straight drive along Interstate 90. Hudler could keep talking and keep me awake. I was a veteran, and Hudler was a rookie with all of seven games of NHL experience. I figured he would want to talk hockey and ask questions the whole way. It might even be fun.

Jiri slid into the passenger seat and was asleep in two minutes, before we even got to the highway! He was just a kid and didn't speak much English. He turned out to be a good NHLer. He won the Lady Byng Trophy in 2015 when he was with the Calgary Flames. But on December 10, 2003, I was the very well-paid chauffeur who drove Jiri Hudler to Buffalo.

I played that night. Didn't play great, but we won 7–2.

CHAPTER 68

The Smell of Burning Rubber

HASEK SAID HE had a groin injury, and so he quit halfway through the season. I was back to the number one position, although they gave Manny Legace plenty of playing time too.

We wound up in first place in the Central Division, with a record of 48–21–11–2, and were heading into the playoffs against the Nashville Predators as the top seed in the West. I went to Dave Lewis and asked him, point blank, "Are you going to play Manny?"

He said, "Oh no, no, no. I'm going to play you."

They started Manny.

He started the first four games and won two. Prior to Game Five, Dave told me, "Okay, Manny can't play anymore."

"Is he hurt?"

"No. Can't play anymore." That was it.

So after this turbulent season, I went in. We won the series against Nashville and then took on the Calgary Flames. In the pre-game skate before Game One in Detroit, Jamie Rivers, a seventh defenceman who had been called up from the Griffins, took a slapshot from close in. A hard one. I smelled burning rubber. That's what happens when you get hit in the head with a vulcanized-rubber puck at that speed. One of the sights and sounds of the game you don't get to experience unless you are on the ice.

I turned my head just as it hit. You never want to turn your head. Goalie masks back then weren't even tested from the side. The puck hit my right jawbone, or lower mandible, and it was like no pain I'd ever felt.

Glenn Healy had retired and was working for *Hockey Night in Canada* as a broadcaster. He had just come in through the back of the rink past the Zamboni entrance and was walking to the glass when he heard a huge *thwack!* and saw me drop like I'd been shot.

About an hour later, Heals called. He told me he'd seen the play and was worried. My jaw was really sore. It felt like the hinges needed oil. "Heals, I can't eat, I can't talk. I can't function."

Regulation time that night ended in a 1–1 tie, but we lost in overtime. After a sleepless night, I went to the trainers and asked for an X-ray. By that point, I couldn't open my mouth. When I talked, words slid out through my clenched teeth. Later, I asked, "Did that X-ray show anything wrong?"

"Nah, it was negative."

I took a few Advils and played the next night. We won 5–2.

We flew into Calgary on April 26, and when I got up the next morning, game day, I still couldn't open my mouth. The pain was excruciating. Some of the guys were giving me dressing-room medical advice. You know, "You probably need a root canal. I had the same problem one time . . ."

I thought, "Yeah, maybe I need a root canal."

We were staying downtown and I found a dentist's office in the Eau Claire neighbourhood. They took an X-ray, but for some reason their machine wasn't working properly, so I went back to my room and took a mouthguard and fiddled with it, cutting away pieces and fashioning it so that it allowed me to bite down when I played.

Word got out about my jaw, and two nights later, Ville Nieminen, a Finnish forward playing for Calgary, skated by the net and punched me right in the face. He got in front of me and gave me a shot. Thank God it was from the front and not from the side. He was a pest. That's what he was there for.

THE SMELL OF BURNING RUBBER

The rest of the series was close. One- or two-goal games, but we lost in Game Six and Calgary went on to the finals that year, losing to Tampa Bay. The Flames were the surprise of the playoffs, going deeper than anybody predicted, a good team with lots of speed and solid players like Jarome Iginla, Martin Gélinas and Robyn Regehr, but most people will tell you that the secret to their success was a goalie named Miikka Kiprusoff.

The playoffs were over, so I headed back to the farm in Newmarket and made an appointment to see my dentist, Dr. Steiner. The pain had subsided a little. He examined me and took an X-ray. He said, "Good news and bad news."

"Good news?" I was hopeful.

"The good news is you don't need a root canal."

I smiled. "Ahhh."

"The bad news is, you've got a broken jaw."

"Wha?"

He pointed to the X-ray on his computer screen. Sure enough, there was a crack right down the middle of my chin. It's funny how the hit to the right side of my lower mandible caused a break down the middle of my jaw. I guess that's the weakest point.

The break wreaked havoc on my jaw hinges on both sides, and it hurt to chew or yawn for about five years after that.

When I showed up at training camp the next year, I was like, "Hey, I had a broken jaw!" It's true fractures don't always show up when the swelling is fresh. But either way, the trainers I told didn't make a big deal out of it.

I missed my trainers in Toronto. Chris Broadhurst was a friend. In Detroit I had all these quirky injuries like the patellar tendinitis and the plantar wart and the extra bone. I think Chris's help could have made a difference. He would even have to protect me from myself sometimes, because he knew I pushed the limit.

In the end, it all worked out. If I had known my jaw was broken, I wouldn't have played in the Calgary series. In the thirty-one games I ended up playing that season, I had a .909 save percentage and a 2.39 goals-against average—decent, but not great. I did much better in the playoffs, even in the series we lost to Calgary. Over nine games, I had a .939 save percentage and 1.39 GAA—both were the best among play-off goalies in 2004. But despite that, it wouldn't be long before I'd be changing addresses again.

CHAPTER 69

Square to the Puck

THE THIRD YEAR of my contract with the Wings was the year the NHL locked out the players for the entire season, including the Stanley Cup playoffs—2004–05. So I wasn't paid for that year. Remember my buddy Steve Thomas? I see him all the time and he always says the same thing. "Cujo! Eight million. Your highest earnings! You lost more than anybody!"

"Yeah, thanks, Stumpy. Thanks for reminding me."

You know what I did that year? I went back to goalie school. I worked on what was then the new way of goaltending, on my knees. It was a big deal and a humbling experience for me to change everything I'd ever known. But it gave me a new foundation and taught me a more efficient way to stop the puck.

I took lessons in Vaughan, Ontario, with my buddy Dave Franco at Franco Canadian, the goalie school he and his brother Marco founded. And I had my own rink in the barn on the farm, so I practised at home all the time.

Dave and Marco taught me how to use the equipment to my advantage. I used to get hit in the knees all the time because I was never facing the puck squarely. I would turn, and my pads would turn with me.

Old-school goaltending was a lot less scientific. Goalies relied on certain skills. For instance, Glenn Healy had tremendous hands. An interesting thing about Heals is that he wore absolutely no knee protection. I am not kidding. He never wore anything underneath his pads.

I asked him about it one time and he said, "Yeah, I asked my dad for some knee pads one time and he told me, 'Forget the knee pads. Catch the puck. Make the save.'" Anyway, Heals played his whole career without them. Shocking. I don't know how he did it.

Before I developed an understanding about the new style of goaltending with the Francos, I'd make saves by going down, getting up quickly with the leg closest to the post or my outside leg, and then I'd push across and go down to try to make another save. Moving up and down like that uses a lot of energy. The Francos taught me that when I was down, I should just stay down. Push off with that outside leg and use my lead leg to leverage myself across the net.

I also learned to square up to the puck when I was down. So, if a shooter was in close, I'd stay down and block with my body, using the angle to my advantage. If the shooter raised the shot, I could use my shoulder to make the save. In this new style, I had to keep my body more symmetrical, both knees down together with both feet out at the sides, instead of just one leg out. It was so much easier on the body because it meant no more diving. No need to go into the splits on saves, and I didn't need my glove as much.

I remember watching a group of kids practising in Vaughan. They were just eleven years old, but I was so impressed by their understanding of the position. I watched one kid execute, and then I got in net and tried to stop the puck using the same technique, but my ankle was underneath my pants, so I didn't get much of a push across. The kid looked at me and said, "Mr. Joseph . . ."

I knew he must be pretty thrilled to have an NHL goalie there with him, so I said, "It's okay. You can call me Curtis."

The kid nodded, then said, "Curtis, you're using the wrong leg. Use your power leg to push. And your ankle is bent. You need to force the lead leg out."

GOING INTO THE 2005–06 season, I got two calls. The first was from Wayne Gretzky. He'd been involved with the Phoenix Coyotes since 2001. The other was from Eddie Olczyk, who was the coach in Pittsburgh at the time. Neither club was a playoff team. Still, I was excited. Thirty-eight years old and I was getting calls. Great!

Wayne didn't give me any guarantees. "Listen, Curtis. We know you're a free agent and that you're older now. Brian Boucher is our other goalie, so you'd have to compete for the job." He told me why he was coaching. "I miss the game, and if you can't be a player, the next best thing's a coach. I'm excited to do some good things here. We do have a couple of other guys under consideration, but I really want you and that's why I'm calling you. I want you to consider us."

I put the phone down and stared at it for a moment. "Wayne Gretzky just called me! On this phone, right here." And as soon as the kids got home from school, I was like, "Hey, kids, guess who called me today?"

One of the reasons I opted for Phoenix—besides the fact I knew what Pittsburgh looked like in the winter—was that I really wanted to make a difference for the Phoenix Coyotes and be a part of growing a championship team. The management team they had there was incredible. There was Wayne as coach, and Mike Barnett was the general manager. On top of that, Cliff Fletcher was senior vice-president in charge of hockey operations. I knew we didn't have a ton of talent and there wasn't enough money. And if you don't have an abundance of great draft picks, it's tough for a team to move up. It's not as though Wayne was working with the 2018 Vegas Golden Knights, an expansion team with underrated and emerging talent picked up from across the league, along with two key veterans, James Neal and Marc-André Fleury. The Coyotes just weren't that deep, but they did have Shane Doan.

Doaner's a great guy, a great captain. He was ultracompetitive on the ice. He was physical, he stuck up for his teammates, and he enjoyed the game. He was happy to be an NHLer every day. It was fun seeing him at the rink. I met his parents, and I could tell he was another Western farm boy who was brought up right. Doaner was like Brendan Shanahan, always learning, always trying to get better. He asked me a lot of questions about his shot. We talked for hours.

I signed for $900,000. I remember my older boy, Taylor, saying, "Dad, you just went from $8 million to $900,000. Wow. What a pay cut."

I laughed and said, "Taylor, that's just a starting point. I'm going to be MVP of that team. You'll see, I'll be their best player."

Our family rented Brad May's place. I love Brad May. We went to the World Championship together. We hired a retired teacher and the kids were home-schooled, which gave them the flexibility to come to every home game. For Taylor and Tristan, that was right up their alley. I'd take them every time we played, and they'd just run around the rink, and then sit and watch the game, and meet me afterward.

What's really interesting is that, although they only went to school for a couple of hours a day, when we returned back home to Toronto they took an equivalency test that showed they were right up to grade level. In fact, one of the testers said, "Okay, who came in and wrote the test for Taylor?"

I said, "I dropped him off here myself. He wrote it!"

The teacher smiled. He was kidding. He said, "I couldn't have given him a higher mark. He's off the charts." Yeah, okay. Proud dad moment, but still.

I'd drive them to the tutor every day. They'd come to hockey practice and games, so we spent a lot of time together. A big reason for that was Wayne. He's a great family person. He would accomplish all kinds of things at the rink despite all the distractions that were around. Kids would be playing ball hockey in the dressing room, families would be coming and going. Wayne was very much a proponent of having family around.

One time, he said to me, "Hey, why doesn't Taylor come on the bench for the game?"

I said, "What? Holy cow, what a thrill for him."

I was in net and somebody tried to rim the puck around the boards to dump it in. Suddenly, it jumped the glass right into our bench, right where Taylor was sitting.

I skated out, craning my neck, thinking, "Oh my God! I hope Taylor didn't get hit!"

At the first TV timeout, I skated over to make sure everything was okay. Taylor had a blood-covered towel draped over his arm and a shocked look on his face.

"Taylor, what happened?"

"Holy crap, Dad. Sean O'Donnell lost his teeth right in front of me. A slapper right to the mouth. And all he did was bend his head, drop them into his hand and hand them to the trainer, who put them in his pocket." Taylor was wide-eyed. "Dad, these guys are tough!"

As a coach, Wayne allowed us a lot of freedom to play creatively, but he expected us to play tough and at a high level. Wayne's work ethic as a player was fantastic. He was always a professional on the ice. He practised hard and he played hard, but it'd be fair to say he had a lot of natural instinct and talent. Not all of the younger players coming in had that high hockey IQ, but Wayne was certainly patient with them anyway.

The problem is, you can only tell somebody so much. Maybe they don't have the talent, or maybe they don't have the courage. You can say, "Listen, go to the front of the net and bang in some rebounds." But if you're afraid, you're not going to do that.

One time, we were working on our power play and I was in net. The defencemen turned their sticks upside down so that the blades were in their hands and the knobs of their sticks were on the ice. It was an artificial way for the power play to practise moving the puck while the defenders couldn't intercept. It was supposed to give the shooters confidence. The defence was pressuring, but they couldn't get hold of the puck. And you know what? Nobody scored. Nobody got a shot on net.

Wayne was so frustrated. He said, "Okay." He grabbed a stick and shooed somebody away and took a position on the point. The puck came back to him, he passed it back to an open player, who immediately passed it back to Wayne. Wayne walked the line and made a magnificent aerial pass right down the centre for a two-on-none, and they scored.

And while he was doing all this, he never looked down at the puck. Not once. He was looking around at guys and explaining what to do. When the puck went in off his great pass, everybody stopped and looked at each other and went, "Oh."

You think anybody else could do that? Make a no-look aerial pass right on the tape down below to the only open guy? In coaching skates—skates that were two sizes too big? No way. There was only one Wayne Gretzky.

Another time, Wayne actually laced up his old skates, the ones he wore as a player with the blue blades. A couple of the young guys who had never seen him play watched him flying around, making all these plays, and their mouths were hanging open.

It was good for him to do that, because they realized he wasn't just telling them this stuff. He could actually do it. It's like a personal trainer being really fit and making you think, "All right, I'll listen because I want to be fit like you." Wayne opened a lot of eyes that day. And it got through to the younger guys who didn't really know who Wayne Gretzky was. They knew the stats, but until you see the performance, it's hard to believe it.

I thought it was an effective way for him to get his message across. He wasn't just a guy in a fancy suit telling you what to do. But he did have some nice suits. I never saw him wear the same pair of shoes or suit twice. I like fashion too, and I remember looking at him and thinking, "Man, that's another nice suit," or "Look at those Italian shoes. Leather as soft as a two-minute egg."

And Wayne would take anyone's call. Moms, dads, agents, he answered every question. Never skirted his responsibilities.

Another thing I respected about Wayne is the amount of enjoyment we had because of his love and passion for the game. You could see it in practice. You could see it on the bench. He was intense sometimes as a coach—just as he was when he was a player. Real fire. It was contagious.

Brian Boucher was the veteran goalie who backed me up the first year in Phoenix. We've become good friends. We used to warm up together, throw the ball and get ready for games. He has a great personality. I really like Bouche. Years earlier, in a Philly–Toronto game, I'd wrestled him to the ice in one of those good old-fashioned bench-clearing brawls. I grabbed him and held him down. It wasn't a real fight—more of a pair off and dance.

But then, when I got to Arizona, he pretended he was mad at me. He was always giving me the stink eye, and I'd ask him, "Bouche, you wanna talk about something?"

He'd scowl. "Yeah, that time in Toronto! Why would you do that? Everybody thinks you put me down, when all I did was trip!" Bouche is a great guy, a wonderful human. He's a broadcaster on NBC. He does the interviews during the playoffs. He's very good at what he does. He knows what questions to ask. Another smart guy.

Grant Fuhr was my goalie coach. Fuhr focused more on the mental side. He had a great sense of perspective, especially when things weren't going well. Looking back on my career, I always played my best when I was needed. Fuhr told me that Wayne would tell him, "The young guys' agents are calling me, insisting I play my younger goalies, but Fuhrsy, I have to play Cujo if I want to win."

As a team, we were below .500, but we had a winning record in the games I played. I actually had a pretty good year. And I played a lot—60 games with Phoenix. I won 32 games, ninth-best in the league. It was the seventh time in my career that I had reached the 30-win mark, and early in the season, I racked up the 400th win of my career. There were 21 losses in regulation time, and three more in overtime. I had a 2.91 goals-against average, a .902 save percentage and four shutouts (tied for seventh in the league). My 1,524 saves were 11th-best in the league.

Just like I had told Taylor at the start of the season, I succeeded. I was thirty-nine years old, still a number one goalie, and was named team MVP.

I might have felt like I was thirty-two or thirty-three, but that was not the reality from the organization's point of view. I remember negotiating with our GM, Michael Barnett, in 2006. He said, "I can give you a pay raise, Curtis, but we're not going to give you any years, any term."

I said, "Michael, have you ever seen me on the training table? I'm never on the training table. I never need to be worked on."

"Curtis, you're thirty-nine. Nobody's going to pay you a number one goalie's salary." And he was right. So I signed for one more year, at $2.2 million.

I loved playing for Phoenix, but I was older and I knew I wouldn't be signed for a third year. They were looking to develop young players, which was totally understandable and necessary for their long-term ambitions. My last game for the Coyotes was on April 8, 2007, when we beat the Vancouver Canucks 3–1. That was my 446th NHL victory, and it put me into fifth place all-time, one ahead of the great Terry Sawchuk.

CHAPTER 70

"Let's Go Have Some Fun"

I WAS HOPING to play for a team in the Eastern Conference when I left Phoenix in 2007. I worried about being too far away from my kids for too long. I felt great physically, with none of the ailments I had in Detroit. But there were no offers. I remember thinking, "I'm forty years old but I still have the itch to play." I was at home on the farm, taking the kids to school, going to their games. But I wondered what I was going to do with the rest of my life.

Kevin Prendergast, a former head scout for the Edmonton Oilers, was working with Hockey Canada, and he called me in November. He's a friend of Donnie Meehan's. They grew up together. He said, "Hey listen, Curtis, if you want to play in the NHL again, there are lots of teams that need a backup for the playoffs. Even a team contending for the Stanley Cup. If you really want to get your name out there again, go play on the Spengler Cup team and you'll get seen."

"What exactly is the Spengler Cup tournament?" I asked. I'd seen it on TV, but I didn't really know a lot about it.

He told me it was the oldest international hockey tournament—it dated back to 1923. It's held in Davos, Switzerland, at the top of a mountain, in just a beautiful rink. It takes place in late December—it's a Christmas tournament for the European club teams. The Canadian entry is made up of guys playing over there, along with a few NHL prospects. He said, "Travis Green is on Team Canada. You'll actually enjoy it. Go over there and play. Doug Gilmour's one of the assistant coaches. He's helping put the team together."

Doug called me a day later. "Hey, Curtis, you should play in the Spengler Cup."

I figured he had probably just talked to Ken. "You're the second person who's told me that. Yeah, Dougie, sure. Let's go have some fun!"

I had to scramble. I hadn't played any hockey since April, when the Coyotes' season ended. I had to start training, but I only had a few weeks to get ready. I called up the Francos and started getting myself in shape.

I headed to the Spengler Cup at Christmastime after skating for a couple of weeks with my goalie coaches, but I hadn't played a lick. In the first practice, I was dying. It was the altitude. Newmarket is about eight hundred feet above sea level, while Davos is close to a mile. I thought, "I'm not ready for this!"

We had two other goalies, Sébastien Caron, a fourth-round pick by the Penguins from Amqui, Quebec, and Wade Flaherty, who had played with the San Jose Sharks and New York Islanders, among other teams, and had been out of the NHL since 2002–03.

Both Sébastien and Wade were good goalies. Sébastien played a couple of games, in and out. I thought he might have to take over, but I got better as we went on. We were outshot badly, which always worked for me. I must have played well in the preliminary games, because they kept playing me.

When I got over there, I saw Travis Green, a familiar face. We'd done battle together in Toronto. He had been instrumental in our playoff series against the Islanders. Any time you have that bond, you pick right up where you left off. I didn't know anything about playing in Europe, and so I asked him about it. He was playing at the time for a Swiss team called EV Zug.

"Hockey's a little different over here," he said. "My first game, I went on and crushed this guy at centre ice, open-ice hit. Equipment exploded, gloves went flying, helmet blows off his head. Just drilled him. I skated back to the bench, adjusting the jersey, feeling pretty good about myself, and one of our best players looks at me and goes, 'Are you fucking *crazy*? What are you doing?'"

I saw quickly that there was a lot of skill but not a lot of hitting on the bigger ice surface. For a goalie, that's a big adjustment. Playing the angles is different. You can lose the net behind you. And the timing—it takes longer for guys to get to the net. Once they pick up the puck, they have to take a few more steps. There's also more room to go wide, so you get more guys sweeping in on you. In the NHL, your defencemen head them off into the corner.

We had a bunch of guys who were great at blocking shots, like Mark Giordano. He's the captain of the Calgary Flames now. Gio was so mature for his age. He was playing for Moscow Dynamo that year because he and the Flames couldn't agree on a contract. Anyway, he was such a nice guy. He played great. He was our best offensive defenceman. We had a good team.

Canada had won the Spengler Cup ten times since we first entered the tournament in 1984, but our last win had been four years earlier, in 2003. We played five games in a row and won all of them. I played a strong game in the final and was happy with myself. It was on TV, and I remember Shane Doan telling me, "Hey, we were watching that in the dressing room in the morning skate!" The Coyotes were cheering for me because I'd been their teammate in Phoenix.

We were the underdogs in the final. We faced Salavat Yulaev Ufa, the top team in the Russian Superleague that year. They had a $55 million payroll, and they were super-talented. Meanwhile, we were just a bunch of guys from Canada. But that's the point, right? You don't get a lot of chances in your career to wear that maple leaf on your chest, and so, when you do, you play hard. You do all the things it takes to win. These aren't games that were going to fade into the night. They're games for the history books.

Chapter 71

Trust

WE BEAT UFA 2–1 in the Spengler Cup final, played on New Year's Eve 2007. Playing in the tournament did get me the attention I needed to sign with a team. Six or seven teams showed interest, but it came down to a choice between Calgary and San Jose.

Mike Keenan called me from Calgary and said, "Hey, Curtis, I know you knew me in St. Louis, but I've changed. I've really honed my craft and I coach a little differently now." He was very impressive. He said, "We've got a good team, you've got a chance to win here." He really sold it to me. He wasn't the Mike Keenan I knew back in St. Louis. Certainly not the Keenan who got me so frustrated that I cleared his desk off and wanted to strangle him. I liked the idea of playing in Canada, because I had had success in both Edmonton and Toronto. So I picked Calgary and backed up Miikka Kiprusoff.

I love Kipper. I'll tell you a story about him and me. Kipper was making $6 million, and he was a great goalie. I was making $1.5 million prorated. I was officially a backup goalie for the first time since about 1990–91. At first, I felt like Kipper considered me his competition. The Flames leaned on him hard, and you can't be 100 per cent every night. I wanted him to feel good around me so that he could be at his best. We were going to ride him like Seabiscuit to the finals. I needed to let him know that I was aware of my role, that he was the guy and I was just there to support him. But you can't just say that to a guy. You have to show him.

About a month after I got there, Colorado was in town. I said, "Hey, Kipper, I'm pretty familiar with all the shooters. I keep all their data in my head. Do you need to know where some shooters go? Because I find it really helps."

Now, a lot of goalies will go, "No, no, you'll mess me up." But Kipper was like, "Yeah, sure."

"Well, Joe Sakic, if he gets the chance and he's in close, he's going to go low blocker. He's got an amazing wrist shot. And if you don't anticipate that, he's probably going to beat you."

That night, on a turnover, Sakic got a great chance in front and took the shot—where else but low blocker. Kipper was ready. He knew it was coming. Joe didn't have a chance. I was on the bench, and the play was down at the other end. I saw Kipper looking over at me, giving me the nod. He came over to the bench on a timeout. "Kipper, don't make it look so easy," I warned. "He'll rip one over your shoulder next time and hit the high glove." That made him laugh.

After the game, I was getting undressed and he came into the room, already dressed in his street clothes. He was carrying two Coors Lights and handed me one of them. From that day on, we were best friends. Trust. You gotta have it.

Remember I told you about how Brendan Shanahan and I would strategize in St. Louis? And in Phoenix, Shane Doan and I would spend hours talking about goalies and shooters? Well, I told Doaner about one move in particular. "It's a great move," I said, "and it's going to work every time. You are a big, strong guy, so when you come out from the corner and take it to the front, a goalie will be afraid you are just going to go around and use your reach to slam it in the side. So you can make it look like that's what you are going to do, and instead, you slide it in the five-hole real fast."

We practised it just the way I described it. He slid it right under my right shin really quickly. Perfect. That spring, the Flames played the Coyotes on the road and I was starting in net. I appreciated the start because I had played for Phoenix in the previous two seasons. Doaner came out of the corner, and I had to get over. I had to give a good push off the post, which meant I couldn't go down early. And then, just like we'd talked about, he slid it under my pad, right in the open end of my five-hole!

He jumped up, waving his arms and celebrating, but he was looking at me. I gave him the glare, as if to say, "Wow, did you really just do that to me?"

He just laughed.

We both laugh about it now, but I didn't think it was very funny at the time.

The Calgary guys were great. My first day there, defenceman Dion Phaneuf came up to me. "I've got your stick hanging above my bed." I gave him a look that said, "Well, that's kind of weird," and he said, "Oh! No, no, no! My bed in Edmonton. Where I grew up."

We had a laugh, and he told me that when he was a kid, I was the first star one night in Edmonton and I handed him my stick when he was hanging over the rails.

Did I feel old? Oh yeah, but that's okay.

Jarome Iginla was a great captain. He played hard. He was a very serious guy most of the time. And everyone told me that Owen Nolan could be mean and grumpy, but when I got there, he said to me, "Hey, Curtis, I know you're by yourself. Come on over to my place. I'll make you lunch!" I'd head over to his place at least twice a week. He'd make me lunch and we'd watch golf. He was such a great guy. I love Owen Nolan.

I sat beside Eric Nystrom. His dad was Bobby Nystrom, who won four Cups with the Islanders and was known as "Mr. Islander," a guy I really respected. Eric was a young guy, and I liked the way he played. He had lots of energy and was physical. I tried to keep him in the lineup by giving him some advice about Keenan. "You've got great speed and I've seen you go to the net hard a couple times, but you have to do it all the time. I know it's painful, but this coach, Keenan, will love you for it. Don't ever pull up. Every time you get the puck, go to the net, run over the goalie and try to score. That's all you've gotta do."

Daymond Langkow was really quiet, but man, he was the fittest guy despite eating McDonald's every day. The guys were shocked he could eat so much junk food and still be jacked. Adrian Aucoin, a defence-man, was a good guy. He played seventeen years in the NHL. He was a right-hand shot, not known for his goal-scoring prowess, and yet he was just great at the shootout. He'd put it high on the glove side and score every single time.

Craig Conroy was Chatty Cathy, always in the mix. He was one of the leaders and scored some big goals. He had scored the winner on me when I played for Detroit in a playoff game against Calgary. I went over to his house for a barbecue one time. His wife, Jessie, was a sweetheart. Craig was out cooking on the barbecue, and she handed me a photo of him scoring that goal in Detroit. She said, "Craig would never ask you, but will you sign this picture?"

I said, "Of course." It was a great goal. The only goal I let in that game. I signed it, "To Craig, great goal. Your friend, Cujo."

I only played nine games for Calgary, over the course of about two months from February to April. All nine were on the road. I missed the welcoming energy of a home crowd.

I wasn't as good as I wanted to be for the first couple of games, but I improved over time. But Kipper was just incredible that year—seventy-six games, and a record of 39–26–10. Third in the league in wins, fourth in saves. He was truly a talented guy. He was taller than me. If I could have changed my makeup, I would have been taller and leaner. My height—five foot eleven—would never cut it these days. An ideal goalie body today is six foot four, maybe even taller, and 185 pounds. Get down in the butterfly when you're that tall, and your shoulders reach the crossbar.

I started one game and played part of another in the playoffs. Kipper started Game Three at home against San Jose, but he got pulled after letting in three goals in a little over three minutes. It was my first post-season action since 2004. I had always had great success against San Jose for some reason. I went in, stopped everything and we won 4–3.

There was some debate whether Kipper was going to play the next game. He had a few years left on his contract and he was their guy. They wanted to get him going. But I had a tremendous record against San Jose—in forty-seven regular-season starts, I'd won thirty-five times. Their coach, Ron Wilson, knew that too.

Still, Kipper ended up playing the fourth, fifth and sixth games, and starting Game Seven. And then the strangest thing happened. Keenan had confidence in me. He knew I could go in at any point. San Jose was up by a goal in the second period. Everything was on the line. Not a time when you pull your goalie. Anyway, Mike looked at me and yelled, "Curtis, get your stuff on! Get in there!" And then in a TV timeout, he gathered the guys together.

I was like, "What? Holy crap." It wasn't Kipper's fault. I looked over, and there was my buddy Brian Boucher, my backup in Phoenix, sitting by the glass on the San Jose bench, looking at me. He has just a great personality, and the look on his face was just too funny. His eyes were wide and his mouth was open because he'd heard Mike tell me to go in.

He pointed to Mike and mouthed, "Did he really just say that?"

I shouted, "Mike!" But he wouldn't answer me because he was talking to the team in the timeout. I tried again. "Mike!"

But he still didn't say anything. I was conflicted, because I knew that if Miikka saw me grab my stuff and put a mask on, he was going to think, "The coach has no confidence in me." Besides, I didn't want to embarrass Kipper. I didn't want to take the heart out of him. They were paying him a lot of money and he had years left in his contract. It wasn't the right thing to do.

I had to be 100 per cent sure, so I yelled again. "Are you fucking serious? What's happening? Mike!" He looked up and waved me off. "No, no forget it!"

I did go in for Kipper, late in the second period. By then, it was 4–2. I let in a goal on the second shot but played well after that. Unfortunately, it was too late. Our season was over.

But you know what? I thought Mike was a great coach that year. Not at all the way he was in St. Louis. With the Flames, he used to sit down in the room and go around and make each guy accountable.

CHAPTER 72

"I'm Going to Play for the Leafs!"

MY CONTRACT WITH Calgary ended, and I wasn't sure whether I would get another offer. I remember Cliff Fletcher calling me in June of 2008. I was at Taylor's baseball game in Nobleton, not far from King City.

"Hey, Curtis, how's it going?"

"Good. Just at my son's baseball game."

"How would you like to come back to the Leafs?"

I couldn't believe it. Talk about a dream come true. "Wow, that'd be great!" Here I was, forty-one years old, with a chance to finish with the Leafs. The team I had wanted to come back to ever since the day I left. I was excited.

I told him, "Yeah, Cliff, that's wonderful. Thank you. Let's do it."

And then I sat my kids down and said, "Hey, guys, I've got a chance to play one more year in Toronto." And they started jumping up and down.

Of course, I played it up. "Are you sure? I'll be busy. I'll be playing."

They were all like, "Dad, are you kidding? We'll do our homework by ourselves! We'll wash the dishes. We'll walk the dogs! Dad, you've gotta do it!"

I knew that would be their response, but I wanted to hear it from them. Let them think they had a say, and let them take credit for giving me the push. "Okay," I said, "I'm gonna do it! I'm going to play for the Leafs." And they were so excited. I was too.

That's why it was so disappointing that I was godawful that year in Toronto. I was terrible.

I couldn't focus. My marriage had broken up after seventeen years, and suddenly, I was single and living on the farm with the four kids as well as two boxers—Phoenix and Arizona—and Madi's chihuahua, Caramel. And we still had horses. Up until then, hockey was my escape. It was my respite from the stresses of everyday life. I could totally immerse myself in hockey. Just like when I grew up.

Listen, the kids were always my number one concern. I hated being away from them. The only thing I didn't like about being in Calgary from January to April was that I didn't see them a lot. I loved being back home. I loved that they were living with me, but I needed help, and so I hired my nephew-in-law Chris and his girlfriend, Felicia. They did a nice job. He was a good cook, great with art projects, a big help with school, and so was she. It was like having built-in tutors and a cook.

I don't even know how people knew I was going through a divorce, but my buddy Marty Harding called me and said, "Hey, I read that you're dating Shania Twain. Is that really happening?"

"What?"

He said, "It's all over the internet!"

I said, "Really? No."

And then Mike Zeisberger of the *Toronto Sun* called. "Hey, buddy, the *National Enquirer* called. What's going on with Shania? You can tell me."

"No!" I like her music, but I've never laid eyes on Shania Twain in person. I still haven't met her. It was just a hot rumour. I can see how rumours spread, because people are quick to believe them. I don't know how that started. I think she might've been going through a divorce at that time too, and people thought they were putting two and two together.

Everywhere I went for a while, I would hear, "How was Shania Twain? You dated her?"

And I'd be like, "Sorry, but . . ."

Except for playing and practice, I didn't go out. I stayed home and hung around with the kids. And then, in September 2008, I was invited to participate in a car rally put together by a group of successful Toronto businessmen to raise money for SickKids hospital. They brought in Kurt Russell and Goldie Hawn to host the event, and they called it the Rally for Kids with Cancer. The idea was that each guy would raise a couple hundred thousand and use the money to bid on a celebrity, and that celebrity would join the winning bidder in a treasure hunt around the city the next day. It was a two-day event, so I stayed downtown overnight.

I met Goldie that night. I knew their son Wyatt was a goalie, so we talked about Wyatt and goaltending. I did end up meeting Kurt later. I saw him at the Water's Edge in Muskoka. We talked about the movie that he starred in, *Miracle*, in which he played the legendary hockey coach Herb Brooks. Kurt was a charming guy. He knows a lot about hockey. I told him I sat with Herb at the Olympics in 1998, and we watched the Sweden–Canada matchup together. It was interesting to hear his running commentary on the game. A pretty cool experience.

A few minutes after I got there, I spotted this girl. She had a long, elegant neck, square jaw, just a beautiful face, and these perfect, really interesting eyes. Green, almond-shaped. And this thick mane of hair. It was blond-brown, a great colour. A natural colour. Perfect posture, perfect body. She was God's art on God's canvas.

When I played, I was aware of everything going on around me. It was the same that night—I was aware of where she was the entire evening. I wanted to talk to her, but I just couldn't bring myself to be that forward. The auction started and she came up to the stage as one of the celebrities. It turns out she was a *Playboy* Playmate—Stephanie Glasson, Miss July 2004. I wasn't into *Playboy*, but I knew there weren't many Playmates—only twelve a year. It's an impressive accomplishment. Danny Ardellini, and his wife, Charlatta, bid on Stephanie to ride with him in his Lamborghini Murcielago for the treasure hunt. I'd met Danny when we were checking into the hotel. I kept my distance at first, because he's a boisterous guy and he kept screaming over, "Cujo! Hey, Cujo! I need a stick!" He and Char turned out to be wonderful people. We're still good friends.

But there I was at first, trying to avoid him, and then when I learned that Stephanie was going to be in his car, I wanted to be his best friend. I made a mental note to make sure to find him in the morning in the parking lot. He'd told me I was his all-time favourite goalie. I thought, "This is good. Maybe he'll pump my tires when he's driving Stephanie around."

So now I knew her name. I saw her standing by the bar with some friends and I worked up the nerve to meet her. I said, "Hi, I'm Curtis Joseph, with the Maple Leafs."

She was raised in Tennessee, so Canadian accents were kind of foreign to her. On top of that, she'd never seen or heard a hockey game in her life. Because it was a charity event for kids, she thought I said I was with the organization. She smiled and held out her hand, "You're with the Make Believes?"

The bar was loud, so I raised my voice a little. "Maple Leafs. I'm with the Maple Leafs."

She shook her head, not understanding. "The Make Believes? You're raisin' money for the kids?"

"No, no! I'm with the Toronto Maple Leafs. I play hockey."

It was obvious she had no idea what I was talking about. We talked for a few minutes. Well, *she* talked. She was very clever and smart and interesting. I could have stood there all night. Suddenly, I realized she'd stopped talking. We stood there for a moment. I had no idea what to say to a girl like her. So I asked, "Would you like a drink?"

She smiled. "Sure."

"Where are you sitting?"

"Over there." She pointed to a table full of her friends.

"Okay, I'll bring one over." I headed to the bar. My heart was pounding as if I was heading into Game Seven of the playoffs. I ordered her a wine and then I marched over to her table and plunked it down next to her. "Here's your drink," I said. And then I turned and ran back to my table. She watched me go, and then said to her friends, "Tell me the truth. Have I got BO?"

I went up to my room and tried to sleep, but I couldn't. I was too busy kicking myself all night for blowing it.

The rally went off the next day. I was riding with a lawyer, a wonderful guy, though I forget what his name was. He was an amazing driver. We were in his Ford Cobra, in the fast lane of Highway 401, but we needed to turn off. Instead of getting in the declaration lane for the off-ramp, he flew over four lanes past a hundred cars and then made a move out of a *Mad Max* movie that left my gut on the dash. I thought, "This is how I'm going to end my life?" I was literally hanging on for dear life.

There was another gala that night. Danny invited me to sit with them, which gave Steph and me a chance to talk a little more. We exchanged BlackBerry numbers.

A couple of weeks later, she messaged me her picture from the rally. She was sitting on a car, wearing a shirt that wrapped around the top of her shoulders. I laughed because you could see me lurking in the background. I looked at the photo again, and suddenly I felt like I'd been struck by lightning. I called her up in Singapore, where she was modelling.

"Oh my gosh, I've seen you before. Did you ever live in Arizona?"

"I did. I lived there three years ago."

I said, "I lived there then as well! Where did you live?"

She said, "Near DC Ranch." That's on the outskirts of Scottsdale.

I couldn't believe it. I remembered seeing her back then. I had a really good memory for people and places, sticks, situations and plays. Let's say Jarome Iginla is coming in on you on a two-on-one, down the left side. I would remember he wasn't going to go to the net. He's a right-hand shot, so he was going to pull up, pass it, move to the other side for a pass back, and then he would one-time it. So I had to be prepared, come out, be big, for a better chance. It was all there, stored in my memory.

Same thing with Steph. I could still picture her floating through Starbucks, so graceful. Shoulders square, head up. Absolutely stunning. As I watched her, I thought, "That is the most beautiful woman I've ever seen in my life." But of course, I was married, so I never saw her again. I just took a mental picture and stored it in my memory along with shooters and plays and sticks.

I told her, "I saw you one time at Starbucks in DC Ranch. You walked by and it looked like you had a book on your head." Smooth, Curtis. Smooth.

We started texting pretty regularly. I didn't aggressively pursue her, but I'm funnier and wittier in texts than in person, so it seemed to hold the relationship together.

Steph was living in Virginia Beach and renting a house. When I was on the road, I'd fly her in and we'd go to dinner. We got to know each other, taking it slow.

Steph is funny and a good person. Once we got to know each other better, I could see she was comfortable and secure in our relationship. One time, she told me, "I'm gonna get an I HATE SHANIA TWAIN T-shirt and start wearin' it!"

She didn't meet my kids, and I didn't meet her daughter, Kailey, for six months, when I finally told the kids I was dating Steph. They already knew something was up. I'd be playing Wiffle ball in the driveway with Tristan, and he'd hit the ball and be running the bases, and I'd get a text from Steph and stop to look at it, so he knew I was distracted.

At first, it was tough for them. I was a good dad, but you know kids. I had never dated anyone other than their mother, and now that they were living with me, they were used to having all my attention.

Once Steph and I started dating openly, I met her daughter, Kailey. She was shy, just like I was as a kid. Quiet and well mannered. I was careful not to be pushy with her, preferring to let her get to know me.

Our relationship developed on the right curve. One thing I do know is kids. I like to observe their different personalities, and I can feel their energy. I took it slow, found out what she was interested in, and then I would ask her about it.

My youngest son, Luke, is three years younger than Kailey, and over time they've formed a big-sister/little-brother relationship. He's a wonderful guy. The talker of the group. Luke's a good hockey player—he's going into Junior A. I watch him out there, talking to the referees and then picking up the puck for them. He collects the pucks after practice too—last one on the ice collects all the pucks and puts them up. He's a real leader. A captain-type player. Kailey and Luke became good friends and remain close. It's been a wonderful thing.

Steph never stayed at the farm with my kids, but occasionally she would come to town. I took her to a team get-together at Shayne Corson's bar in the Distillery District in Toronto. I was kind of like an elder statesman on that team. We had a lot of young guys on the team, so they weren't like my buddies. It wasn't like the dynamic I had with Chaser and Twister, where we were all the same age.

My teammates didn't know me so much as they knew *of* me. They were a little more respectful and didn't really give me the gears. Except for guys like my buddy Jamal Mayers, another veteran. Jamal's funny. I respected him and it was nice getting to play with him. He was a warrior and a great guy, a smart college guy. He was pretty big, and he played tough.

The night I took Steph to the team party, Jamal came up to me and said, "Man, you bringing Steph in here. She's so beautiful, the whole room stopped and looked. In fact, man, she made you look like Tom Cruise when you walked through that door. I heard somebody's wife say, 'Is that what happens when you get divorced?'"

I laughed and thought nothing more about it.

And then at practice the next day, I was in the training room, getting ready to ride the bike—and remember, I was a rookie at all this dating stuff. I forgot something, so I ran back through the locker room to my stall, which was at the far end. I grabbed my stuff and then walked back through the dressing room, and honestly it was like a beer commercial. One guy started this slow clap, and then another joined in, and another. It got faster and louder until every guy on the team was up on his feet, giving me a standing ovation.

CHAPTER 73

Riding into the Sunset

I HAD SO many great teammates that last year, like Jamal and Brad May. Brad and I had villas across from each other in Muskoka. Great guy. We played together that last year in Toronto. One of the first things Brian Burke did when he came in as our GM was to trade for Brad. Burke wanted a more physical team, and Brad had played for him in both Anaheim and Vancouver. Brad's from Markham, Ontario. It's a big deal to play for the Leafs, especially if you are Toronto boys like Jamal and Brad and me.

That last year, I was backing up Vesa Toskala, a thirty-one-year-old goaltender from Finland. That's the transition. From a star player to backup. As a team guy, you have to embrace it.

The benches in Montreal were too small, so I was sitting across the rink, on a folding chair near the penalty box, on January 8, 2009. After a faceoff, Brad got into a fight at centre ice with Francis Bouillon and was tossed from the game. He was laughing and all jacked up thanks to the testosterone rush you get after the fight. I followed him into the dressing room and noticed a little of Bouillon's blood on his shirt. I said, "Hey, Mayday, first fight in a Maple Leaf uniform. Hold on a minute." I went over to my locker and grabbed my phone from my suit. "I've gotta take a picture of this. It's gonna last forever. Your first fight and a blood-stained jersey."

We still laugh about it. See, these are the things you do once you're a backup goalie. You don't have to think about performing in the game. You're thinking more about making a contribution as a good teammate. There's only real pressure on the days you start.

For me, it was the end of the line. Everybody knew it. I didn't play much, and as I said, I didn't play well. But I did have one unforgettable game, my "riding off into the sunset" game. It was against the Washington Capitals at home on March 24, 2009. Martin Gerber was in goal for us, but it was kind of like my Mick McGeough situation. Brooks Laich scored in the last minute of the third period to make it 2–2 and Gerbs felt he had been pushed into the net. When Gerbs came out to argue, he made contact with the referee, Mike Leggo. When I saw him push the referee, I thought, "Ooh, that's it. He's gone." Meanwhile, there was a melee. Everybody was screaming and yelling, and I was looking around for my equipment, thinking, "I'm going to have to go into this game."

It was tied 2–2 with fifty-six seconds left. Gerber got a game misconduct, so I went into the game, and the fans were great. I faced a couple of shots right away, including a slapper from Alexander Ovechkin. Saved it. We played a five-minute overtime. Again, Ovechkin was taking shots, one-timers. The crowd was going crazy because the Capitals didn't score. Neither did we, so we went to a shootout. Jeff Hamilton scored on José Théodore, and I stopped their first two shooters, Nicklas Backstrom and Alexander Semin, both of them highly skilled guys. Ovechkin had the last shot and a chance to tie the game. I remember looking around, taking it all in. The crowd chanting, "Cujo! Cujo! Cujo!" Both benches up on their feet, players craning their necks. The refs on either side were ready for the call. I looked down the barrel at Ovi. He bent over and stared back. Measuring me up. Envisioning what he was going to do.

I had already pretty much decided I was going to retire at the end of that season. It had been a terrible year, but now, with this chance, I could turn that around. I smiled to myself, confident. "How cool is this?" I thought. "I'm going to make this save and we're going to win this game. It's how I am going to end my career."

At that moment, I started zipping through my data files. "All right, Ovechkin likes to go forehand. I haven't seen him go backhand ever, because he's got that big hook on his stick, which means he can't get the puck up. He'll fake a shot and then go forehand." I kept going through it, breaking it down. "I'm not going to fall for the fake. I'm going to be patient."

Ovechkin came in, faked a shot and went to the forehand. I made the save and we won.

All the guys were so happy because here's this old goalie that they grew up watching, who never gets to play anymore, and he stops the greatest goal scorer of this era. Nice way to go out.

Chapter 74

What Wayne Said

I PROPOSED TO Steph the old-fashioned way. We were at her place in Virginia Beach, looking for seashells on the sand at sunset. I held her hand, and as we walked up the beach, I surprised her. I got down on one knee, pulled out a black velvet ring box from my pocket, opened it and said, "Steph, will you marry me?" When she said yes, it was one of the happiest days of my life.

A year later, we were married on a beach in the Turks and Caicos Islands. I remember my son Tristan saying, "Dad, you've only dated two women, and you married both of them."

Steph and I gave the kids a little sister, Kensie Shayne, in 2014. Steph says Wayne Gretzky is responsible for Kensie Shayne's existence. We were at his hockey camp in Vegas. I was standing nearby while Wayne was signing autographs at the rink. He was asking about the kids when, suddenly, he said, "You know what? You guys should have a baby. A baby will blend the two families."

If anybody else had said it, I would've shaken it off, but I had never known Wayne to be wrong, so . . . a year later we had our little spark plug. She's like her mom. And athletic? Beyond belief. She wasn't even walking yet, just barely sitting up, when I started to play catch with her.

My kids mean everything to me. Steph says I love them the way I wish I had been loved. My whole life, I had my walls up just to protect myself. I was always embarrassed about my childhood. My family wasn't like other families. Other families protected each other, loved each other. I was ashamed that nobody loved me. And so, I hid it and built the walls.

It's just so great because people see a different me now. Totally different. I think all the guys I played with would be a little shocked if they knew me now. I try to be that friend who calls if somebody's going through a terrible time, like an illness or a death or a divorce. I would never have taken that initiative when I was younger.

But Steph made me understand it was okay to talk about my childhood, which in turn made me feel it was okay to talk about it in public. She's made me extremely comfortable with it. I've done some public speaking. I tell my story. The story about how I grew up and some of the obstacles I faced. I'm not embarrassed about it anymore.

It wasn't until I met Stephanie, when I was forty-one, that I was able to bring my walls down. She made me feel safe and accepted and loved. The only other time I felt that way was with my teammates. Especially when I played for the Leafs.

People ask me all the time, "Do you wish you hadn't left Toronto in 2002?" Going to Detroit, well, it's easy to answer that now, because you can see how it played out. I was unsuccessful. Going to a new team had never been a problem for me before. But maybe because I was leaving Toronto, maybe because my heart was still there, maybe because when I heard Bob Cole and Joe Bowen broadcasting games, I missed it. Maybe it was because of the injuries and the ankle surgery. Maybe it was because I was thirty-five years old at the time. But hindsight's 20/20.

My first stint in Toronto was a great time in my life. We had a team with nine guys who could've been captains. There was a ton of leadership, a ton of alpha males in that group. We were so confident and we had a really good coach in Pat Quinn. That's why we were so close those years to going to the final. There was no salary cap in those days, so you could pretty much build a team the way you wanted to. And our fan base was fantastic. You're not going to find better fans than in Toronto. Walking to playoff games and receiving the appreciation from people on the street, they just adored that maple leaf on the front of your sweater.

So I would tell my younger self, and I'd tell Freddie Andersen if he were about to become a free agent, "Freddie, you're successful here. The grass isn't always greener. Be proud of the battles you've waged and the battles you've won. Learn from them and make yourself stronger for your team. Stay here, Freddie. They love you in Toronto, and you love them back. Stay, and win a Cup for the Leafs."

CAREER MILESTONES

Ontario Junior Hockey League Most Valuable Player (1986–87)

Saskatchewan Junior Hockey League First All-Star Team (1987–88)

Centennial Cup championship with Notre Dame Hounds (1988)

National Collegiate Athletic Association West Second All–American Team (1988–89)

Western Collegiate Hockey Association Player of the Year (1988–89)

Western Collegiate Hockey Association Freshman of the Year (1988–89)

Western Collegiate Hockey Association First All–Star Team (1988–89)

First NHL game: Edmonton 6 at St. Louis 4 (January 2, 1990)

First NHL win: St. Louis 2 at New York Islanders 1 (January 30, 1990)

First NHL shutout: San Jose 0 at St. Louis 4 (December 19, 1991)

Best save percentage (.911) among NHL goalies (1992–93)

Third in Vezina Trophy voting (1992–93)

Played in the 1994 NHL All–Star Game

Fourth in Vezina Trophy voting (1993–94)

Top First-Year Oiler Award (1995–96)

Team Canada (silver medallists) at 1996 World Championship

Team Canada (finalists) at 1996 World Cup of Hockey

Fifth in Vezina Trophy voting (1996–97)

Zane Feldman Trophy—Edmonton Oilers MVP (1996–97)

Edmonton Oilers Most Popular Player (1996–97, 1997–98)

Edmonton Oilers Molson Cup winner (1996–97, 1997–98)

1998 Canadian Olympic Team

Second in Vezina Trophy voting (1998–99)

Fourth in Hart Trophy voting (1998–99)

One of five finalists for the Lester B. Pearson Award (1998–99)

Toronto Maple Leafs Molson Cup winner (1998–99, 1999–2000, 2000–01)

Played in the 2000 NHL All–Star Game

King Clancy Memorial Trophy (1999–2000)

Third in Vezina Trophy voting (1999–2000)

2002 Canadian Olympic Team (gold medallists)

Phoenix Coyotes Three-Star Award (2005–06)

First goaltender to reach thirty wins in a regular season with five NHL franchises (2006)

Team Canada (champions) at 2007 Spengler Cup

Fourth in NHL career wins with 454 at retirement (2010)

St. Louis Sports Hall of Fame Inductee (2015)

Ninth among NHL goalies in assists, 31 assists in 943 regular seasons

CAREER STATISTICS

League	Seasons	GP	Min	GAA
NHL Regular Season	19	943	54054	2.79
NHL Playoffs	14	133	8106	2.42
NHL All-Star Game	2	2	39	10.77
AHL Regular Season	1	1	60	1.00
IHL Regular Season	2	38	2115	3.09
Olympics	2	1	60	5.00
World Cup	1	7	468	2.31
World Championship	1	6	349	2.06

W	L	O/T	SO	GA	SA	SV	SV%
454	352	96	51	2516	26795	24279	.906
63	66	—	16	327	3927	3600	.917
0	1	0	0	7	39	32	.821
1	0	0	0	1	21	20	.952
22	10	3	1	109	1100	991	.901
0	1	0	0	5	25	20	.800
5	2	0	0	18	203	185	.911
4	2	0	1	12	156	144	.923

Curtis Joseph's Career Ranking Among NHL Goaltenders

(to the end of 2017–18)

Regular Season
943 games played—6th
454 wins—5th
24,279 saves—6th
51 shutouts—23rd

Playoffs
133 games played—7th
63 wins—13th
3,600 saves—5th
16 shutouts—3rd

Acknowledgements

KIRSTIE AND I would like to thank the following people for their friendship and help in writing this book:

My wife, Stephanie, our girls, Madison, Kailey and Kensie and our boys, Taylor, Tristan, Luke and Jason, who are all such a big part of my story. I'd also like to thank my biological mother, Wendy Graves. I admire her strength and courage. Finally, thank you to Wayne Gretzky for writing the foreword. No matter what, Wayne is always there for all the guys who played.

This book couldn't have been written without my partner Kirstie working with me to tell my story the way it needed to be told. Thank you to Kirstie's content team—her husband and partner, contributing writer and editor Larry Day; hockey expert and fact checker Ron Wight; Steve McLellan, our number one transcriber, with help from Paul Day and Charlie Day; Tom Braid, Sheila Rae, Kaitlyn Kanygin and Evan Adlington on photos; Len Glickman from Cassels Brock Lawyers. Kirstie also wants to thank her family for their encouragement and support, Buddy, Kristin, Téa, Jaxon, Griffin, Charlie, Lundy, Geordie and Paul, and the entire McLellan clan, Bud and Joan, Paul and Deb, Hugh and Bonnie, Jan and Doug Folk, Julie and Jay Sinclair.

From HarperCollins, Jim Gifford, our editor, for his mentorship, constant ear and wisdom; Lloyd Davis for his excellent work on the edit; Jeremy Rawlings and Alison Woodbury for their legal advice; Noelle Zitzer and Stephanie Conklin for fantastic editorial assistance; Patricia MacDonald and Lesley Fraser for having a careful eye; Leo MacDonald, senior VP of sales and marketing; Michael Guy-Haddock, senior sales director; publicist Mike Millar; Cory Beatty, senior director of marketing; Alan Jones, art director; our great advocate Iris Tupholme, senior VP and executive publisher; and CEO Craig Swinwood who believed in this book and made it happen.

I also want to send a special thank you to my family members Karen Eakins, Jeanette Turner, Munimah and Freddy Joseph for sharing their memories with us. So many others spent a ton of time helping us out, including: Barry MacKenzie; Bijan Pesaran; Brad Isbister; Brett Hull; Brian McDavid; Chris Broadhurst; Connor McDavid; Cory Cross; Craig Adams; Dave Manson; Don Cherry; Don Meehan; Eddie Besnilian; Garth Butcher; Gerry Isbister; Gina Casey, executive assistant to mayor and council, Town of East Gwillimbury; Gino Cavallini; Glenn Healy; Guy Govis; Harvey Libby; Irene Libby; Jeanette Chapman; Jeanette Turner; Joe Bowen; Joe Persechini, councillor with the Town of East Gwillimbury; Joe Weiler; Kari Leivo; Kelly Chase; Ken Dryden; Kevin Lowe; Lisa Barry; Mike Ham; Mike Hinton; Martin Harding; Cory Wright; Paul Torkoff; Rob Weiler; Rod Brind'Amour; Ron Low; Ron MacLean; Shayne Corson; Stephane Gauvin; Steve Thomas; Terry McGarry; Tim Francis; Tom O'Rourke; Tony Twist; Travis Green; Tyler Stewart; Virginia Hackson, mayor, Town of East Gwillimbury; Wayne Thomas; and Wendy McCreary.